UNLEARNING ARCHITECTURE

UNLEARNING ARCHITECTURE

Louis I. Kahn
Graduate Studio and Office

Cengiz Yetken

Library of Congress Control Number: 2021901293
ISBN: Hardcover 978-1-6641-5401-8
Softcover 978-1-6641-5400-1
eBook 978-1-6641-5399-8

Front Cover Photo Credit: Louis I Kahn by Beverly "Sasha" Pabst, The Architectural Archives, University of Pennsylvania
Background photo: Fort Wayne Theater by Craig Kuhner

Print information available on the last page.

Rev. date: 02/25/2021

To order additional copies of this book, contact:
Xlibris
844-714-8691
www.Xlibris.com
Orders@Xlibris.com
816338

Contents

BOOK 2

Office of Louis I. Kahn

BOOK 3

Transition to Practice

To my colleagues and friends whose work gives us
the places we live, we learn, we question.
And to the students of art and architecture, who delve deep
into thoughts of design.

PREFACE

Throughout my years in architecture, both as a professor of design and a practicing architect, I have frequently been asked about Lou Kahn—arguably one of the most distinguished architects of the twentieth century. Such inquiries multiplied following the release of the documentary film *My Architect*, although the curiosity the film generated had less to do with his architecture or his teaching than with his rather tumultuous personal life. Many friends have also encouraged me to write about my years associated with Kahn, first as a student in his graduate class at the University of Pennsylvania, and then as a young architect working in his office at 1501 Walnut Street in Philadelphia.

At first, I considered composing a series of letters addressed to my children about my experiences with Louis Kahn and the reasons his buildings are so special. Then I realized I should address these reflections to students in architectural schools and to my colleagues in architectural practice. That would be the best way to communicate the sense of design embodied by these buildings, and the convictions that gave birth to them.

I began this by simply documenting events and anecdotes from my years with Kahn. The more I wrote, however, the more I realized I was discovering new things and writing with new insights. It became increasingly evident this was going to be more than a collection of memories; it was going to shed light on the very act of designing. It was also going to be a personal journey to rediscover my own design thinking. In this journey, I recalled many rewarding and poignant experiences that helped me during my early years of studying architecture. Above all, I fondly remembered what being with Kahn had taught me, and its effects on my professional life.

Architecture is a curious profession. Everyone seems to be interested in it, and it evokes a certain kind of respect, even some adoration. People know it is about making buildings, but not much more than that. Many are scarcely aware of the nature of that magical process of architectural design. It was this process that I began examining through these recollections. How do I come up with a spatial realization, and how do I put "the first line on paper," as Kahn used to say? And how does that help the flow of relevant ideas for comprehensive spatial statements along the way?

While visiting the Dhaka Assembly Building in Bangladesh recently, I was invited to speak to architecture students about Lou. The questions from these bright-eyed, beautiful young men and women made me aware of how thirsty they were to find out about Kahn, his personality, his study habits, his comments in the class, and even his reaction to deadlines. They were, in short, looking for that magical process of design. I am not sure how revealing my answers were, but I felt, then and there, that new discoveries were opening for them—and for me as well.

In the book, I wrote what I remember vividly—those memories that still hang in the wrinkles of my brain. These are the ones that gave me direction. These are the ones I voiced frequently to myself, to my students, and to my colleagues whenever they seemed relevant and meaningful.

My intention is to tell my own story—my own understanding, development, and conclusions. I gave examples of my projects and studies in Kahn's class and in his office, relating them to his comments to help explain further my understanding of design and Lou's way of guiding.

This book is not about Kahn's approach to architecture, nor is it an attempt to explain his point of view. These memories are what I have learned from being with Kahn—in his class, his office, and his buildings—and from being in the profession for so many years. I am attempting to answer a more elusive question: What did I learn from Kahn?

I am certain that each student in Kahn's class and each of one of us who worked with him at his office learned their own lessons, derived their own understandings, and reached their own conclusions about his comments and ideas. Read this book not as a memoir but as an inventory of experiences in architecture. I am not describing a person or a period, nor am I telling a story. I am simply exploring, through the memory of Kahn, that same magical process of architectural design. Looking back now, some fifty years later, I can see clearly what still shines in my mind. "A good building," Kahn said in class one day, "does not impress you at first sight. It comes back to you as a recollection years later. Then you remember and say 'That was a good building.'" It is now, for me, that time of recollection. And I say, those were good years—very good years!

Cengiz Yetken
Chicago

BOOK I

Kahn Graduate Studio at Penn

It is the offering of the mind. … A man motivated not by profit of any kind—just a sense of offering—he writes a book, hoping that it will be published. He is trying to—he is motivated by the sense that he has somewhere in there, whether it is deep, deep in the silence, or whether it is already on the threshold of inspiration. He must be there to write it, and what he draws here from here, and what he draws from there, somehow, he motivates his writing a book. And he gets it also from another beautiful source, and that is through the experience or the Odyssey of a life that goes through the circumstances of living.[1]

[1] Kahn, Louis I., 2003, *Louis Kahn: Essential Texts*, ed. Robert Twombly, WW Norton & Company, New York, p. 239.

PART I

A Foreign Student

Philadelphia

One fine sunny day in May ’65, I took a Pan Am flight from Ankara to Rome. My plan was to stay two days in Rome and then proceed to New York City. I had completed five years of architectural education at Middle East Technical University (METU) in Ankara. Following graduation, I was asked to stay and teach design, which I was pleased to do. After a year of teaching, I received a Fulbright travel grant and a scholarship from the University of Pennsylvania. So there I was, an exchange student, traveling to Philadelphia to pursue another master’s degree, and this time I was to study with the master architect himself, Louis Kahn.

On the way, I wandered around Rome for a few days with no objective. I visited all the places I remembered learning about from Introduction to Architecture class at METU. I visited the Trevi Fountain, the Rome Termini train station, the Spanish Steps, and the Pantheon. However, none of those places meant much to me. *Rome is meaningless when you are alone,* I thought. I had limited money in my pocket, and Rome was very expensive.

A strange thing happened to me while I was there. I was sitting on a bench at the train station designed by the structural engineer Pier Luigi Nervi, and while I was observing the design, a beautiful young girl approached and sat down next to me. I was startled by her sudden appearance and the fact that she opened a conversation by asking all sorts of questions, such as where I was from, where I was going, and where I was staying. She said she was an American, living in Rome for a while. She was very friendly and slightly drunk or high, I thought. I noticed her naked arms were full of needle marks. *Yes, she must be a drug addict,* I thought. We talked some more, and then I excused myself and walked away. I saw her again the following day, this time at the Spanish Steps, where she approached me once more in a very friendly manner. After a brief conversation, I left and continued my tour alone. To this day, I don't know if those needle marks were real or made up to check if I was bringing contraband to America.

I should be honest. We all feared coming to America, particularly New York City. Those of us who were born and raised in other countries often heard very wild stories about the dangers of life in the United States. We read about street muggers, drug addicts, corrupt police, and dark and dangerous subways. It seems only sensational news is reported on, and travels across national borders. We were fed mostly negative news, such as catastrophic events, murders, and upheavals, as they happened in the United States.

The flight from Rome to New York City was frightening; air turbulence was not something I took lightly. Plus, the flight was the longest I had ever experienced, as we had to fly over the Atlantic. Pan Am's huge plane was practically empty. The response to my request for a pillow was a long throw from a beautiful flight attendant.

Friends of mine from METU who graduated with me and came to NY a year before to study at Pratt Institute met me at Kennedy Airport. We spent a few days together, seeing the sights. We visited MoMA, the Metropolitan Museum, the Whitney Museum, Forty-Second Street, Broadway, the Seagram Building (Mies Van der Rohe,

1958), the Lever House (Skidmore, Owings, and Merrill; 1952), the Guggenheim Museum (Frank Lloyd Wright, 1959), and Central Park (Olmstead, 1873). I remember also going to an Ella Fitzgerald concert with them at an outdoor theater in Harlem.

Then I traveled from New York to Lewisburg, Pennsylvania, a small college town along the Susquehanna River. I was required to take summer school classes at Bucknell Institute, for English Language and Orientation to American Culture. There were lots of students from Aramco (Saudi Arabian and American Oil Company). The campus buildings were relatively new, but the air-conditioning in one building smelled bad, like sharp human sweat. It was ironic that one of the student assistants instructed us to use deodorant, saying, "Americans do not like to smell body odor."

I was there for eight weeks. We all stayed in dormitories and ate in a university cafeteria. We went to language laboratory classes six hours a day. We learned to say *wader*, not *water*. We were given exercises to improve our pronunciation: "Betty Botter bought a bit of bitter butter." "what did Betty Botter bought?" "Betty Botter bought a bit of bitter butter." "Repeat after me. 'Betty Botter bought a bit of bitter butter.' Repeat after me …" And so it went. We also had a social dance class, as well as other "cultural" activities.

At the end of summer, I took a flight to Philadelphia. I was met by Yildirim Yavuz, another friend from METU. He'd just completed his master's degree at Penn. He hosted me for a few days and then arranged a place for me to stay. This was a house with two other Penn architecture students, Jim Auster and Phil Goiran. Phil had a Harley-Davidson. Cool.

The small brick house was located on the east side of the Schuylkill River on Naudain Street (fig. 1). Phil and Jim had arrived earlier and had taken the best bedrooms. My bedroom was the smallest and happened to be the coldest. It was on the second floor and had windows facing the north and west. From my windows, I could see the river in the distance and a small yard below (fig. 2). That first night, Jim cooked us a meal of spaghetti. After that, he regularly suggested ice cream for dinner. The house did not have heat. We could have started the coal heater on our own if we wanted to; however, none of us felt the effort of shoveling coal could be justified by the comfort of a single night, so we just wrapped ourselves in blankets to bear the cold, moist air.

Figure 1. A house in Naudain Street.

Figure 2. Backyard on my bicycle (1965).

Even though I had both master's and bachelor's degrees in architecture from METU, G. Holmes Perkins, Dean of the Graduate School of Fine Arts, who had been instrumental in establishing METU in Ankara, did not allow me to get into Louis Kahn's class. I was very disappointed.

So it was. I was not allowed to go to Lou's class for that first semester. I guess I had to be tested to see if I was good enough. Instead I registered for an undergraduate 401 design class for the fall semester. This turned out to be a valuable experience for me; I was expanding my English language skills, discovering architectural terminology, and getting accustomed to Penn's handsome campus and to this great American city.

Everything was new to me that autumn. We did not cook regular dinners at home. My roommates showed me places to get a meal, such as the cafeteria at Eero Saarinen's dorm on the campus, small shops along Forty-Second Street between Chestnut and Walnut, and a place called the Dirty Drug, located at the corner of Walnut and Thirty-Fourth streets. I seldom ate at the Dirty Drug. It smelled like alcohol, was noisy, and lived up to its name. Houston Hall and, later in the year, the law school cafeteria at Thirty-Fourth and Sansom Street became my lunch and dining halls of choice. I watched films by Pier Paolo Pasolini, Federico Fellini, and Michelangelo Antonioni at the Irvine Auditorium. I was fascinated by the Center City in downtown Philadelphia. The City Hall central area was always filled with groups of four to five people singing in harmony, like those in some subway stations in New York City.

This was a foreign land to me; everything was new and different. I learned to enjoy hamburgers, pizza, sliced bread, egg noodles, cookies, doughnuts, and coffee. I also learned to cook spaghetti, wash my own clothes at a neighborhood Laundromat, and select and buy food sold in cardboard boxes.

I was fascinated by the area along the Schuylkill River. Seeing two or three railroad bridges crossing the river at the same location puzzled me. They all looked well-built, but I could not understand why there should be more than one railroad bridge crossing the river at the same location. This was before I figured out that in America, companies and people do not share things. Sheer abundance! It was an interesting historical and economic fact, but it seemed like too much waste and useless production. Seeing so many different churches had the same impact on me. There didn't seem to be a sense of sharing for the common good. These things made me think that America was full of lonely people.

I know I was. Foreign students are very lonely during their first year in the United States. It takes almost a full year to establish a community around you—to make friends; to learn your way around; to find the post office, the library, and decent food shops; and most especially, to learn to interact with the values of the new society you are now part of. During those first few weeks in Philadelphia, I felt terribly alone. But then we received our telephone service in the house, and a week later, we bought a used black-and-white TV set for our living room. Soon afterward, I had enough money to buy a small portable tape recorder/player. These things helped little by little, and I was not lonely anymore. Now I could listen to Turkish music, songs I longed to hear, and I could make and receive telephone calls from friends living in New York. I could watch television and learn about life in the States. I was constantly learning new words and was able to better understand the social norms and values that were prevalent in America at that time. I called these the three *Ts* of civilization: telephone, television, and tape player. Those were magical.

I was in this brand-new world—in America, in Philadelphia—and everything was opening up for me. As the early days of my first year drew to a close, I realized I had begun to get my bearings. I had figured out what to do and how to live in this new environment, and I was happy. Still, I was a newcomer, a foreign student with limited income. I went to such places as the Army Navy surplus store, the stationery store, and the clothing stores, and I did a lot of window-shopping. What a lot of things you can buy in America! I guess it is human nature to acquire possessions that make you feel safe and comfortable and that remind you of home. Some of these material things made me feel more at ease in my new surroundings.

I was warned not to walk too far south on South Street, nor to go too far west, and certainly not north beyond Thirty-Eighth Street. I was warned not to walk north of Chestnut as well. I was told these areas were dangerous. Well, OK, I was also told I shouldn't walk on the South Street Bridge, but it was my only way to get to school. Philadelphia was an ideal city for bicycling, so I bought a used bicycle. This was my only means of transportation. I would ride my bicycle to school, so I was obeying the warning "not to walk on the South Bridge." It also made it a lot easier to come back home after a late-night study session at school.

* * *

The fall semester started during the first week of September 1965. The undergraduate architecture studio was located at the Old Fine Arts Building along Smith Walk, across from the Towne Engineering Building. Our project was the medical health center in West Philadelphia. Our studio critics were Professor Mario Romañach and another practicing architect. In an early discussion of one of my concept design diagrams, he said something like "Don't work with these forms. Do something like Turkish gardens with fountains and pools, and buildings with domes and arches." This was puzzling to me. I wanted to say, "No one makes buildings like that in Turkey anymore. I started my architectural education in 1959, and we learned mostly about Le Corbusier, Wright, Aalto, and Mies. Besides, I believe in universal values. Have you heard of minimalism, sir? About true forms, clean expressions, and honesty in material?" I felt insulted by his comment. *Do you think Turkish medical centers have only Turkish viruses and Turkish medicines?* I mused. Human bodies, whether they are Turks or Americans, are the same. Medical treatments for all human beings are the same, and medical knowledge is shared by all. Why should a medical center designed for West Philadelphia express sixteenth-century Ottoman gardens? However, I was thankful the semester ended successfully, as Professor Romañach recommended me to Dean Perkins, who allowed me to join Louis Kahn's class the following spring semester.

* * *

I had heard the Foreign Student Office at Penn was planning a trip to California for foreign students during the Christmas and New

Year break. The plan was to show foreign students Middle America. We were to visit St. Louis, Albuquerque, the Grand Canyon, Los Angeles, Hollywood, and Disneyland; see the Rose Bowl Parade and San Francisco (fig. 3); and then come back through Chicago. My friend from METU, Fikret Yegul, and I thought we had to see Chicago. The trip was sponsored by the First Presbyterian Church of Hollywood in Los Angeles. It cost thirty dollars for a round-trip ticket by Greyhound bus. The bus trip would take a week. We also learned we could travel the same distance by air for sixty dollars. But we could only stop at Chicago if we traveled by bus, so that was what we did.

Figure 3. Group of Penn students in San Francisco (December 1965). Author is standing at the back row, third from right.

I became very sentimental looking out of the bus window while riding through California. I was seeing telephone and electric lines with wooden posts, very much like those found in my country, near Ceyhan. I wrote it in my journal: "California, Salinas Valley—thinking of *The Grapes of Wrath*. Reminds me so much of my sweet home, Cukurova." In Los Angeles, the First Presbyterian Church of Hollywood found an American Armenian family to host Fikret and me for the night. We stayed there and had dinner with them. Our host didn't smile or talk much, but he said he was involved in construction work. *A dark home and an unhappy man,* I thought.

The next night, the church invited us to a dinner. We were given miniature Bibles in our own native language before being allowed to go sit at the dining table. That night, we all slept on cots in a high school gym. British Prime Minister Harold Wilson's son was rumored to be in our group, and they pointed out a tall blond fellow. *Good to know,* I thought. The next morning, they woke us up very early and took us to the Rose Bowl Parade. I wasn't too impressed. Afterward, we were taken to the Rose Bowl Game. I don't think any of us were familiar with American football, so that wasn't much fun either. It was more like a handball game than football.

Both Fikret and I were looking forward to our first visit to Chicago. We considered it to be an architectural mecca. We arrived in Chicago on a very cold, cold winter day. This must have been the last few days of December 1965. None of us had proper winter wear, such as coats, shoes, or hats. We walked around the Loop (downtown). We were very cold. We wanted to see Robie House (1906–1909), the outstanding piece of architecture by Frank Lloyd Wright (1867–1959). We did not know where it was located, but we had been told to take the train. And so we did. We walked and walked, asking for directions at every turn. Robie House (fig. 4) seemed miles away from the last train station. By the time we finally reached it, the sun had gone down, and it was bitterly cold. I was so tired and cold that I did not have a good impression of it. By then, there was nothing that could impress me besides a warm room. Unfortunately, the house was being restored, and we could not get in. We were freezing and in pain—it was the end of me—and we had to walk back to the station! I turned to Fikret and said, "Remember this, because it is not something I do very often, but here and now, I swear I will never come back to Chicago if I live!" And I meant it too. Still, today, having lived in Chicago for over thirty-five years, I remind myself frequently of the Turkish proverb "Buyuk lokma ye buyuk laf soyleme" ("Big promises will choke you").

We returned to Philadelphia a few days before the start of the spring semester.

Figure 4. Robie House (1906–1909), Chicago.

* * *

In my design classes at METU, I tried to make the most direct and simple buildings. I also tried to make the most distinguished designs of anyone else in my class. Our design teachers were all educated in the West, mostly graduates of US schools, and trained with the examples of Saarinen, Neutra, Aalto, Philip Johnson, Mies, Le Corbusier, Niemeyer, and even SOM. I don't remember hearing any talk about Kahn.

Modernism was very attractive to me. With ornamentation, I thought, one can hide a lot of odd relationships, sloppy proportions, and clumsy and oppressive details. But in modern design, there is no place to hide ugly joints and sloppy details. One should be very careful and attentive. Architectural space must be pure and clean. It should enclose or envelop life in its fullness. A building's ultimate success shows when it gives credit to life rather than to frozen ornamentations. The purity of a design does not allow for the cover-up of an odd placement or incoherent connection. Modern architecture is pure, and its success comes from its intolerance of anything that might be out of place or out of proportion. I cared about hearing inspiring ideas, new ways of making things, and new ways of shaking one's mind.

During my year of teaching design at METU, I asked our most respected, experienced professor, Fritz Janeba, about Lou Kahn. "He is a formalist," he said in his heavy Austrian accent. That was it. That was the end of the conversation. A formalist is one who imposes geometry and forces life to fit into it. Well, I would learn later that our well-respected professor Janeba did not bother to scratch the surface much!

My first introduction to Louis came through Vincent Scully's book *Louis I. Kahn* (1962); I was fascinated looking at the plans and photographs of the Trenton Baths (1954–1959)—four squares (fig. 5) touching at corners, with simple gable roofs; U-shaped walls enclosing private areas; and passages between rooms. The walls also acted as columns, the roof supported at the corners by simple concrete-block walls. But in its simplicity, I saw a spatial dynamism, a powerful response for its projected use. It was repetitive but ingenious in its conception, as if someone had taken its smallest denominator and brought it forth with a gigantic heroic and overwhelming confidence. *This act, this design,* I thought, *shows a great respect for the builder*. This project gave the builder an opportunity to show the mastery of his art and skills. It indicated clearly and powerfully what the architect had in mind—that the act of building is the art of architecture. To me, it was fair, it was justified, and it was right. It described the primary character of this modern age, period. This was a new way to design a building, the most honest, truthful, and confident architectural statement made for a brand-new world.

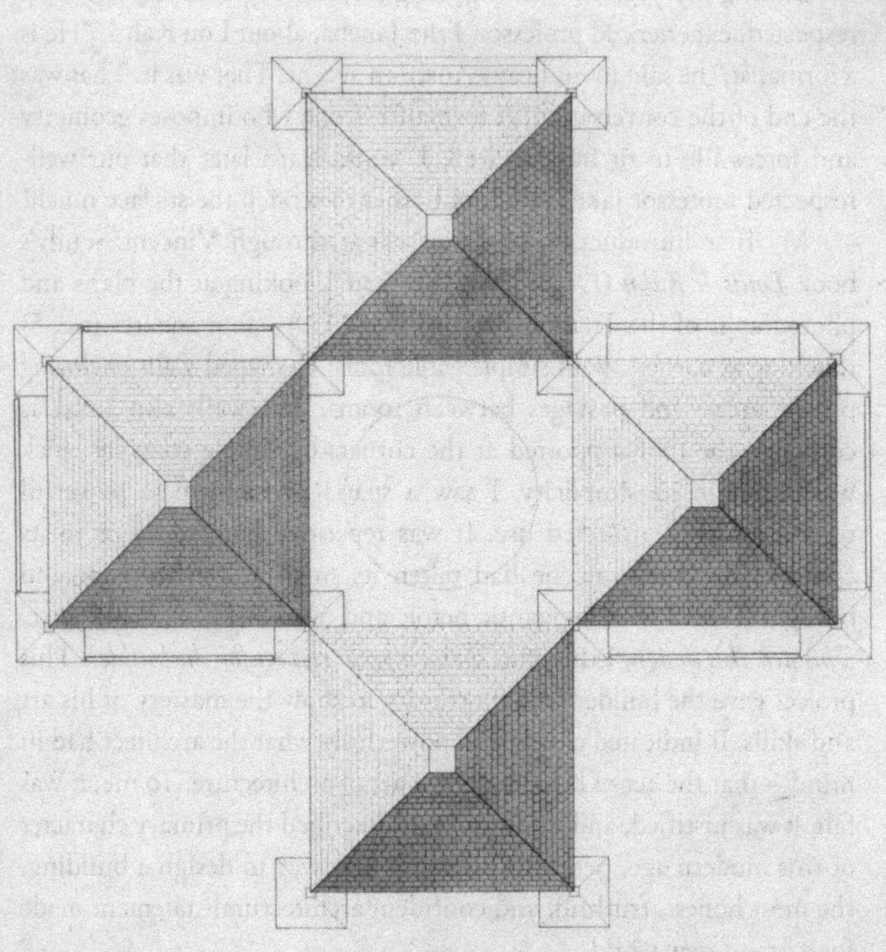

Figure 5. Trenton Plan.

PART 2

Graduate Studio at Penn I

And I would say the desire to be, to express, exists in the flowers, in the tree, in the microbe, in the crocodile, in man. Only we don't know how to fathom the conscientiousness of a rose. Maybe the consciousness of a tree is its feeling of its bending before the wind. I don't know. But I have a definite trust that everything that's living has a consciousness of same kind, be it as primitive. I only wish that the first really worthwhile discovery of science would be that it recognizes that the unmeasurable, you see, is what they are really fighting to understand, and the measurable is only a servant of the unmeasurable, that everything that man makes must be fundamentally unmeasurable.[2]

2 Kahn, Louis I., 2003, p. 237.

Louis Isadore Kahn was sixty-four years old when I first met him. He was a distinguished professor of architecture, teaching in the Master of Architecture studio at the University of Pennsylvania. He was at the top of his professional and academic achievements.

Philadelphia was damp and cold that January day. This was nothing new. It was the spring semester of the 1965–1966 academic year, my second semester at the university and my first in Kahn's class. Finally, that very afternoon, I would be able to sit in the same room and listen to this great architect.

I was not sure what to expect from all this. I was not yet fully aware of the status a master's degree from the University of Pennsylvania would provide. I was not familiar with the concept of an Ivy League school. But I was curious to discover how my career might develop, and I was excited by the prospect of being able to learn more about the important issues related to my profession, a profession I dearly loved.

Under the Tree

The upper studio (fig. 6) in the Furness Library Building (currently named the Fisher Fine Arts Library; designed by architect Frank Furness [1839–1912] in 1890) was where Kahn met with his graduate students. I was so proud to climb the long staircase (fig. 7) leading up to Louis Kahn's studio. This was a large U-shaped room. It had windows on curved walls. The straight wall (fig. 8) had a blackboard. There was a high curved ceiling and a narrow balcony on all sides. The room was full of drafting tables, with some display panels shoved in between.

Figure 6. Kahn's studio at the Furness Library (currently named the Fisher Fine Arts Library) at the University of Pennsylvania.

Figure 7. Stairs leading up to Kahn's studio.

Our class roster had twenty-five students for that semester: eleven students from the US, one from Canada, six from India, two from Thailand, two from England, one from Germany, and two from Turkey.

Figure 8. Author's sketch of the studio.

My friend and fellow graduate from METU, Fikret Yegul, was already in class. He was in his second semester with Louis, and it was my first. Seeing him there calmed my fear and excitement.

There was a large conference table, maybe 7×20 ft (2×6 m), along the blackboard wall and three comfortable chairs at the table. It was obvious those were reserved for professors. The students sat around the other three sides, on drafting stools. I sat on the outer fringes of the front row of students (fig. 8).

At two o'clock sharp, Kahn walked in. He was a short man with a friendly smile. He was wearing a black suit with a white shirt and a black bow tie. He had an apple in his hand. He sat in the middle chair at the long side of the large table. To Kahn's left sat Professor Le Ricolais,[3] a

[3] Robert Le Ricolais (1894–1977) was born in 1894 at La Roche-sur-Yon. His university studies in math and physics were curtailed by World War I, in which he was wounded and decorated, and were resumed after the war. As a practicing hydraulics engineer as well as a painter and poet, in 1935 he introduced the concept of corrugated stressed skins to the building industry and was awarded the Medal of the French Society of Civil Engineers. Then in 1940, his work on

French structural engineer, and to his right sat Professor Norman Rice.[4] This was to become a familiar pattern at the start of every class.

As everyone settled down and the room became quiet, Kahn allowed the silence to deepen. Then he looked all around at the students, and with a deep glance from side to side, he began the class with a thunderous voice and a stunning story.

> Schools began with a man under a tree,
> a man who did not know he was a teacher,
> discussing his realizations with a few others
> who did not know they were students.
> The students reflected on the exchanges between them and
> how good it was to be in the presence of this man.

---

three-dimensional network systems introduced many architects to the concept of space frames. After years of research and many patents and the 1962 Grand Prix of the Cercle d'Études Architecturales, he was well established as the father of space structures. In 1951, at fifty-seven, he came to America to conduct "experiments in structure" workshops at Illinois (Urbana), North Carolina, Harvard, Penn, and Michigan. In 1974, Le Ricolais succeeded Louis Kahn as the Paul Philippe Cret Professor at GSFA, holding the prestigious chair until his death in 1977. [Wikipedia]

4 Norman Rice was a classmate, colleague, and longtime friend of Louis I. Kahn. He was born in Philadelphia. He graduated from Central High School and studied architecture at the University of Pennsylvania with Kahn, where they both earned a B.Arch. degree in 1924. Mr. Rice worked with Kahn on the Sesquicentennial Exposition while both were in Monitor's office. In part because of the frustrations of the experience of watching city corruption in action, traveling widely throughout Europe, the Middle East, and North Africa, Rice landed in the Paris office of Le Corbusier and Pierre Jeanneret, working there with José Luis Sert, among others, between 1929 and 1930. Rice returned to Philadelphia in 1931, revitalized by his exposure to Le Corbusier, and joined the firm of Howe & Lescaze during the seminal PSFS Building project. In 1932, Rice established an independent practice in Center City, Philadelphia, which lasted for some fifty years. Rice returned to Penn as a teacher in 1963, continuing there until 1977; he co-taught a master's studio with Kahn and Robert Le Ricolais until Kahn's death in 1974. Rice also taught at the Philadelphia Museum School of Art in the 1950s. [Wikipedia]

Soon the needed spaces were erected,
and the first schools came into existence.

I was hearing things I had never heard before. Kahn was not talking about any of his architectural experiences, nor was he speaking about constructing buildings. This was so very different. His poetic story was a step into the minds of the students. *A quite unconventional way of teaching design*, I thought. Kahn was provoking his students to build their own mindset about architecture.

This description made a lot of sense to me. A place didn't have to be brick-and-mortar to be a school. Most of my education, I remembered, took place in buildings that were not built to be schools. Even during my years in architecture school at METU, while the academic campus was being built, our classes took place in service buildings designed as Laundromats, maintenance spaces, and mechanical rooms of yet unoccupied spaces of the new parliament building in Ankara. Our cafeteria was in a space designed to be a garage for maintenance trucks.

What I heard from Kahn lingered in my mind. I understood the message: one should ask "What makes a place a school?" before thinking about the needs program and the list of required spaces. Kahn's point was clear: the architect should look first to the essential purpose, the sense of coming together, the sense of being there, before making sketches and drawings to arrange areas, before thinking of seductive, fashionable, and artsy new spaces.

I realized, of course, modern schools would need not only classrooms but also playfields, gymnasiums, performance spaces, and laboratories. These are also part of education. But first and foremost, it is important that there will be people who want to learn and people who want to teach. And this all comes from the sharing of ideas and experiences.

I always thought that the character of a place is formed by the human activity. Now I was hearing that it is also the inclusion and overall sense of it, and that this sense may be present even before it becomes a building, a recognizable place. An architect must understand and acknowledge the basics of that dimension before attempting to design and make a place for it. The sense of being there and the spiritual meaning of coming together are the most significant factors in making a place.

"Schools began ..." *This is going back to the beginning,* I thought. *This must be the center of the undeniable characteristics of a place to learn. It is important to discover its essential principles, leading the architect to find its simple and pure means, forming the art of its essence.*

What a unique experience this was. The students' intense respect for Kahn was clear. He was sharing a genuine and serious reflection of his knowledge and experience with his students. *This relationship inspires learning,* I thought. *This is Louis Kahn. This is real.*

Our project was to design a junior high school in North Philadelphia.

* * *

I kept thinking how different it was from my previous education.

Our design classes always started with a given program or needs program or space program. This was a list of required or needed areas to be built for the project. (In some schools, this was called a brief, a friend reminded me recently.) And this would be the only reference to begin and develop design studies.

Then table crits would start. Instructors would begin talking about their experience with a similar project—on students' drafting tables. "If you make it this way" or "if you make it that way" type of suggestions would guide students. The instructor would try to impress students with his own talent and knowledge, explaining the functional aspects of each place in the program. The whole reference for students of architectural design would be the program and need through these studies.

I kept thinking how different Kahn's approach was from my earlier design education. Kahn was drawing out students' understanding along the way to help them realize the architectural setting.

Desire/Need

The introductory phase continued. Kahn talked to us all afternoon about subjects ranging from his beliefs and views on architecture to the character of spaces in a junior high school.

"Do we need music?" he started his talk that afternoon. "No, we don't. Did we need Mozart? Did we need Bach? No. The *need*, the need is out of circumstance. We desired music." He explained that a need is something prescribed, merely a list of quantities. But desire is more. It encompasses the need and goes beyond. An architect's work must not be merely a response to a prescribed list. An architect must understand desires and be able to make a place for desires. Desire is beyond measure and quantification.

"Remember the Pantheon" Kahn continued. "Did the Romans need a large room? No. It was a desire that brought the Pantheon into existence."

Figure 9. Pantheon, Rome.

I remembered the Pantheon (fig. 9). It is a huge circular room with a great dome. It has a unique spatial character. It is a temple for the gods of Rome, built by the emperor Hadrian (AD 126). A clear image was forming in my mind. Architects translate needs and desires into spatial realms, into physical and spatial experiences.

Richards

I heard that the only Kahn building on the Penn campus had recently been completed and that the construction wall around the building site had just been removed. I walked over to see it.

The Richards Medical Building (fig. 10) reflected the reality of architecture, I thought. This was not a photograph, not a drawing, not a lecture. I was seeing the real thing, not a black-and-white picture I had admired a year ago in Ankara. This was in full living color. It was full of light and life, a world of structural expression, of a prestressed, precast modular concrete system. The laboratories were stacked. Towers separated clean air from dirty air. Kahn was helping me define architecture, not in some class discussion, not in a talk, but right here in front of me.

Figure 10.
Richards Medical Building (1957–1965).

Struggle

At the end of the third or fourth class meeting, Kahn mentioned he needed help in his office to finish some of the work for his upcoming one-man exhibit at MoMA. I was excited by the prospect of seeing his office. The next Saturday, eight to ten of us met in his office at 1501 Walnut Street (figs. 79–82). I had never been in such an architectural office. It was a warm and accepting place.

It had a welcoming feeling; it looked like an architectural design studio/classroom. There were large drafting tables, lots of reference drawings spread around, model studies on tables, and lots of daylight. I felt privileged to see Kahn's work during its design stage in his own office.

I became part of the team working on the model of the assembly hall (fig. 11). "The Capital of East Pakistan, Dacca" was its project name (as it was spelled) in the office.

The model was not complete, but I could see its powerful presence. It seemed it was sculpted from a massive eight-sided block. It was full of geometric cutouts for daylight along the perimeter wall.

Figure 11. Top view of the assembly hall model I worked on.

My task was to cut out the complicated roof shape and fix it on top of the already built side walls. I wondered why it was not made from thin gray chipboard rather than white Strathmore board, in order to express its exceptional character. The walls were lightly scored with sharp blades, and talc powder was applied on scored lines indicating horizontal concrete-poured joints with marble.

Kahn was circling around, saying "Thank you, thank you" to us, while we were trying to complete the model. It was hard to believe he was thanking us. As for me, I was thrilled to be in his office and that we were asked to come and help finish the presentation models for the MoMA exhibit. And we were getting paid!

I was working alone later that night, trying to complete some miscellaneous parts of the model. Kahn came walking around the model, looking at it from various angles, with his hand on his lips. Then he turned to me. "Everyone wants to see this," he said as he pointed to the model. "But I want to show them my struggle. No one is interested in that."

I thought about this later. What did he mean by "struggle"? Could design be a struggle for Kahn? Could that be because he was so talented that he must have had many design options available with such a creative mind? Among so many options, he needed to choose one. Was that why he took a lot of time to reach his final scheme, and why he felt the urge to question his choice and explain his thinking, not only in class but also in his public talks —not so much what he had done but how he had reached his conclusions and how he had conceived the ultimate design? Kahn's poetic writings and the talks he has given over the years at various schools and professional institutions attest to this. Could this be his struggle?

Around the Table

His talks in class were poetic and abstract. I thought students were also trying too hard to impress him by presenting their concepts in a way that was philosophical and abstract, and that they were pretending hard to be poetic and mystical. It made me wonder how those abstract/

philosophical thoughts could translate into architectural forms or if they could be represented as architectural formats.

The introductory phase of the project continued in the studio. Students sitting around the big table presented their ideas about their concepts. These were mostly on yellow tracing paper. To me, they all just looked like words, lines, and bubbles. Kahn would patiently listen and carefully examine sketches and be very serious in responding to them. He was careful not to say anything negative. In those conversations, I noticed there was some significant advice or some examples from his life, such as "I grew up when horses were pedestrians." Or he would complete his review by saying "Architecture must not be concerned with expressing the limits of technology." Technology should not be the deciding influence for the art of place-making. Technical excellence alone is not enough. He was providing students with opportunities to make the connections, and there was always a lot more in what he did not say.

Painted Stripes

In the studio, one could learn so much about the nature of the project by just listening to Kahn in these discussions. I kept my attention mostly on his odd comments. Some reminded me of an event from my past, with interconnected thoughts and images.

In the middle of his talks, he would stop and say something like "A striped painted horse is not a zebra." It made me wonder if he meant "Deal with the inherent nature of something before dealing with their appearance" or "Be careful to realize a genuine act, as opposed to a pretentious one" or "Keep your eyes open to see a deeper understanding of the essence rather than of the shallow and stylistic gesture."

I found myself repeating this phrase frequently to my friends, using it to mean "Simple appropriateness is more important than the shallow architectural thrills or seductive shapes."

No Typical Site Analysis

There was no pressure to do a typical site analysis for our current school project. This was usually a must in any project in most schools; there was pressure to visit the project site. I realized later that this was consistent with Kahn's primary interest of studying the inner workings of a place first and foremost.

As the old habit still lingered in me, I visited the school site. It was a wide-open area. There was a low wall all around the site, with a few houses at the edge. It was a slightly sloped site, with few large trees. *Not much influence on the design,* I thought.

Life Stories

He would frequently refer to life stories. "The right thing done badly is greater than the wrong thing done well." I was fascinated by such comments. To me, these represented Kahn's way of life and way of seeing architecture. Those reverberated and provoked considerable thought and reflection in me. I have no doubt that this was exactly what Kahn had intended.

The Piano

His love for Philadelphia was obvious. He referred to it as a great place for a child to grow and figure out what to become. He loved music. At home, his room was so small that there was not enough space for a bed and his piano, so he slept on the piano.

He used to earn income by playing piano for silent movies, and he had to run from one theater to the other to catch the show times. Those times—"when horses were pedestrian," he would add—delivered big changes over his lifetime. Horse-drawn streetcars must have been common during his childhood. Horses are carried in vehicles now.

Maquette

I was working hard to show something that would receive his comment. Our formal studio meetings with him were on Monday, Wednesday, and Friday afternoons. Tuesday and Thursday afternoons were for student studies. Other students seemed familiar with Lou's expectations and presented their architectural concepts and listened to his comments about essential concerns. This was their third project with Louis. It was my first.

I decided to build a maquette (a small preliminary model of a building) rather than present a drawing, for two reasons. First, I myself wanted to see and understand my concept in its totality. A model shows the architectural concept more clearly than a drawing. The second reason was my discomfort with the English language. I did not want to depend on words to explain my project. I felt I should not depend on the spoken language so much in words. I practiced this in all my previous years in METU, where the academic language was English. Even in early stages of study, I presented my studies as maquettes rather than sketches.

In my maquette (concept model), I brought certain groups of activities together. They would share the same floor level and would be easily connected to one another. A central garden captured their being "together." The students' arrival area, the area for buses and cars, an open-air theater, the administrative offices, a gymnasium, and the parking areas would be located on the ground level. Spaces for academic activities, like classrooms and laboratories, would be one level aboveground. This would provide students with a pleasant view of the city. The land would remain in natural form. There would be large ramps connecting the classroom level to the garden. I thought students would enjoy coming to a school like this. I knew I would.

It was our third or fourth class meeting. Most of the students had already presented their ideas about their projects. I had my maquette on my lap. Perhaps I was the only student who had brought such an insanely simple maquette (made of four pieces of wood, some glue and Plasticine) to present to Kahn in his graduate class. There were no others left to present in class. I had to go through with it. With a tremble, I moved my stool between the front-row students. I put my maquette (fig. 12) on the table and slowly pushed it toward Kahn.

Figure 12. Maquette (January 1966).

1. Classrooms
2. Administration
3. Labs
4. Amphitheater
5. Ramps
6. Girls' gym
7. Boys' gym

In my shaky voice and simple English, I explained that the classrooms were around a large square open-to-sky courtyard, with large ramps leading to the classrooms from the central garden. The land moved freely underneath the classrooms. The auditorium and the gymnasium were all at grade level. Ramps provided access to the sports fields. The courtyard was the recreational garden and outlined the academic world.

I did not have much more to say. A big silence followed. Kahn was looking deep into my eyes. Behind his thick eyeglasses, I could see his eyes had widened. I wondered if I had said something wrong. I was glad that it was over, that I had done my presentation. Everyone was quiet. Then Kahn spoke. He said something about certain aspects of my presentation that he did not agree with. It was hard to understand him; maybe he was commenting about raising the classrooms above the ground level and making them float in air. Nonetheless, I nodded in agreement. Then a thunderous phrase came from him. "But I admire your sense of architecture." Now this I understood. It was very clear.

It was 5:00 p.m., the end of the class. I stayed frozen for a few seconds. I looked at my maquette again, as if searching for a meaning in it. I was elated and did not know what to think or say. I lowered my eyes. I pulled my maquette toward me. I was happy; it was a good comment from Kahn. It was the end of class. Kahn pulled his chair back, and students followed, pulling away from the edge of the table. "This is good," I whispered to myself. "This must be good, isn't it?" Kahn looked toward me. I repeated his words in my head.

I collected my stuff, put it away, and walked out. Then I ran home to Naudain Street and wrote it all down in my diary. I was in Louis Kahn's class. I was in the graduate school of architecture at the University of Pennsylvania.

Poetry

Poetic expressions and metaphors were always present in Kahn's talks. These expressions were full of meaning for me. He talked in short phrases, like reading poetry. Some of those phrases were simple and easy to understand; at other times, the words would crush you.

In my family, anecdotes, stories, advice, and recommendations were often expressed as poetry or proverbs. This is not only true of my family; I think it is true of Turkish culture in general, which uses proverbs and metaphors in daily speech to convey a richer meaning. Maybe this is another reason Kahn's words resonated with me. Sometimes what one does not say makes a better point.

I loved poetry and abstract ideas. His stories and his talks were fascinating. They inspired deeper awareness in me, creating a life of their own. Sometimes, seemingly unconnected and apparently illogical phrases stayed with me longer. Words building on words brought out a sparkling sense, and they kept showing their brilliance and relevance even years later.

Kahn used the term *timeless* frequently. He did not feel the need to explain it. He probably thought the word defined and explained itself. *Timeless* means "to be above and beyond cultural values, as well as the constraints of time and place." To be timeless is to be beyond geographic or regional limits, beyond consideration of age. I had not heard this term before. A new concept was installed in my thinking. *Timeless* referred to qualities that would stand the test of time, those essential characteristics that are defined through decades and that still contribute to life. *Timeless* is the best way to qualify a piece of art, a statement, or an expression.

I looked at these poetic statements as a kind of foundation for architectural thinking. I believe these were the ones he himself was guided by. They provide the framework; they are not something to walk away from, but something to walk toward. They were all tied to the importance of human values, human life and relationships, and a sense of putting oneself in others' shoes.

All throughout my career, both in the professional and the academic world, some of these expressions would creep up in friendly or sometimes hostile discussions. What is "structure is the maker of light"? Or what is "asking a brick"? Or "Why did Kahn use short phrases, and why was he so poetic?" These poetic statements were steps into the students' minds. Kahn was using an unconventional teaching method. He was provoking students to think of architecture. My answer was that I liked it. I was ready to hear some poetry, some abstract ideas. Isn't it like the story of Eve giving an apple to Adam? There was no apple, nor was there a snake. They were symbols of their realization of their togetherness as a couple; it was not about a boy eating a girl's apple. Kahn's anecdotes, stories, and poetry were symbols to spark thinking about architecture.

Stradivarius

"Is the auditorium a Stradivarius?" he asked the class one afternoon. "An auditorium wants to be a violin, that it may be keyed to Bach or Bartók." Kahn was explaining the "what it wants to be" concept. An auditorium should be an acoustically perfect place for human performance, so that it may be tuned to the purity and beauty of the human voice, from a whisper to a cry, with complete integrity and its detailing, not just rows of seats.

By saying "the concert hall wants to be a Stradivarius," Kahn added another mystic, emotional, and meaningful dimension to its architectural realization, to its form, to its existence, to its architecture, and to its meaning.

Belief

Belief, *order*, *agreement*, *aura of commonness*, and *existence will* were frequently used terms in his discussions. He'd use these without a moment of doubt, with full confidence and a solid sense of certainty, as if everyone would know what was meant. But what is belief? How can one know, learn, or develop belief? Architecture schools teach mostly construction knowledge. Curricula are filled with structure, history, mechanical equipment, methods of construction, and materials. Teachers would describe architecture through decorations, historic styles, building materials, construction methods, 3D renderings, or doctored photographs published in magazines - not through their way of life, generated experiences, or any spatial characteristics. Not as settings for living. But for me, Kahn's most intriguing term was *existence will*. In English, it sounded to me like its character is brought up by its existence or its meaning is created by being what it is. My translation of it into Turkish is "varolusunun getirdigi karekter, yarattigi anlam."

Review around the Table

There were two sessions in every afternoon meeting. The first session was from 2:00 to 3:15 p.m. Kahn would talk about the general realm of architecture. Professor Rice or Professor Ricolais would rarely make any comment. I never heard them partake in the design discussions. I always wondered why they were there. On one occasion, Rice distributed the project needs program (brief), with schedules, due dates, jury dates, etc. I heard Kahn did not give grades to his students; Rice did that. The story that went around the class was that Rice was Kahn's classmate in Penn's architecture school and was selected to be sent to France to study with Le Corbusier, although Kahn was the one who was better in design. It was a typical administrative decision in academia; a similar thing had also happened to me.

At 3:15 p.m., the class would have a break for about fifteen minutes. Then the same arrangement would begin again and continue until 5:00 p.m. This time, students would ask questions in relation to the subjects discussed in the previous session, and discussion would continue.

The projects were given in class as a base for discussing architecture, to delve into the essential themes of design. After a project was issued, discussions turned into idea/concept-generating sessions. Some students would talk about ideas; some would present loose pencil sketches. The term *design* was not used much; it was *realization* in Kahn's terminology. Loose sketches, or sketches scattered with words on tracing paper, would be presented around the table. These always seemed too abstract, almost to the absurd, and too meaningless to me. I could not see any architectural sense in their words and sketches. There was no pressure to present a complete set of drawings or any particular scale. Everyone was free to choose their own expressive style.

Review on Boards

I was hesitant to present any new scheme that could erase my first good impression. I was not rushing to present my next proposal.

Figure 13. Class discussion around a typical display panel. Kahn is in the lower middle section of the photo (1966).

From left: Unidentified person, Rice, Kahn, Ricolais, unidentified person, Michael Bednar, unidentified person, Yukio Sano, Cengiz Yetken, unidentified person.

At the fourth or fifth class meeting, the students started to present their work with scale drawings pinned up on studio panels. All three professors moved from panel to panel (fig. 18), listening to the students' explanations and prompting students with references, directing them to discoveries. The whole class followed these exchanges and moved from project to project. Kahn defined architectural elements in the most understandable and simple terms. He would point out people's actions in such places.

He interacted with each student, patiently listening, examining drawings and sketches, questioning assumptions, and explaining conflicts. Conversation would flourish between the students and the master. Everyone learned from everybody else's experience. Principles became clearer using this dynamic process, reviewing spatial composition and realizing how lives would be lived within those spaces. Every line, every space would be read back to the student, and what it meant would be explained. Kahn would explain architectural space as a human experience. He would give examples and refer to human stories or reactions that might take place in each setting. He would not use big, obscure philosophical terms or complicated definitions. There was a keen sense of experience, knowledge, and observation in his statements.

He would speak softly but firmly. Solid ideas were voiced with conviction and authority. There would be no hesitation. Sometimes a controversial comment would slip through his lips, like the one about the David Smith sculptures exhibited in front of the Furness building. "Architects throw away things like that every day," he said, noting his displeasure with them. I agreed with him in silence.

Figure 14. Project review in studio.

Do Not Copy Kahn

Students who did sharp-angled buildings like Kahn's recently published forty-five-degree chamfered corners did not receive any sympathy from him. Any superficial or stylistic gestures, such as tilting walls, ceilings, or windows that were long on shock value but short on substance, also received his wrath. Kahn's message was clear: architecture is not shape-making. Understand what makes them be what they are. Do not copy Kahn.

A Symphony

"Here are the violins." I saw Lou point to a certain part of a student's plan. Making violin sounds, he moved his arms. "Then an oboe enters," he exclaimed, making a different sound and pointing out a side segment of the plan. Showing the row of rooms, he started pounding—"bum, bum, bum"—and pointed to the columns in the structural grid. Harmony, timing, and emotions came together. An architectural studio critique had turned into a music lesson. This kind of criticism could only have come from someone with a great understanding of music. Kahn was examining the plan as if he was looking at a musical score. He was describing a musical composition. Kahn was a conductor of an orchestra. He was hearing every instrument and following every move. He was teaching us to have a conversation with our drawings, to listen to the spaces we bring to life. He was telling us that every instrument has a role to play. Every note is essential; every part is important in the composition. Nothing is less or more important than the next one.

I was aware of the relation between composing music and designing, but it was not so clear to me in architecture. I did not think how close the acts of composing music and composing places were. *There must be a lot to learn from music,* I thought. A designer must have a strong understanding, awareness, and appreciation of music. Kahn wanted architects to be composers.

Corridor

"Not corridor," he would say whenever someone used the word *corridor*. "A corridor is just a narrow and meaningless space," he explained, raising his voice. "These should be galleries." A rich life takes place in these connecting spaces. These are the primary connectors. These spaces are full of life; everyone passes through them. Students learn more there than in classrooms. Those are places of interaction, and they are places of learning.

"No double-loaded corridor," he added. Kahn despised the term and made fun of it. "What does *double-loaded* mean?" He explained that galleries must be open to the garden, with classrooms on the other side. Students must be able to see outside, to connect to the city, to know the time of day, to figure out the weather outside. He criticized the current fashionable(!) concept of a windowless school. How could anybody think of such a stupid idea?

To and Through

Tuesday and Thursday afternoon studio classes were free for students to study on their own. Those days and evenings were very enjoyable. My fellow students and I would visit each other's work and repeat Kahn's peppered comments. During the many late nights and weekends working in the studio, we would listen to the peace and protest songs of Pete Seeger, Phil Ochs, Joan Baez, and Bob Dylan.

One night, a classmate, Miguel Angel Roca, pointed at one room in my plan and jokingly asked, "Is this a 'to' place or a 'through' place?" I had not thought about architectural spaces defined like that before. This was something exciting, and it opened up a new way of thinking for me.

I identified "to" places as spaces along the paths of "through" spaces. That strength of spatial realm lies in the to/through concept. In other words, it makes the destination places (which are "to" places) properly relate to one another. This creates the essential architectural character in any spatial composition.

Some identify architecture by its "to" spaces, paying too much attention to how the individual rooms are made, shaped, or ornamented, without giving much attention to how such rooms are interconnected. My belief and experience dictate that primary attention should be given to "through" spaces. One's primary efforts in architectural design should be focused on how the interconnecting spaces are to be made. How well is the building integrated to its life setting? How clear is it to navigate through the building? Are they meaningful, enjoyable, and inspiring?

The essential architectural character comes from the "through" spaces, I thought. It became clear to me that all great works of architecture, such as the Pantheon, Guggenheim, Kimbell, Unity Temple, Ronchamp, and Farnsworth, are based on this architectural understanding. Kahn's *street* and *room* definitions also related to this. I remembered all those bubble diagrams we used to make in my earlier education. Bubbles indicated "to" (destinations), and thin lines indicated "through" (interconnecting) spaces. Thin lines eventually became corridors. At that level, we were not sufficiently equipped nor knowledgeable or experienced enough to understand that the shared characteristics that give architectural distinction are not through rooms but through streets. However, also keep Kahn's words in mind: "A street is a community room" and "A street is not a road; a street is a human agreement."

Don't Ask Komendant

There were a few instances when Kahn was negative about student work. Once, a student was insistent on his own correctness, rejecting Kahn's comments, saying that Kahn did not understand his culture and that people in his country (South America) would love it the way he insisted. Kahn responded, "We have that here too. We call it bad architecture."

In another instance, he pointed to the lack of structural indication in a student's plan. "Structure brings an order to your plan," he said and reminded him an architect must make structural design decisions. With a smile, he added, "Don't ask Komendant. He thinks everything is possible."

"I hear your reasoning," Kahn said after one student's explanation. "But you see, this is *ar-chee-te-chure* and not,"—he rounded up the sound—"*arc-he-tek-chure*." He meant the project wasn't quite at the level it should be. His mispronouncing the word *architecture* demonstrated a misunderstanding of it on the student's part.

Sound

I was struggling to come up with the design concept for our junior high school project. I did not know much about life in a junior high school in America. The junior high I attended in Adana was a single two-story building with only six classrooms (fig. 20). It was built as a residence for a cotton factory owner around the turn of the century and was used as a single-family residence (as a wedding gift to his only daughter) for a long time.

Figure 15.

Adana Istiklal Orta Okulu. I attended between 1951 and 1954. It is still used as a junior high school.

Our given building program was very detailed and had many parts besides classrooms; there was a gymnasium, a theater, a library, and laboratories. I had no clear concept of how or where to start.

Describing life in school, Kahn pointed out the noise generated by students during recess. He summarized *two disciplines* that generate two different kinds of noise. One is where the teacher's presence is strongly felt. He called this *classroom discipline*. The other is *gym discipline*, where the teacher's presence is not as strong, like around the gymnasium, auditorium, music studios, and art classrooms. I held on to this idea and wanted to see if this could be brought into architecture and if it could lead me to acceptable design work.

Intersections

I prepared a hardline drawing of a floor plan of a junior high school in scale, complete with all the areas in the given needs program, for my first review and placed it on one of the class presentation boards.

That afternoon, Kahn came directly to my board. He looked at my plan, and a few seconds later, he said, "This is not a corner." It was where two rows of classrooms intersected at 90° (fig. 19A). The class was all around us. I looked at it again, and I was not sure what he meant. I was not expecting such a comment. I was expecting something more general and maybe about its architectural composition.

I looked at my plan again. Did Kahn mean there was no axial symmetry? Did he mean the corner was lopsided? The stairs were on one side, and the toilets were grouped on the other. *This is just a corner,* I thought. There were other important areas in my plan I wanted him to comment on.

"This is not a corner." *What does he mean? Why isn't it a corner?* I was frozen. Kahn walked away. "This is not good," I mumbled to myself.

That night was hard for me. I kept asking myself the same questions. *Why is it not a corner? How can a corner be? What makes a corner? Two segments of equal value coming together? What is the nature of coming together? Is it a test about the geometry of the intersection of two equal parts?*

I spent Friday night, Saturday, and Sunday thinking nothing else but *Corner.* Friends, on seeing my hard face, worriedly kept asking, "What are you thinking about?" For the next three days, my answer was the same: "Corner."

Finally, late Sunday night, I decided I had to do something for Monday's class. Kahn must have been referring to the continuation of each wing over the midpoint they intersected. One side should not be favored over the other (fig. 19A). A corner must be the resolution of their common enterprise (fig. 19B). A corner must indicate the recognition of each side, their individual character, while acknowledging the act of their coming together.

For Monday's presentation, I made a drawing of my new "corner" (fig. 19C). I was not sure, but at least this was going to clarify if I understood Kahn's comment or not.

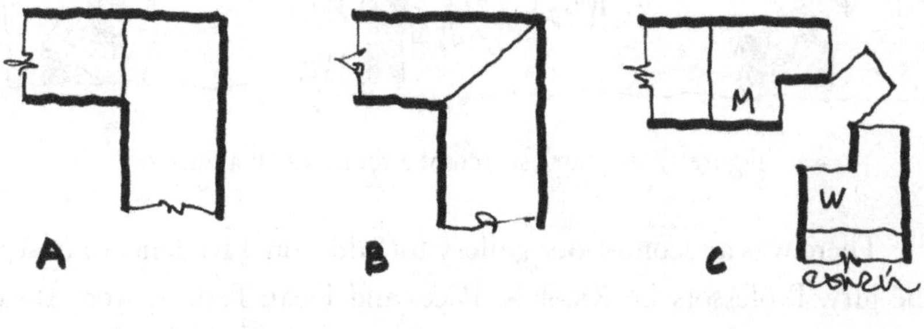

Figure 16

Upon entering the studio on Monday afternoon, Kahn came directly to my panel. He looked carefully at my drawing. "Now," he said, "this is a corner."

Final Review

Graduate school final juries were quite formal. They took place at the front hall of the Old Fine Arts Building on Smith Walk (currently Hayden Hall). This building also housed the undergraduate architecture school. The front hall was a two-story-high space designed specifically for exhibitions and jury presentations (fig. 17).

Figure 17. Author's sketch of a room for final juries.

There was a second-floor gallery for additional students to observe the jury. Professors Le Ricolais, Rice, and Dean Perkins were always present in graduate juries. In addition, Kahn might invite one more faculty member, who would join as a visiting faculty. Kahn would guide the jury and allow only important points into the discussion. No one would say anything before Kahn would comment on a project. No one would question or make a judgment for fear of exposing their own limited understanding of architectural principles. Students would present their projects in alphabetical order.

I was the last one to present, because of my last name. I explained my project with simple sentences—arrival sequence, parts of the plan, two courtyards, stairs. The courtyards were open, clear of any architectural articulations. These areas were the students' playground, their place to come together, their place to be together, their neighborhood, their garden.

There may be trees and hills. I would figure out its character after observing school life, their plays, their games, and their desires for recess periods.

Two open stairways cascaded down from the third floor to the ground floor where the two courtyards join. The stairs would start narrow at the top level and become wider at the middle level and even wider from the second level to the ground. I responded to all the space needs and area requirements stated in the program. Every section received plenty of daylight (fig. 18).

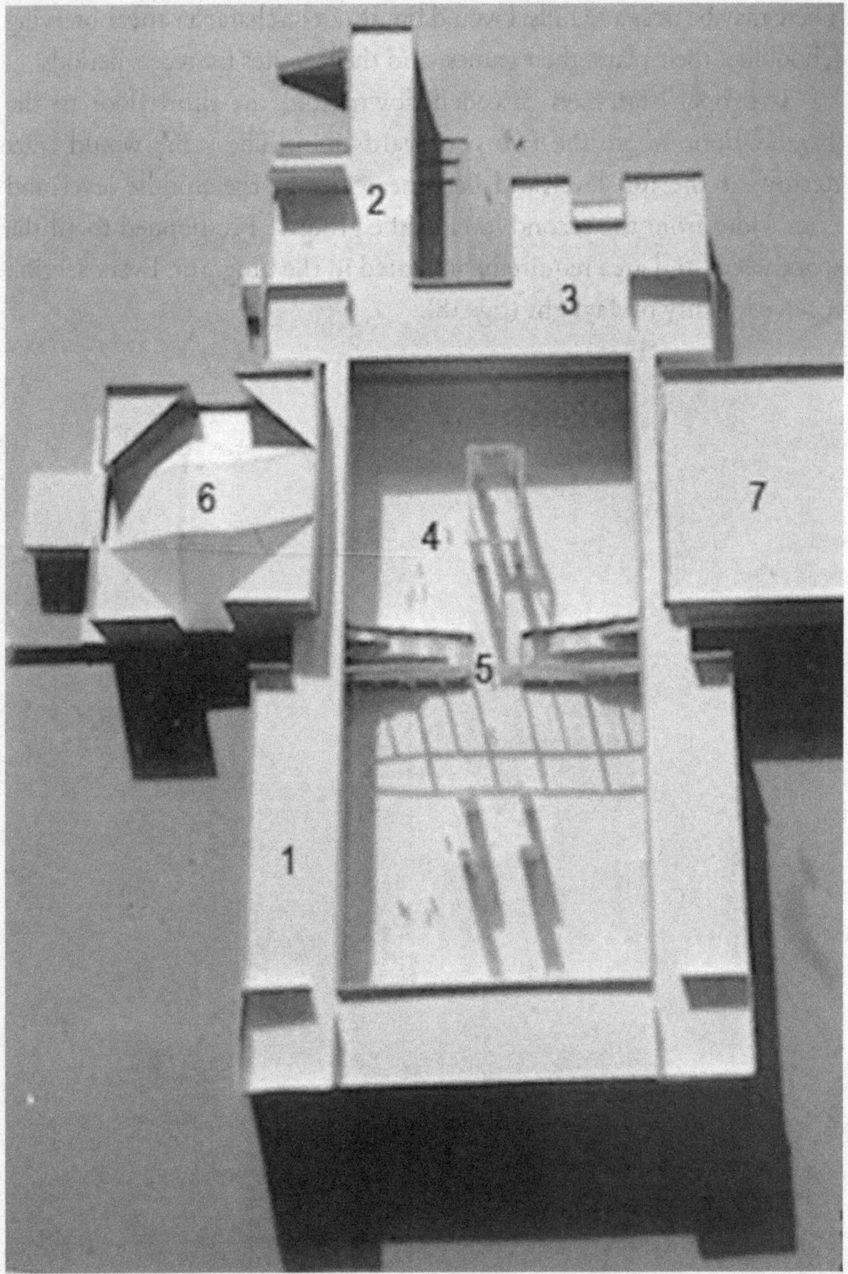

Figure 18. Final scale model of junior high school.

1. Classrooms
2. Administration

3. Cafeteria
4. Courtyards
5. Stairs
6. Auditorium
7. Gymnasium

First, Rice said something like "Beautiful articulation around the perimeter of the building." Everybody else remained quiet as they examined my model. I thought they were waiting for Kahn to say something. Finally, Kahn, turning to Dean Perkins, said, "Look, ingenious stairs." Dean Perkins agreed. They all smiled. And that was the end of the jury.

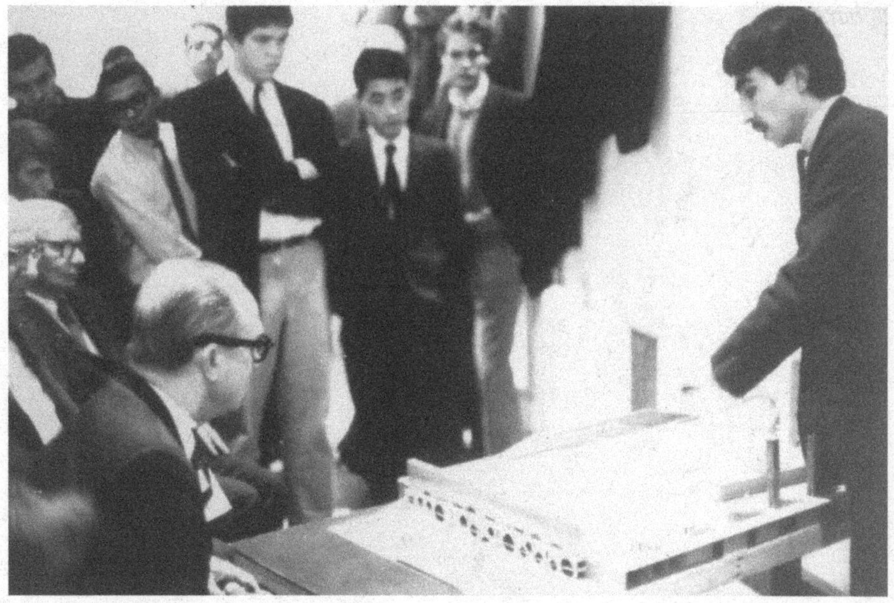

Figure 19. Yetken presenting his project at a final review (December 1966).

Seated, from left to right: Norman Rice, Louis Kahn, and August Komendant.

Back row: Craig Kuhner, Vincent Rivera, Gosh Summit, Peter Dominick, Yukio Sano, Jim (roommate).

Collecting my project, I was thinking that I was not happy with my work. Mine was a building done just for the building program. It did not have any architectural sense. It was just an organized construction, if that. It did not have any architectural soul. It was not an inspiring place to come to learn. It did not nourish learning, understanding, or even playing. It did not have any particular character that made this building a place to come to learn. It was just a grouping of classrooms, labs, offices, etc. It did not indicate their reason to be together or even a reason to be in the same spatial organization.

I should have explained the courtyard garden in more detail. *A lesson learned,* I thought. *The solution came to you easy, which could not have been the best answer. Pay attention. Watch out for the striped painted horses.*

PART 3

Graduate Studio at Penn II

I wish to distinguish between design and form and I cannot help but to start feeling wonder and, as they say, wonder is the beginning of knowledge and knowledge seems to be unsatisfied without the sense of order. Knowledge is almost worthless without a sense of order. The sense of order or the sense of harmony of systems in physical nature comes to realization in a form, and form has no shape or dimension. It is a realization of the difference between one thing and another, the inseparable parts of something. … Therefore, what to do is form, it lies, it lies in form; how to do it is design. Often, we turn to design somewhat too quickly, because we have no information as to the form.[5]

5 Kahn, Louis I., 2003, p. 139.

Project Introduction

FDR Memorial

Figure 20. The Tidal Basin, cherry trees, and the Washington Monument in the distance in DC.

Our project was a memorial for the thirty-second president of the United States from 1933 to 1945, Franklin Delano Roosevelt (1882–1945). The project site was the land between the Potomac River and the Tidal Basin in Washington, DC. The site was open at the time. (The current memorial by Lawrence Halprin had not been commissioned or built yet.) Maps and photographs were provided to the class. Kahn talked about the cherry trees (planted in 1912) at the site, which became the major attraction around the Tidal Basin in later years.

I had never been to Washington and was not familiar with FDR. There was a lot of talk about the beauty of the cherry trees on the site. I do not remember seeing a live cherry tree up to that time, just photos. I listened to descriptions of how people in DC enjoyed them every year, beginning in mid-March and throughout the early weeks of April. The trees were gifts from Japan before the Second World War. *How civilized, sweet, and delightful,* I remember thinking. The site looked flat in photographs; there were no rolling hills to establish a backdrop for the cherry trees (fig. 20).

My knowledge about the history of the United States was limited. In public schools in Turkey, particularly during my student years, we primarily studied the history of Seljuk and Ottoman Turks (from the sixth century to the 1923 War of Independence). The Seljuk and Ottoman history is so vast and detailed that the school years always ended before we could reach the history of the New World.

Fountain

I don't recall what prompted Kahn to tell this story. It was at the beginning of the class. He turned to Rice and asked if he had told the story before. "No, not to this class," Rice answered. "It is an old Jewish story," Kahn said, and with a smile, he turned to the class.

> Once upon a time, there was a bright young man, a thoughtful and meditative man. He crystallized his questions into a simple one: What is life? His friends couldn't answer this. After a while, a trusted friend said he had heard of a wise old man living in a faraway land who could answer this question.

The young man traveled to this faraway land and found the wise old man. "I have a question," he said.

"What is it, my son?"

The young man answered, "What is life?"

The old man sighed deeply. "Oh, I cannot answer this question," he said, "but I know one who could. He lives on the other side of high mountains. He is wiser than me."

So the young man walked and walked to find this wise old man, and upon finding him, he asked his question. "What is life?"

The old man looked up, looked around, took a deep breath, and said, "Oh, what is life? This is not easy to answer. But I know one who would know the answer to your question. He is a lot wiser than me. He lives across the blue sea and on top of a high mountain. Go and ask him."

The young man walked for days, weeks, and months. He sailed and rode, and finally, he found the wise old man and asked his question. "What is life?"

The old man rubbed his long white beard, looked deep into his face in a wondering pose, and took a long and deep breath. He said, "What is life?" He repeated it. "What is life? Life. Life. Life." He stayed silent for a while. "Life," he said. "Life is a fountain."

The young man was shocked. "What?" he yelled, with an unbelieving look. "A fountain?" He gave the old man a hard stare.

"Well," the old man calmly replied, "then it is not a fountain."

There was silence in the studio. Kahn was quiet; he did not say any more. He was looking at the students' faces. I could imagine the smiles in their eyes and them smiling and turning to one another behind me. What? This is about human nature, isn't it? Isn't this about being human?

Around the Table

Every Monday, Wednesday, and Friday, the students would gather around a large table, and Kahn would walk in and sit at the table. With a deep glance from side to side as everyone quieted, Kahn would start with a thundering sentence like "Light is the maker of structure" or "Architecture does not exist"[6] or "Science is a servant of art." Then he might stand and draw on the blackboard and continue with his talk.

Mozart in Greece

Near the end of his discussion in class one afternoon, in a crisp and clear voice (as if there was no need to say more), he said, "Many Mozarts died in early Greece." I had a funny image of a man in a toga walking along a marble street in the ancient city of Ephesus (in Western Turkey), mumbling tunes. I thought he meant that talent requires nurturing and development at the appropriate time and place to grow. It brought

---

6 A similar line has been published in many publications. "There is no such thing as architecture."
"Architecture has no physical presence. You can't touch it. You can touch a work of architecture but not architecture itself. When a work of architecture touches the spirit of architecture, it becomes part of the treasury of architecture. Only a small percent of buildings are architecture." (Louis Kahn, quote from *The Furnishings Daily*, New York, NY, 3/5/68)

a smile to my face, thinking how odd and unlikely the circumstances were that had brought me to Philadelphia and to Kahn's class.

Silence and Light

"Architecture is born between silence and light," he said on another afternoon. "Light is the giver of all presences, and silence is what one feels near the pyramids." This had the greatest influence on me. I get emotional when I repeat this, thinking of how deeply and strongly Kahn felt about architecture.

I remembered the Selimiye and Suleymaniye Mosques done by Sinan (1570–1575) and the Sultan Ahmet Mosque (Blue Mosque) by Sedefkar Mehmet Aga in 1616. Then there was the Ayasofya by Isidore of Miletus and Anthemius of Tralles in 537, some 1,430 years ago. My memories were filled with Kahn's words. "Light is the maker of structure." "Architecture is born between silence and light." Could that be what they had felt and done centuries ago?

Figure 21. The Blue Mosque in Istanbul.

Figure 22. Ayasofya (Hagia Sophia) in Istanbul.

Kahn was also talking about that sense of awe when he mentioned the pyramids. That completeness, that strength, that clarity of expression, that purity—what a wonderful way of thinking about architecture. What a wonderful way of seeing architecture.

I also thought of "silence" as an inward-looking condition, listening to an inner voice, searching through the inner self. "Silence" is intuition. "Light" is comprehending, figuring out.

Our inquisitive mind is awake; we listen to our inner voice and distinguish our inner voice from others, accepting some and rejecting some, reasoning in silence.

* * *

I primarily worked at the Furness studio, building models, sketching, thinking, and drawing. I also made lithographs, etchings (fig. 25), woodcuts (fig. 24), and wood sculptures (fig. 26) in the studio of the Furness, in Professor Robert Engman's class. I was happy.

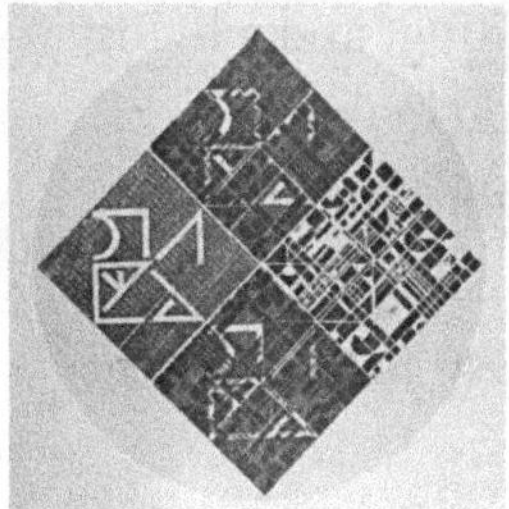
Figure 23. Woodcut.

Figure 24. Etching.

Figure 25. Sculpture.

"Nature does not make art," Kahn said once. "Nature deals with rules and laws. Only man makes art."

Kahn's statement was beautiful, but I felt strange about the "making art" expression. Could art be a personal thing? Art is us. Art does not belong to a person. Making. Art is not made; art becomes. Art happens, art forms, and it forms in the observer, in the perceiver. It becomes; it happens in others. I do not think Picasso sat down and said, "I am going to make art now."

I understand the word *artist*, but not *art maker* or *making art*.

Art is timeless. Art becomes, happens, in a song, in a poem, in a scene, in a look, in a sound. Suddenly, it becomes. It vibrates. It forms a sense, a feeling, an emotion.

Form Comes from Wonder

As architecture students during the late fifties and early sixties, we were drilled with "Form follows function," which was made popular by architects Louis Sullivan (1856–1924) and later Frank Lloyd Wright (1867–1959). We used this frequently to show off our deep(!) knowledge and understanding of architecture. "Form follows function." This affected our understanding and approach to everything, including architecture.

Like others in my class, and as some still might, I understood *form* and *function* to be clearly defined terms. *Form* was the shape, like a building shape or a room shape. *Function* was the use—the function of a dining room is for dining, a waiting room is for waiting, and a living room is for living. As students of architecture, we would look at the title of a project and figure out its function. When I thought about it a little deeper, I found there were functions that were not easily describable or even definable, and that were certainly not so easy to respond to architecturally.

Now I was hearing from Kahn, "Form does not follow function. Form comes from wonder."

What happened to "Form follows function," the most well-known phrase in architecture? I mused. We were all trying to do functional architecture, but it was quite hard to figure out which form followed what function.

Frank Lloyd Wright's buildings were special. We were being taught architecture through beautiful slides, mostly of exterior views, and maybe drawings, elevations, and plans copied from some publications. None of my teachers had been near or inside those buildings, and I did not hear any definition or description of their actual character and the aspects of living they provided in and around their neighborhoods.

It was hard to understand Kahn, and it took a long time for me to understand his definition of *form*. It started with his phrase "Form comes from wonder." Maybe he meant it is an idea, a thought, an emotion, or a desire, long before it becomes a poem, a building, a painting, a book, or a movie.

The meaning of *form* is also "to make up; to constitute; to start to exist." My mother tongue was a good help in clarifying all this. In the Turkish dictionary, I found that it is "teskil etmek, olmak, bir seyin istenilen ve olmasi gereken durumu" ("to be; being; to become a desired and required condition"). I thought the closest Turkish word to it could be *OLUŞUM*. A new concept started working for me. And if Kahn said *OLUŞUM* comes from wonder, then it must come from wonder.

Of Eh

I loved expressions with moving images. I bought a Bolex 16 mm camera and completed a 16 mm film, edited it myself, and put in an optical sound track (figs. 26–29). I named it *Of Eh.* There was no plot, no theme, just a series of curious moving human images. The sound track was made up of scattered words. A viewer had to continually and carefully watch and listen to combine images and words to pull out its message.

Figure 26

Figure 27

Figure 28

This film won second prize in the Foothill College Experimental Film Festival in California in 1967. My involvement with the art of filmmaking continued (1968–1972) later in Turkey. I made numerous 16 mm experimental movies, and one was accepted to participate in a UIA Biennale in Varna, Bulgaria. But it never reached there. It was censored in Turkey. Other short films received awards from TRT (Turkish Radio and Television).

Sanctuary

Kahn started his class one afternoon with "Architecture does not exist." *Wow, did I hear that wrong?* "There is no such thing as architecture," he went on. "You cannot touch architecture."

There was a silence around the table. He continued, "What exists is an offering to the sanctuary of art."

For years, I have carried this in my thoughts. *Sanctuary of art.* I wondered if this sanctuary was the human soul. Should music, poetry, and literature be regarded as offerings to the human soul? Could this be the essential spark that qualifies art and architecture? Was I to understand that architecture is not to be merely an enclosure, a completed construction, but an offering, a thrilling and awesome gift to the human soul, to life, to feelings, to emotions?

I thought this was not too far from the Turkish word *mimar*.

I do not know when, how, or why the love of architecture was instilled within me. I had wanted to be an architect for as long as I could remember. There was not a single architect in my surroundings—not in my neighborhood, not in my town, not in my state or in my large family. There were doctors, lawyers, and engineers in my family, but not a single architect. Growing up, my only reference was Mimar Sinan (architect Sinan). I grew up hearing praise for Mimar Sinan (1490–1588). The Turkish word for *architect* is *mimar*. The word has an Arabic root, *imar*, which means "to render prosperous or to improve; to improve a place by construction, of roads, of public buildings, of public improvement." I guess with this, I defined architecture as a force to advance society for its betterment, and an architect is a person who achieves this betterment for society, for the culture of civilization.

I never thought of architecture as a business or a means to accumulate personal wealth or fame. Architecture was a social cultural service, and one must be best in its realization and application.

New York, New York

It was mid-March 1966. Spring was moving in. The days were getting warmer, and things were looking good for me. My METU friends living and working in New York City frequently invited me out on weekends. I would take the train to New York; we would go to the Village and listen to folk music in small cafés and bars, or we would go to Central Park and visit MoMA, art galleries, and museums. Life was good.

FDR in My Mind I

I was trying hard to think about the FDR memorial, something simple and suitable for a nation's president. I thought of those I was accustomed to seeing in Turkey. I looked at photographs of other memorials around the Tidal Basin for presidents Jefferson, Lincoln, and Washington. My first thought was to make a large room that was open to the sky, with high walls on three sides. Here ceremonies could take place. Visiting dignitaries, kings, and presidents from other nations would come and lay wreaths. Military bands would play, flags would fly, national anthems would be sung, soldiers with guns would march, and so on. Yes. This was a good concept for it.

Three Walls

I built a maquette for my concept presentation (fig. 29). It was a simple room that had high walls on three sides and that was open to the sky. Wide steps, but not high-risers, would lead visitors, slowly rising, to the end wall, where there would be patriotic reliefs with FDR and his well-known words. The memorial would be in the middle of this peninsula, at the end of a long processional walk starting at the northwest edge. It would be a refuge from the surrounding cherry trees and other attention-grabbing views. It would be a place to remember, a place of serenity and peace, inspiring respectful reminiscence.

Figure 29. First maquette (1966).

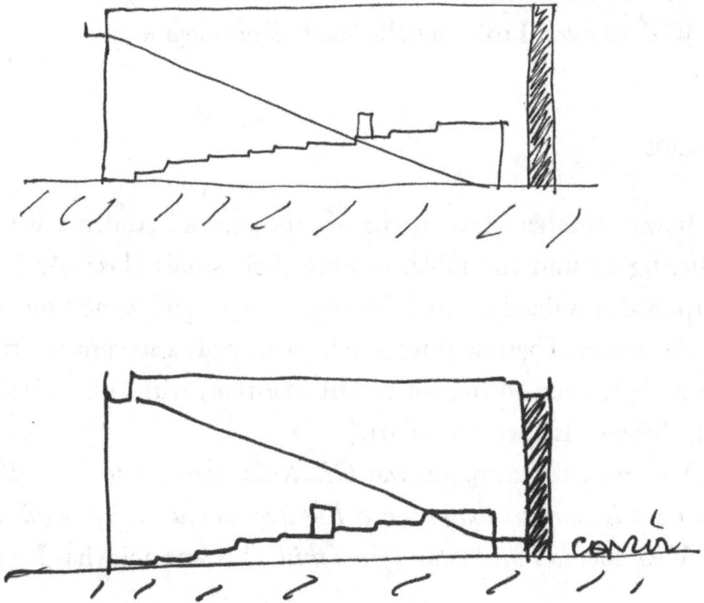

Figure 30. Sketch for the "three walls" concept.

Kahn went around the classroom, reviewing and commenting on other concepts. Then he came to mine, looked at my model, and then looked at me. I did not say anything. He smiled, and with perfect pronunciation of my name and the name of Atatürk,[7] he said, "Cengiz, FDR's life was not as dramatic as Atatürk's." I was surprised to hear this from Kahn. "FDR was a very friendly person," he continued. "He acted like an ordinary citizen, and everyone liked him." I nodded. I was astonished he could read drama and sadness in this simple maquette.

I did not know much about FDR. But this was just a memorial, right? You just had to prompt people to remember him, and then leave it up to them to remember. All that was needed was to indicate the location and mark the name of the person. Visitors would do the rest. What one remembers is one's own responsibility. A memorial. One just needed to mark the spot, right?

Soon I realized, through listening to Kahn's reviews in class, that it was not so. I struggled with this. Maybe it should be a special place—not as anonymous as a headstone, but a unique headstone, a memorable and monumental one.

Well, go back, I told myself. *Start all over again.*

Servant

It was another class in the afternoon, and students were slowly gathering around the table, pulling their stools close. At 2:00 p.m. sharp, Kahn walked in, took his regular seat, and waited for silence in the classroom. Then he thundered, "Science is a servant of art." There was no hesitation in his voice. Just like that, with full conviction, he said, "Science is a servant of art."

My immediate thought was *OK, Kahn wants us to think like artists. Our work is more art than science. But why would science be the servant of art? What should I understand from this?* This was not what I was taught

---

7 Atatürk (pronounced [äˈtäˌtyrc]; May 19, 1881 [conventional] to November 10, 1938) was a Turkish army officer, revolutionary, and founder of the Republic of Turkey, serving as its first president from 1923 until his death in 1938. His surname, Atatürk (meaning "Father of the Turks"), was granted to him in 1934.

in school. Science was the king; art was easy. Wasn't art what one did in one's spare time? There had to be something else in Lou's words. What did Kahn not say? Once again, the internal exploration of trying to understand his phrases was set in motion.

Scientists observe and then interpret their observations. Their interpretation is guided by their intuition. Interpretation is where art creeps in. Maybe Kahn was pointing out the value of intuition over intellect. He must have been telling us that our intuition is more trustworthy and more coherent with life. "Art has always been in front of science," I whispered to myself. Art transcends time. Think of Alhambra; the Moors are long gone, but their presence is still fresh.

Science is learned; art is sensed, felt. "Science is a servant of art." It is an understanding that what is learned serves what is sensed.

Mozart's Kitchen

> "A dish that has fallen in Mozart's kitchen is a beginning of a symphony." Hearing Mozart's name sharpened my attention. *What a great way to describe talent,* I thought. The "talent" of the receiving soul—not what it is, but what it will become.

In one other sense, Kahn was reminding us that an architectural composition should be realized and constructed as carefully, as sensitively, as emotionally, and as artistically as a musical composition. He wanted us to see architecture as having the same elegance, the same nobility as a piece of classical music. Likewise, a designer of places must be attuned to surroundings, discovering meaning and inspiration in the world around them.

FDR in My Mind II

Was Kahn seeing and describing the memorial as a place of reverence, a place of meditation? Maybe. That can bring out emotions, without pushing one into the drama of dying or suffering. Kahn was seeing the memorial without any flags, wreaths, or military bands.

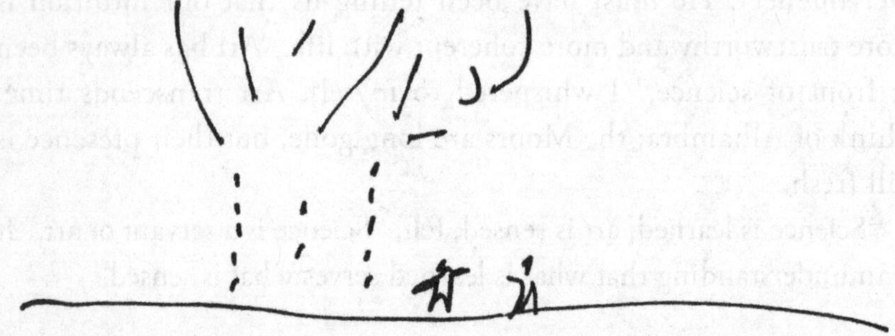

Figure 31. Yetken's sketch of the memorial.

A Torch

I built another maquette. This one was an impressive torch-like structure that floated overhead (fig. 32). This was memorable and unforgettable. The various load-carrying walls at the ground level opened to one another with carved images of soldiers, words, and FDR's accomplishments. It was open at the ground level, and one could walk under this impressive structure, slicing the daylight with dramatic shadows (fig. 33). When lit at night, it would look like a starship hovering overhead.

I was confident of my work. I built a large cardboard model mounted over a 30×30 in (75×75 cm) plywood base. This was the biggest model in class. I placed it in front of my display panel and waited for Kahn.

Figure 32. Second concept maquette for FDR memorial (1966).

Upon entering the classroom, Kahn came directly to my panel, looked at my maquette, and then with a smile, held his hand across one of the high-flying wings angling into the sky. "What if I don't build this part?" he said.

I looked at the model. I realized it didn't make much difference. I thought he was right. Taking away a single piece did not make much difference. Kahn was pointing out the whimsical aspect of its shape. It was just personal shape-making. In fact, it didn't matter how it was shaped. It did not have any meaning in particular to anything or anyone.

I shook my head. My lesson was clear: Taking a piece out should have made the design collapse and should have made it incomplete. But in this case, it did not make any difference to the setup. I was back to the drawing board, as they used to say in the studio.

What Was Kahn Pointing Out?

My first two attempts were fruitless. What was it I was not understanding or was wrongly interpreting? What was I not hearing in class? Was Kahn seeing the memorial as a place to question? To bring out emotions? A place to be learned from, or a place to question?

I could see three principles he had been pointing out for effective architecture:

1. Find its form. Look for its story of existence, its form.
2. Think of its beginning.
3. Search its nature. Ask what it wants to be.

Search its form.
To find its nature, search its beginning.
To search its beginning, question what it wants to be.
To get to what it wants to be, question its nature.
To learn its form, learn its essence.
To reach its essence, clear it from its circumstances.
Understand its institutions. Be alive.
Learn its form. Learn its essence. Reach its roots.
Separate it from its circumstances.
Make it a human scale, a place for memories.
Recall an event. Think of what kind of human relationships it will create.

1. Prepare yourself to remember.
2. Not a person, but a series of related events, a time in history.
3. In order to remember, prepare yourself to ask questions.
4. Maybe this is a place not to be pressed with flags, wreaths, reliefs, or military bands, but a place to learn from, a place to question.

Boullee and Ledoux

With a paper in his hand, Kahn started the class one day by saying, "I was asked to write a dedication for a book on Boullee and Ledoux." He went on to read what he had written:

> Spirit in will to express
> can make the great sun seem small.
> The sun is ...
> Thus, the universe ...
> Did we need Bach?
> Bach is ...
> Thus, music is.
> Did we need Boullee?
> Did we need Ledoux?
> Boullee is ...
> Ledoux is ...
> Thus, architecture is.[8]

In 2002, I traveled to France. I visited an exhibition of their works (figs. 32–34). I was startled. I was seeing pure emotions and pure desire. Was that what Kahn had been saying to us? Those were not what were needed, but they were what came out of the *will to express*.

Boullee and Ledoux were French visionary architects of the eighteenth century. Most of their works were expressed in drawings. I saw *the desire* shining in their work.

---

[8] This text was also published in *Louis Kahn: Essential Texts* (2003). Ed. Robert Twombly, WW Norton & Company, p. 223.

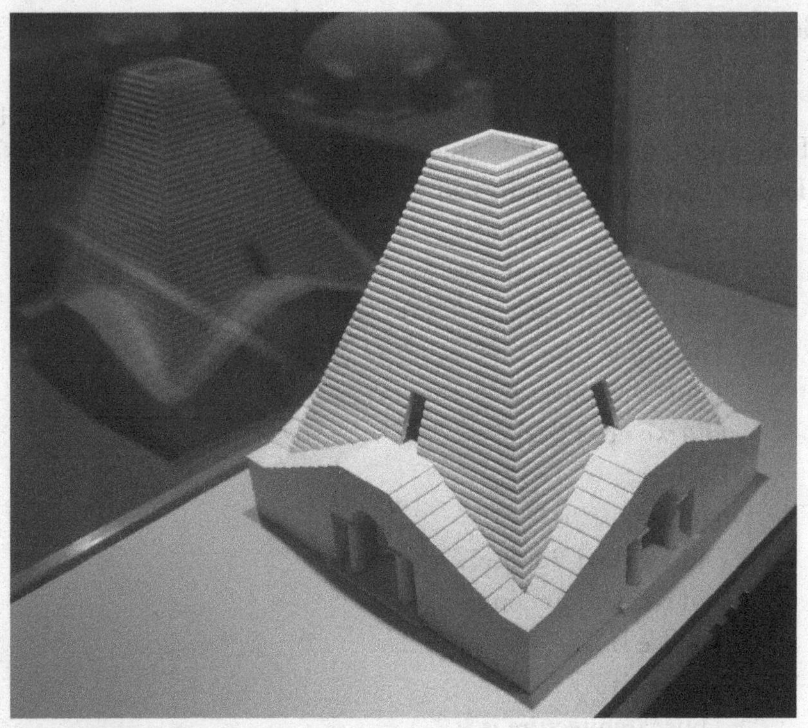

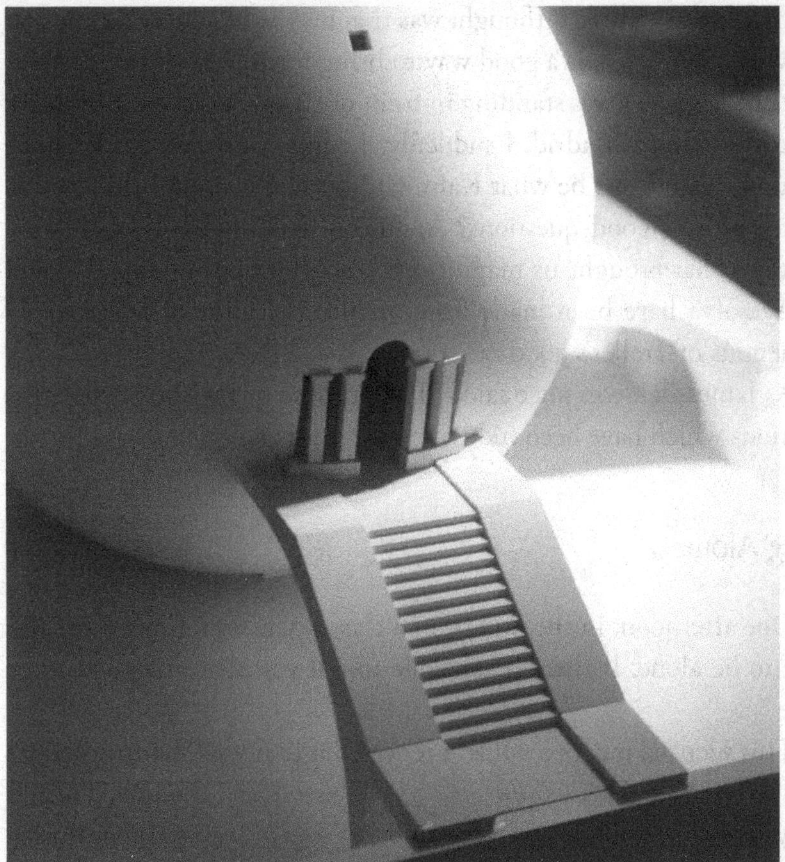

Figures 33, 34, and 35. Some of Boullee's and Ledoux's models at the Royal Saltworks at Arc-et-Senans.

A Good Question

Kahn did not talk about the specifics of designing his buildings. His comments were all very general, more about understanding architectural thinking. During all those, he would add a comment at the most appropriate time. "A good question is better than the most brilliant answer." Then he would continue with his talk.

I could understand that there must be a right question to arrive at the right answer, but this was peculiar and contradictory. What did this mean, really? It sounded wise. But how could I explain this to my future students? My first thought was that maybe he simply meant that knowing what to ask is a good way to bring forth clear answers.

Years later, as I was standing in front of Picasso's *Guernica* in Reina Sofia Museum in Madrid, I suddenly thought *Guernica* was Picasso's question. Could this be what Kahn had been referring to that day? Is it art that asks good questions? Architecture. Could it be architects' questions that brought us magnificent and glorious buildings? Could the Ayasofya have been made from architects Isidore of Miletus and Anthemius of Tralles's good questions?

As James Baldwin once said, "The purpose of art is to lay bare the questions which have been hidden by the answers."

Being Alone

One afternoon, in the middle of a class discussion, Kahn said, "It's good to be alone. If there is someone to tell you that it is good to be alone."

This silenced me for a while. I repeated it to myself many times: it's good to be alone. *This is funny, but it is very sensible,* I thought. There is always one other side to any story, another way of seeing things. I used Kahn's phrase humorously in discussions with my friends, my students, and my professional associates in later years. Kahn was describing a life story. This was his advice on living.

Stone over Stone

"I start sketching from the base, like I am building it step by step, stone by stone." Kahn was describing his sketching technique. I remembered the Richards Medical Building and how clear it was to see, to follow, and to understand how the precast structure was designed and put together. Seeing the flat arches in Exeter or the round arches in Ahmadabad, one could read how they were put together and how they hold the weight.

FDR in My Mind III

Maybe it should be just a pile of stone, like the most ancient memorial would be. Maybe a mound (fig. 36). Make something modest but distinguished, something that would simply appear among the trees.

Figure 36. Stone over stone; a mound.

Stone on stone, like a pyramid. It should be a memorial that is raw and pure, something basic to symbolize the core meaning of remembering, of honoring. It does not require flags, lights, wreaths, or rituals. It is just a place to be, a place that touches the human soul. It should have a poetic presence, no need for drama to remind visitors why they are there.

What is the desire to make a memorial? Why would we desire to make a memorial? Is the FDR memorial a place of sadness, or is it a place to celebrate life—not only FDR's life but life in general?

From Where I Stand

Kahn described places in terms of the way of life it provided. *Evoke* was a word he used frequently. Places *evoke* certain senses in us. Use them to inspire, not to force and expect them.

I had to build the life story for such a setting.

People may come here for the setting, to be around the blossoming cherry trees along the Tidal Basin or to lie down to read a book or to play with their young children. The park setting should be kept.

Make a place that will have a life in their memory—not necessarily to remember FDR, but to remember being there, in the setting. It will be all right if someone reminds them months later that this place is a memorial for FDR.

Make it pure, no decoration or distractions. Life around it should enliven it, not ornamentations. FDR was a president during austere times (the Great Depression and World War II).

Do not make a place that expects people to act a certain way. Do not make a place that expects people to come. It may turn into an insult if no one shows up.

Four Freedoms

I don't know why I did what I did. I woke up one day and started building this model (fig. 37). I don't know if I was thinking of the beginning of a memorial as a pile of stone. I did not think of any reason; I just sat down and built the model. My listening to Louis in class was working silently in me. This was a man-made hill cut into four pieces, all at the same height. They were part of the cherry trees, part of the Potomac River, and part of the Tidal Basin, arranged in an axial path. Two of them had seven steps, and the other two had nine steps. The steps were about forty inches high (one meter) and wide enough to sit on or lie down on. There were no flags, no sculptures, and no place to put wreaths. Two sides had steps, and the other two sides were vertical surfaces that went straight to the ground. The unit at the east looked to the Tidal Basin and cherry trees, the next one looked north to the Lincoln Memorial, the third one west to Potomac River, and the fourth south to the Jefferson Memorial.

I took a long time to decide on the distances between them and on their orientations. I thought they should not be very close to one another, that there should be a neutral zone in between to be free to just wander around and be away from others.

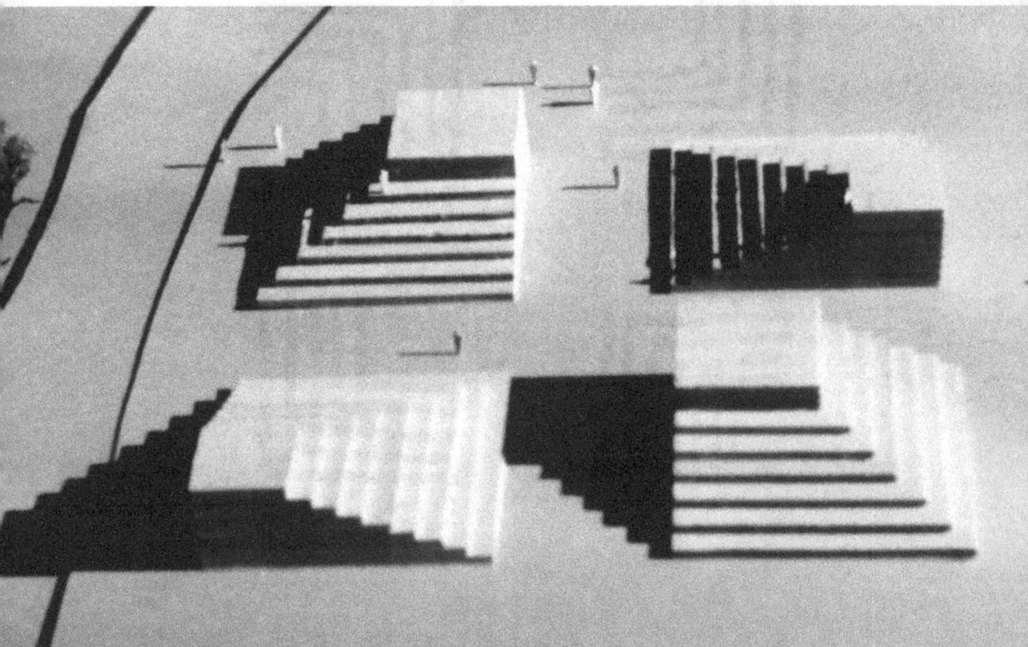

Figure 37. Final model for FDR memorial.

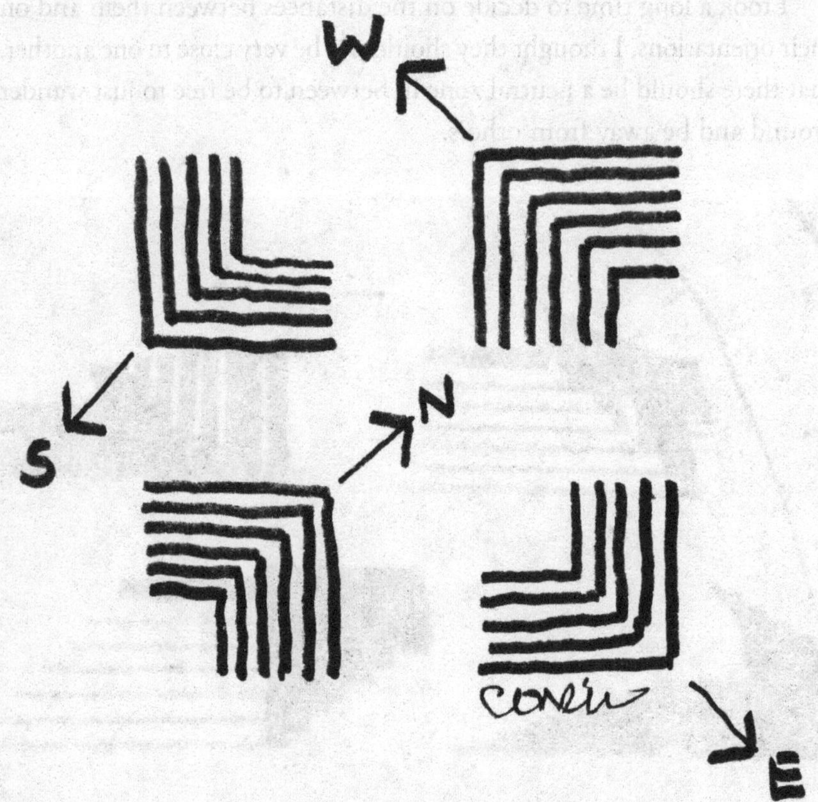

Figure 38. Orientation and setting.

Upon entering the classroom, Kahn came directly to my panel. He looked at the model from right to left and smiled. "Now! This is a memorial," he said. I was pleased but also puzzled as to why he thought this was the right one. He turned to the class. "This is a memorial," he continued. "You can make sparkling pools, marble waterfalls, jumping lights. But this is a memorial."

To this day, I don't know what others in my class thought of it. Maybe some considered the thirty-two steps as representing FDR's being the thirty-second president, and perhaps the four units as representing his election to president of the US four times. Maybe some thought the four pieces represented his four essential human rights: *freedom of speech*, *freedom to worship*, *freedom from want*, and *freedom from fear*. Some may have wondered whether the exaggerated steps were an expression of the pains and challenges facing a person who was unable to walk, stand, or climb, or whether it represented the brutal memories of the Second World War and the painful austerity people went through during the time of the Great Depression.

Perhaps Kahn had responded to its overall simplicity, its abstract quality, the crispness and cleanness of it. A truncated mass cut into four and arranged in four directions, brought together to create a question or to form a meaning of coming together. A man-made hill chopped along the north, south, east, and west axes to find a coherent unity within its sameness, within its oneness, reminding the vistas of the power of their inescapable and essential unity and identity.

Final Review

In the final jury, Rice suggested I better make each unit a different height. Kahn responded promptly, "No, Norm, there is no reason for that. They are and should be all equal heights." After a short silence, Lou turned to Dean Perkins and confirmed his evaluation. "Turkey has a damn good architect."

This became a strong turning point in my understanding of architecture. I was learning to define architecture not through a structure, not through materials or construction styles, but through how it would provide a life setting, how it would inspire a sense of place, how it could bring out and keep values and experiences.

Mid-May

The spring semester of '66 was ending. I had another semester in Kahn's class after the summer break. For the summer months, I needed a job. I approached Kahn in the studio and asked if I could work in his office during the summer. He said yes.

"When may I start?" I asked.

"Whenever you can."

I was very happy. I had a job in Kahn's office for the next three months (June to August '66).

Fall Semester

Soon it was September. Summer was ending, and the fall semester was set to begin. For the next four months (September to December '66), I was going to be both a student of Kahn's class and an employee in his office. My classmates from the last semester had all graduated in May. I was going to be with a new group of students who were starting their 1966–1967 academic year at Penn.

Project Introduction

Exeter Library

In 1966, the fall semester project in Kahn's studio was *the library of Exeter Academy* in New Hampshire. Professor Rice distributed copies of the program to the students in class. This was the same as the original program Kahn had received for the project he was designing in his office. I can still hear his raised voice. "Read the program to make architecture. Do not build the program. Make architecture. A library is where the books are. This is your program." He went on talking about libraries. Books are heavy. Reading rooms must be filled with daylight, with large tables full of open books.

In saying "where the books are," Kahn was pointing out its core essence and focusing on its smallest common denominator. This is similar to him saying "A concert hall is a violin." Think of a concert hall as a musical instrument, not just a facility of brick and mortar. It is an instrument that brings life to musical compositions. An architect must see it with a sensitivity that adds a mythical/human value to it. Similarly, a library is also a temple of sacred knowledge. Kahn usually described books as priceless items; we pay enough only for its printing price.

He stood up in front of the board and drew two circles, one inside the other. "Books are in the inner circle, away from the direct sun." He pointed to the outer ring. "Reading rooms are here. This is where the daylight is."

Someone asked if they could see Kahn's own design for the Exeter project. "No," he said. Suddenly I realized I was the only one in class who knew Kahn's design. The past three months, I had been working in his office. Hideki Shimizu sat behind me at Kahn's office and was finishing the Exeter Library design documents (see part 4).

During the break, Kahn called me to the side, near the window. "I forgot that you are still taking this class," he said. "You graduated, as far as I'm concerned. Do you mind working on this?"

"Oh, no," I said. "Thank you for asking, but I don't mind at all."

The challenge in front of me was grand. My library had to be different from Kahn's, and it had to be good. It had to be original so he would see I did not copy his work. And it had to show him that I was a good architect.

Libraries were spatially confusing to me. I had problems finding books. I often ended up with books other than those I came for. But for this project in class, I had to work hard to make it an exciting and inviting place to visit—with large reading rooms for a quiet and comfortable place to work, to read, and to study; open and with full daylight and a view of the campus; and with clear circulation to make it impossible to get lost in the stacks.

Fish

With a smile on his face, Kahn started class the next meeting by saying, "Do you know when the library started? The library started when the first man caught fish." There was a short pause. "And he did not know how to eat it."

This was funny. I could see ripples of smiles going around the class. Kahn was referring directly to shared knowledge and experience. The beginning of the library. *Stay away from preconceived ideas and images,* I told myself. *Think of experiences and expressions. Define its life. This is a place where sacred treasures are being protected.*

Education

Education is not the learning of facts but the training of the mind to think.

—Albert Einstein

In the middle of a discussion around the table, Kahn roared, "I can't teach you what you don't already know!" I looked around the class. *Did someone question his way of teaching? Did someone say something to get him upset?* "I am not teaching you," he said. "I am teaching myself." *Oh, yes. Someone has irritated him.*

Kahn was right. He wasn't teaching. He was showing us ways to think about architecture. He was showing us opportunities to learn to think. He was sharing his thinking with us. We were supposed to understand things to the extent of our willingness and capacity.. His class was more about learning than teaching.

This reminded me of Louis Armstrong's reply to a lady who asked what jazz is: "If you have to ask, you'll never know."

Review around the Table

Figure 39. Class discussions.

"One entrance." The discussion was about the lobby for the library. In particular, it was about whether there should be more than one entrance to the library. Kahn pointed out that the entrance to a library is an important reference point on a campus. Everyone would know it and pass by it every day. He added a story with a smile. "If you agree to meet your girlfriend in front of the library and she waits at another door, you'll miss her." He went on to describe the spatial character of the lobby of a library, with large windows facing the campus. "You can wait, as long as you anticipate."

Feathers Ruffled

There was a young girl who used to come to class, as some of the wives and girlfriends did in those days. They would sit at the outskirts of the big table and listen to the discussion. The girl was a girlfriend of one of my classmates. She had long black hair, an angelic face, and a big dog.

One day, after Kahn walked out of the studio, this young woman suddenly turned to me and started yelling in my face. "Why does he like you people from India and Asia, and not Americans?" She was yelling at the top of her lungs. She didn't look so beautiful anymore. "What is it with you people? There are so many beautiful designs done by American students, but he always praises you people."

Her fury was sudden and shocking for me. I did not know what to say. "I'm sorry," I whispered, and I slowly walked away from the large drafting table and toward the door. Her boyfriend was holding her back, touching her shoulders to calm her down. The dog did not bark at me. I left the studio.

I thought about this later. Maybe she was right. Perhaps it was students from Asia, Japan, and India that tended to work primarily with basic shapes, like squares, rectangles, and circles. Students from the US, Europe, and South America usually started with complicated shapes, masses, and volumes; with forty-five-degree slanted walls; and with cutouts and circles with cross diagonals. Kahn usually reacted negatively to those characteristics. It had nothing to do with our national or racial heritage; it had to do with the way we had been taught to design—with simple shapes that do not lose their character when joined with others.

* * *

My job at Kahn's office continued. Sitting a few tables behind me, Hideki would be hard at work, finishing the Exeter Library project.

My Scheme for Exeter Library

Reading books is not easy for me. My mind slips away while reading. I agreed with Kahn's comments that books have to be kept away from direct sunlight and that they are heavy and so must be carried by a concrete structure. Unlike books, reading rooms should be full of daylight, with spacious, warm, and friendly spaces. A story for the library was building up in my mind, and some images were taking shape. I started with a simple rectangular plan, a concrete frame structure that had book stacks with frequent columns. This part was set up to face the northern exposure (fig. 38). The southern half of the rectangle would be reading areas. Between these two parts would be a straight, long stairway (fig. 40) connecting every floor. The stairway would receive daylight from above. I thought I would be able to easily find my way around this building and would enjoy being there.

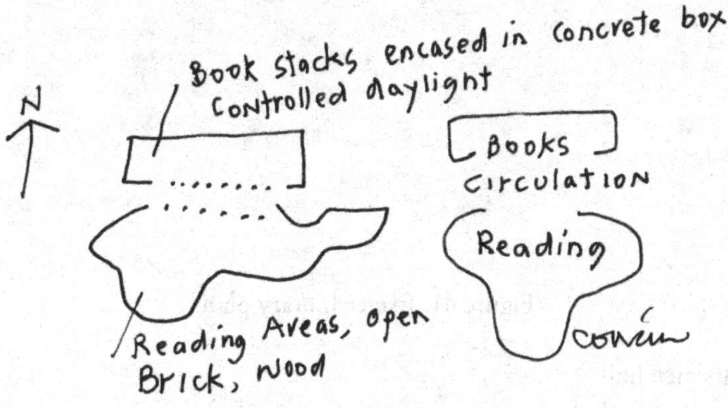

Figure 40. Early concept diagram.

I had four segments in the building composition.

1. The circulation space at the center (fig. 38): It was clear and direct. Wider at the ground floor and narrower in width at each floor above.
2. The north segment: It was for book stacks. A heavy, strong concrete structural grid, cool and away from direct sunlight.
3. The south segment: It was for reading rooms. Load-bearing brick structure. Lively, friendlyspaces, with large windows that let in daylight and had a full view of the campus.
4. Offices, sections for rare books, meeting rooms, research and service areas, passenger and freight elevators, toilets, and repairs and storage areas with easy access to the loading dock.

I worked out the refinements and made hardline drawings.

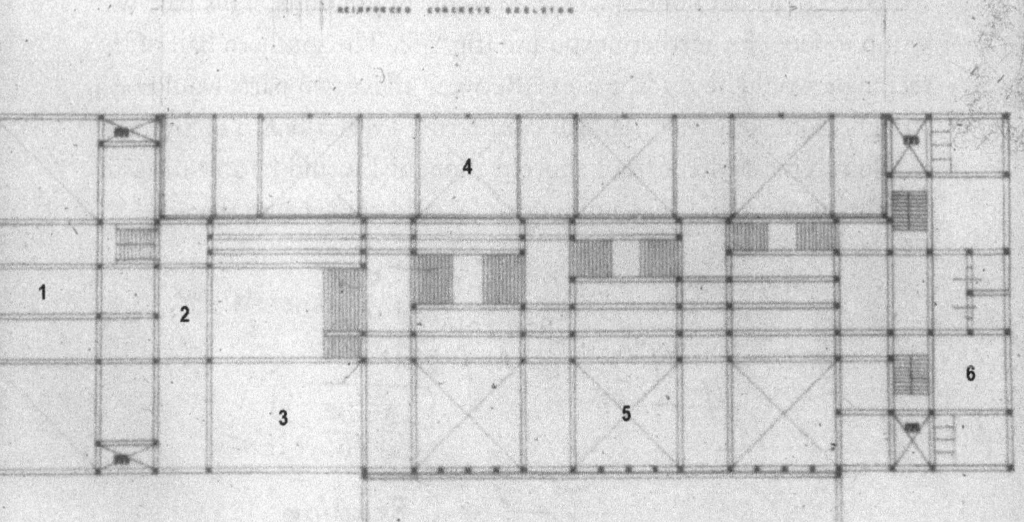

Figure 41. Exeter Library plan.

1. Entrance hall
2. Circulation desk
3. Card catalogs
4. Book stacks
5. Reading rooms
6. Service areas

This was a simple plan. I thought this was the cleanest, clearest spatial organization—almost an archetype—for a library building. It was "where the books are," with clear circulation and a direct way to reach them. On the north side were prestressed concrete beams with short spans carrying the heavy loads—not very friendly spaces. One would not like to linger there more than necessary.

The large reading rooms on the south side, with ample daylight and a campus view, had high ceilings. It had a brick structure and wood finishes for the floor, furniture, windows, and doors. It had inspiring spaces for one to come to study and research, with large tables with open books.

Final Review

I was the last to present in the final review. A strange and unexpected incident occurred. One of my classmates presented a very similar project to mine before me. Wow, what nerve!

I was upset. I had not seen his work in class. No one in class had seen him do these drawings. Kahn did not say anything during his review. Finally, my turn came, and I presented. The first comment came from Professor Robert Engman, the sculpture professor at the Fine Arts School. In a harsh tone, he said, "This is a bad copy of what we saw before. It is not worth commenting on."

I was afraid this would happen. During the last few weeks, Kahn had pointed out to the class that my scheme was his favorite. I had worked on this project as a challenge to myself. And here I was. I turned my eyes away from the jury. Kahn turned to Robert Engman. "No, Bob," he said. "He is the original." Then he turned to me and asked, "How does this compare to the form diagram I drew in class?"

He was testing me. "Not very different," I said. I drew two squares, one within the other. Then I drew two parallel lines slicing these squares. I pointed to a cut segment. "I am just cutting a slice."

It was the end of the jury. Everybody was collecting their drawings. Kahn came toward me. "Are you OK?" he asked.

"It is not fair," I replied. "He could not explain well."

"No harm, Cengiz," he said and added something like "Remember, imitation is a compliment."

I nodded with a sad smile.

My friend Peter Dominic approached me and asked what Kahn had just said to me. Collecting my drawings, I responded, "He said something like 'Imitation is a compliment.'"

Peter smiled and corrected me. "Yeah, he probably said 'Imitation is a sincere form of flattery.'"

That classmate of mine never uttered a word to me about the incident. Years later, I stayed with him and his wife in their home. His wife, who had been at the jury that day, volunteered an explanation about that afternoon. She told me he was so limited in the English language at the time, he could not understand the project assignment or any of Kahn's comments in class. He was so afraid to be unsuccessful and to be kicked out of the graduate program that he decided to draw my scheme, because he knew it was Lou's favorite. I could understand his fear of humiliation, but he had made a bad choice. Haven't we all, at one time or another? I decided that Kahn had been right and that I should simply recall the incident as one classmate complimenting another.

Project Introduction

Philadelphia Urban Study

The last project was an urban study for Center City, Philadelphia, an area bordered by Vine Street, South Street, Schuylkill River, and Delaware River. I remember Kahn posed for a picture in front of my model after my final review (fig. 41).

Figure 42. Kahn standing in front of my Center City model after the final jury (November 1966).

BOOK 2

Office of Louis I. Kahn

PART 4

Office

An architect expresses things a certain way, as a musician expresses them a certain way. A musician sings the song of the soul. You can feel it. You don't have to use language for it because all language is inadequate when you speak of art.[9]

—Louis Kahn

9 Fort Wayne Theater promotional brochure in 1964.

People Seeing People

After spring semester classes ended, I went to Kahn's office at 1501 Walnut Street, to the fifth floor. He was not in. I met Louise Badgley, a nice lady who was Lou's personal secretary for many years. She took me to meet David Wisdom. David was also an architect. He greeted me and gave me some sepia sheets[10] and told me to erase the marked areas. I set to work, and after a while, I noticed the sepia eraser smelled bad. After doing that for some time, I started to wonder if I could enjoy doing this for the rest of the summer in the office.

An hour later, Kahn returned. Passing by, he saw me erasing sepias. "What are you doing?" he asked. I showed him the sepias I had erased. "No, no, no. I have a project for you. Come with me."

We walked down to the fourth floor. He did not see the need to introduce me to anyone on that floor. He pointed to a drafting table along the windows and asked if that table was empty, and they confirmed that it was. "That's your table," he said to me. He asked those in the room, "Where is the Fort Wayne drawer?" They showed him the drawer. He opened it, took out some drawings and placed them on the empty table.

"I want you to work on this project," he said. It was a civic theater in Fort Wayne, Indiana. I was to look at these drawings and acquaint myself with them. The seating was for nine hundred people. "Theater is a plaza." He looked at my face and added, "Theater is people seeing people." He looked at me again to make sure I understood. Then he turned back and left the floor.

"People seeing people." Kahn's words struck me. I was quiet for a while. I thought about what he had said. I looked around. A few tables in front of me sat Anant Raje (fig. 43), an architect from India. He was looking at me with a friendly smile; he nodded as a welcoming sign. Hideki Shimizu (fig. 44), an architect from Japan sitting a few desks behind me, waved and then returned to his drawing. I did not know then that they would soon become my best friends.

---

10 Sepia–semitransparent sepia-colored paper. Original drawings were drawn on a fabric sheet or on vellum with pencil, and copied on sepia-colored paper for consequent revisions.

Figure 43. Anant Raje (1966).

Figure 44. Hideki Shimizu with Cengiz in Tokyo (2006).

I turned my attention to the stack of drawings on my table (fig. 45). *This is good,* I thought. *I have my own project. Isn't this what I wanted?* I thought Lou would come back later, make some sketches, talk to me, and then I could begin some hardline drawings and build a model. Kahn did not come back. I was alone on the project. I waited and waited, until I finally asked Raje, "Will he come back?" "He will come," Raje said, confirming with a few nods.

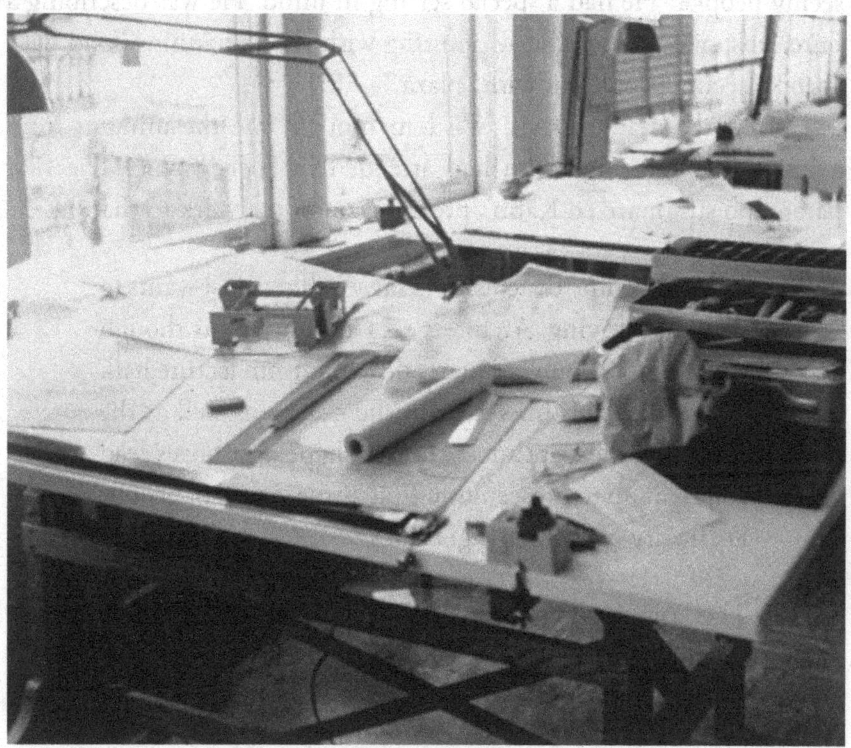

Figure 45. Author's table at the office of Louis Kahn (1966).

The background of the project was not very clear. There were no architectural models of earlier studies. The project had started some time ago, and the last person who had worked on it was gone. I read the documents I found, including some initial letters and some meeting memos. This theater was also going to function as a community center. Besides theatrical performances, concerts, ballets, and dances, it would also be used for award banquets, graduations, public lectures, and maybe even political debates.

To draw a typical plan for a theater is not hard. References to look at to learn some dimensions and critical distances, sizes, and relationships are all available in architectural standard books. Stage types, such as modern, Noh, black-box, street theater, proscenium, and thrust stages, are all well-known. But Lou meant something when he said "people seeing people." He had a special setting in mind. He was describing a pure, unspoiled sense of it by pointing with the "beginning" and with "people seeing people" or with "plaza."

A few days later, David Wisdom brought me the minutes from a June 1966 meeting Kahn had attended in Fort Wayne. The first paragraph summarized Kahn's presentation of the work to that date.

> Kahn: Nothing conclusive so far. Architect just wants to show his striving. Architect sees auditorium as though it is a non-flat public square, different from lecture hall. The audience is interested in themselves as well as the play. The most intimate theater shape and boxes lead you right up to proscenium. Epidaurus, a wall of people. Difficulty of above is sight lines …
>
> The large section, entire ceiling (scene) is in a sense a stage—light actively a part of stage itself …
>
> There can be 700 good seats within 60' depth …
>
> The workhouse (stagehouse) could be behind the stage and as deep. Rehearsals could be held in separate building.
>
> There could be clerestory light at stage.
>
> Architect concerned with what players see …

Additional comments from the building committee included the following:

> Many of the architect's ideas are exciting, but purpose of theater is for the audience and focus is strictly on stage. Ideas of actors' reaction should not be high priority …
>
> The committee likes steep angle floor …

Kahn did not come down to talk to me. Days had gone by. I started sketching on my own and then started building simple models, thinking of the basic characteristics of a theater—the audience arriving, finding their seats, enjoying the performance, and leaving. I did it all in gray chipboard and not in any scale, just to initiate a primary concept (figs. 46–47).

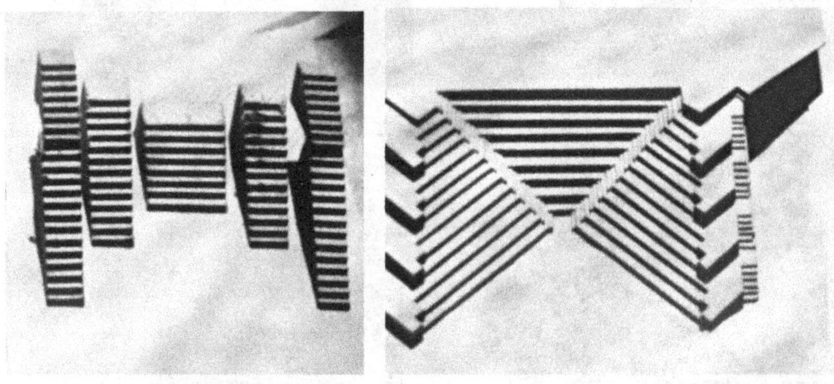

Figure 46. Yetken's first maquette study.

Figure 47. Yetken's second maquette study.

"Theater is a plaza" kept turning around in my mind, but I could not seem to pull myself away from all the conventional theater images. Straight rows, angular rows, curved rows. I kept trying to make them seem original and geometrically interesting.

I liked the continental seating in the theater, without the central aisle (fig. 47). The center aisle, which takes out the best seats in the audience hall, was not my favorite. The cross-circulation that would allow performers to go in and out among the audience was exciting. Comfortable cross-circulation would allow the audience to arrive and exit before and after the show, as well as during the intermission. There were several circulation challenges to be carefully organized and orderly arranged in a theater.

Over the next two months, I made ten to twelve study models (fig. 52). I was trying to grasp the concept of "people seeing people." Making so many models was my way of keeping up the intensity of my involvement while struggling to find inspiration for the architectural reflection of the phrase "theater is a plaza." These model studies were my way of nurturing the creativity one would need to delve deeper.

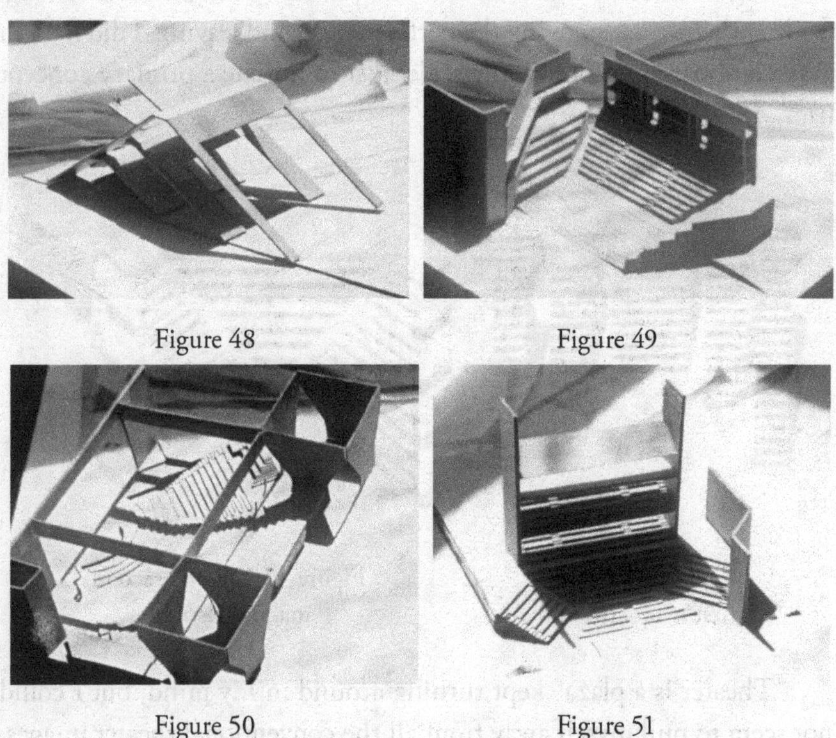

Figure 48 Figure 49

Figure 50 Figure 51

Study models of the theater, by the author (1966).

These study models also show how capricious the process of design is; there is always a long and inescapable gestation period in a designer's mind before any meaningful end is achieved. These also show the struggle of a young architect striving to reach an understanding of a simple verbal statement in architectural terms (figs. 48–51). Design takes considerable time and energy to bring out a good, appropriate, and suitable architectural statement—in this case, to make a spatial/architectural expression out of a verbal statement.

My objective was to make a brand-new, completely unique sculptural arrangement of seating. The auditorium and the stage were two other entities; the backstage area and the lobby would come later. The movement of the audience and the sight lines were most significant. My focus in these studies was to see if any of these would fulfill that notion of "people seeing people."

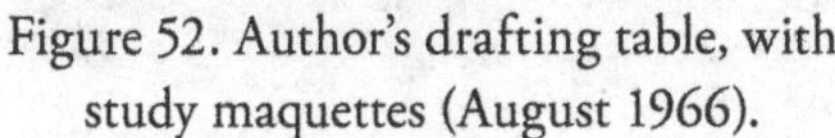

Figure 52. Author's drafting table, with study maquettes (August 1966).

Figure 53. Circular theater maquette (August 1966).

Occasionally, Kahn would come down to the fourth floor, but only to review the Exeter Library project with Hideki. There were times, as he would walk to Hideki's desk, he would slow down near my table. He would look at the study model I was currently working on and offer a gentle smile and shake his head from side to side, as if to say "Not yet," and he would continue on his way to Hideki.

I must admit that if any of these studies had received Kahn's approval, I would have advanced its development. To me, they were good enough. But not for Kahn. I guess "they don't have behind them the kind of belief that made the first [theater], when established, becomes an inseparable part of the way of life."[11] [see original quote at beginning of Part 5] maybe a paraphrase is better? How do you attribute it then? … they didn't have behind them the kind of belief that made the first [theater] to become an inseparable part of the way of life.

Wall of People

It was almost July when Kahn came to my table again and looked at my study models. "Remember La Scala," he started. "Wall full of people." He was referring to his recent visit to Italy. "Think of La Scala. A wall of people," he said again. He looked deep into my face, smiled, and left the fourth floor.

La Scala is probably the most famous opera house in the world (fig. 54). It is a place where well-dressed people are possibly more interested in watching others and showing themselves off than in watching the show. *La Scala is primarily a place to see and be seen,* I thought.

Figure 54. La Scala.

But this new phrase, "wall of people," is different from "people seeing people," I thought. "Wall of people" suggests a very formal relationship

[11] Kahn's words from the promotional brochure for the Fort Wayne fundraiser.

between the performer and the audience. In such a setting, the audience might seem to be held captive in loggias, whereas "people seeing people" indicates a more active place of participation—one that might also be suitable as a community center and as a place for graduations, banquets, or political debates.

I started the "wall full of people" study. I drew a circular plan and placed balconies around the perimeter. I sketched a square seating for the ground floor inside the circle (fig. 53). *Kahn is going to like this,* I thought. *He likes simple geometric shapes.* And I set about making a small model.

I waited, hoping Kahn would come and make some comments before I developed it further. But he did not come. After a while, I decided the circle scheme was not worth pursuing. I started another model. This time, the "wall full of people" was inside a rectangular volume (figs. 55–56). Seating at the corners was troubling. I started yet another model, this one with the troubling corners cut out and left as light wells and stairs (fig. 56).

Figure 55

Figure 56

Maquettes (photos by author, 1966).

It had been over two months since I started working at Kahn's office. None of the work I had done seemed to be going anywhere. Here I was among the most talented people, but I could not seem to get a breakthrough in translating Kahn's direction into an architectural presence.

This was my very first design project in the real world. I was doing my best, but none of it was good enough. It had to be vivid; it had to be pure. It had to show the "beginning" as a place for the art of performing, as a palace of performance, with its spatial and architectural character. It had to be extraordinary; it had to be outstanding. But none of the models I made had the architectural punch, the architectural significance. This needed rethinking. I had to build its story. What would take place here?

Hey, Theater, What Do You Want to Be?

A playwright shares his/her observations with the audience. The audience looks on, reviewing and evaluating the story, watching the actors, and listening to the words in amazement and appreciation.

Actors act in the presence of people. The actors and audience are engaged in the performance, in the play, in their story, in the author's work. This is how performers bring the play right to the audience. Actors watch the audience. The stage, the auditorium, the actors, and the audience are all together.

A live performance requires an engagement of the audience with the performers. A performance is never the same twice; a play never repeats itself.

The proscenium is the window opening into life. Plays extend the human experience, and they tell of joy, bring out fear, and resolve conflicts.

The stage, the setting, defines the extent of that "life." Directors, technicians, and actors bring this life to an audience. Background sets, lights, and costumes build that life onstage in addition to being a place for civic activities, like debates, graduations, award presentations, and the like.

In those years, theater was struggling to figure out its own identity. Theater was trying its best to get away from being merely a proscenium production. "Theater is dead" was a slogan heard frequently. Plays were being directed and produced outside the stage, outside the prosceniums, and even among the audience. Aisles also became part of the stage.

Theater-in-the-round and street theater were very popular. All who were present in the theater, the audience and actors, were considered performers in the plays.

Kahn was right when he said that *theater is a plaza*. A plaza was where human stories would be told to an audience. Theaters were storytelling places. Plays, like literature and poetry, forced us to look at ourselves. I realized how clear Kahn was when he said "people seeing people." With a simple sentence, he had compacted the thought into its simplest sense.

Theater wants to be a public square. Theater, the performing arts, literature, poetry, and even minimal art (and minimal architecture) force us to look closely at ourselves. Writers remind us of human values and our own feelings, and they teach us about ourselves over and over.

What was the primary desire that brought this theater to be here in Fort Wayne? Fort Wayne desired a stage for performing arts, for the various kinds—musicals, ballets, concerts, etc.—where formal seating was preferred. Fort Wayne desired a place for political debates, for graduations, for public presentations, for celebrations, for dinner theaters, etc., with informal seating, freer circulation, with easy access and egress.

A Postcard

Summer was ending. I was not getting anywhere. My earlier studies did not make any sense to me. They looked ordinary; they had no life in them, no excitement, not even a spark of creativity. I had built them with the hope that they might generate some higher connection to something bigger, something better. None of them could inspire anyone to write or direct a play.

Figure 57. Postcard from Portugal.

My METU friends in New York City had decided to return home to Ankara. In mid-August 1966, I received a postcard (fig. 57) from them, from Portugal. In the picture, there were three women wrapped up in black cloaks, their backs against a wall on a local street. A note (in Turkish), poking fun, said:

> Greetings from Portugal. We saw your mother, aunt, and grandmother here, waiting anxiously for your return.

It was funny. I looked at the photo again and again. I did not know why I was fascinated with the image.

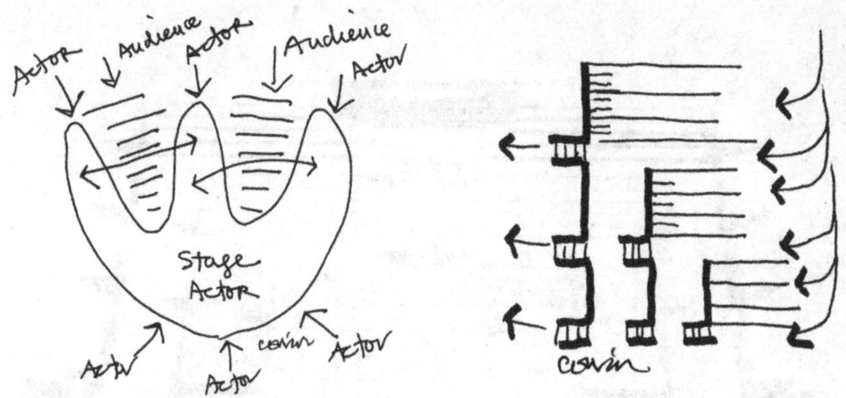

Figure 58. Author's sketches. Diagram for actor-audience relationships, audience entrance/exit, and sight line possibilities.

I made a few line sketches (fig. 58) to figure out the level changes in the photo, then I sketched the totality of it for the theater. This could resolve the cross-circulation in the theater. *It will work,* I thought. The idea excited me. I decided to build a model (fig. 59). I did not want Kahn to come down and see it before I had finished the model. I worked late into the night.

The setup could give equal and freer access for actors and audience. There would be freedom to perform outside the limits of the stage and the proscenium.

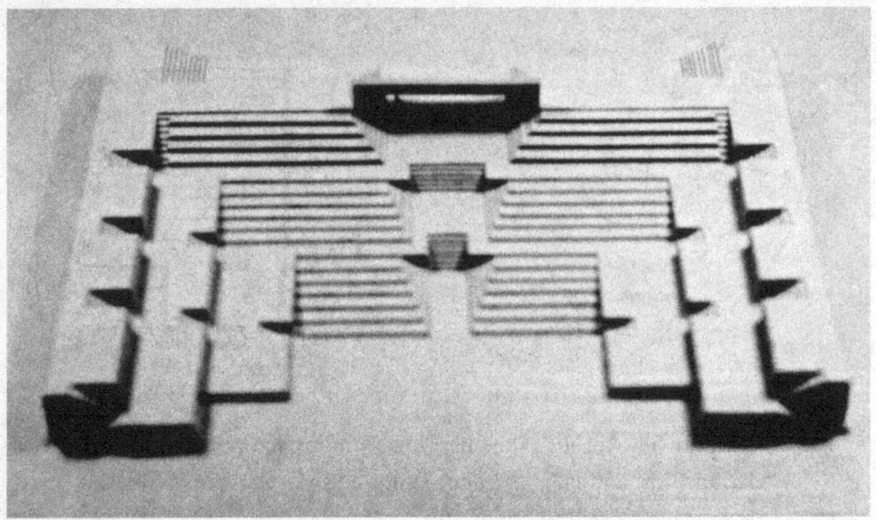

Figure 59. Model from 1966 (photo by author).

The scheme had straight rows of seating and a wide performance aisle at the center. The side piers could be stage extensions to bring actors to the audience or, as in dinner theaters, debates, graduations, or celebrations, to be used as loggias. It seemed the actor-audience relationships were shaping up well. *Actors would enjoy performing here, and directors would enjoy directing their new interpretations,* I thought. This was "people seeing people." The audience would be watching the audience as well as the performers, while the actors could easily watch the audience watching them.

The next morning, I went up to the fifth floor and asked Louise if Kahn would be available that day. He was not in the office. I returned to my table. Of course, then I started to have mixed feelings about it. On one hand, I sensed the study was good. On the other, I could be blinded by my own feelings, and Kahn might not see it the way I saw it.

Kahn was not able to come to the fourth floor for the next few days, and I had plenty of time to increase my anxiety and build my confidence about the scheme. The more I looked, the more confident I felt.

The scheme achieved a few things at once.

- It was something new.
- It engaged the performer and the audience.
- Performing could extend toward the audience.
- Side piers could be part of the performance or the audience hall.
- The audience would be an integral part of the performance.
- All would be able to see and be seen within the auditorium hall.
- The proscenium was fully open to the audience hall.
- Cross aisles provided easy entry or exit for actors, as well as for the audience (fig. 60).

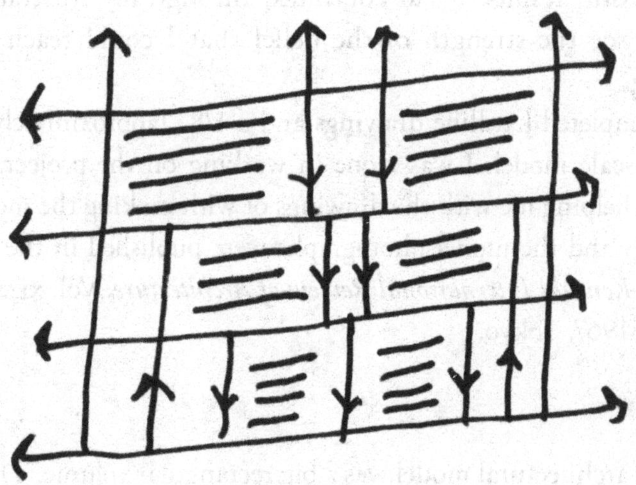

Figure 60. Circulation within the theater.

I would like to write or direct a play in this theater, I thought. It provided unlimited opportunities for different interpretations for a performance director. A set designer would find endless opportunities to develop creative and engaging stage designs. The setting was established. The rest of the theater—the ceiling, lobby, and stage—could be worked out later. This was a place made for the art of performance.

Kahn finally came down to the fourth floor. He talked to Raje first. Then he walked to my desk. I did not say anything; I pushed the model to the upper corner of my table. He looked at the model, and then he looked at me and smiled. "Good," he said. "Let's develop it more. Build a larger model, and I'll take it to Fort Wayne."

I had a good feeling. Finally, I could understand and work with Kahn. I had reached his concept of theater and found its architectural representation.

The next eight weeks, I worked to complete plans, sections, and the 1/8" scale model (figs. 61–65) and to be ready for the next meeting in Fort Wayne. During these weeks, I was also a student in Kahn's class, attempting to design our studio project, the Exeter Library.

I was glad I did not deviate from my studies of a plaza concept. I had kept my belief through many dead ends and divergence and unsuccessful results. I had continued through my frustration, and I could see the strength of the belief that I could reach a bright opening.

I completed hardline drawings and a 1/8" (approximately 1/30 in metric) scale model. I was alone in working on the project. No one else was helping me with the drawings or with making the model. The drawings and the model photographs were published in the Japanese *Kekusai Kentuki International Review of Architecture*, Vol. xxxiv, No. I, January 1967, Tokyo.

* * *

The architectural model was a big rectangular volume. The overall height was the height of the stagehouse. The scenery workshop had a lower ceiling attached to the stagehouse (fig. 61). There was an open-air theater at the roof above the audience hall. At the roof theater, there were large circular openings on the side walls, opening toward the city. The greenroom, actors' lounge, and dressing rooms were in a rectangular volume attached to the audience hall at the eastern wall, and rehearsal rooms were located under the audience hall.

The seating was in straight rows, out of an understanding that any performance could be at any spot or zone on the stage. The proscenium had an extra wide opening for ballet, orchestra performances, and civic activities. Ballet performances could extend from stage right all the way to stage left. And whenever desired, the sliding partitions or heavy curtains could reduce the proscenium opening to the required/desired size.

Autumn

In the middle of this work, the fall semester started at Penn. For the next four months (September through December), I was both a student of Kahn and an employee in his office.

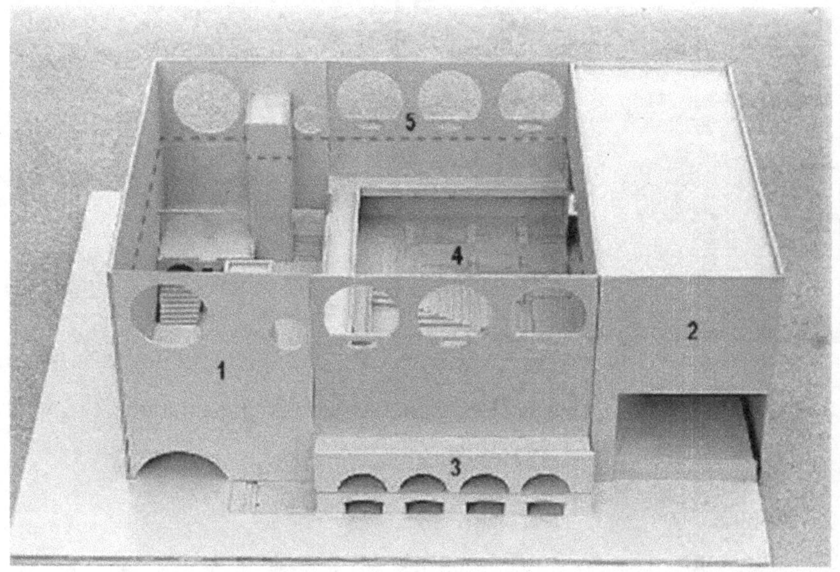

Figure 61. Kahn presented this model in Fort Wayne (October '66).

1. Lobby
2. Stagehouse
3. Stage entrance to greenroom and rehearsal rooms
4. Lobby
5. Stagehouse
6. Stage entrance to greenroom and rehearsal rooms
7. Audience hall
8. Roof theater

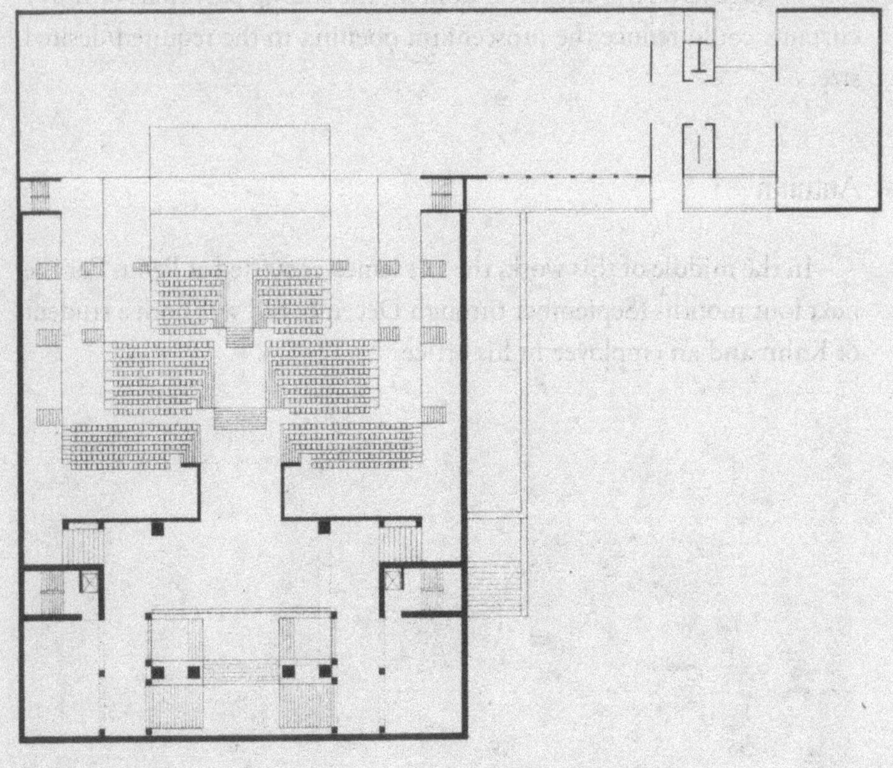

Figure 62. Theater floor plan, October '66 presentation.

1. Entrance
2. Lobby
3. Side stage
4. Scenery workshop

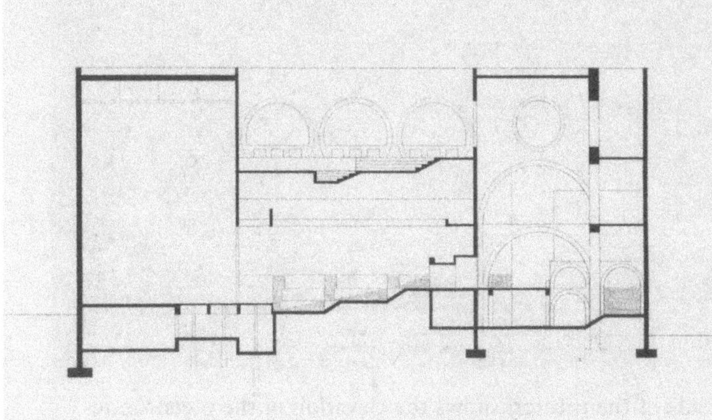

1. Entrance
2. Refreshments
3. Lounge
4. Projection booth
5. Stage traps
6. Makeup room
7. Roof theater

Figure 63. Theater section.

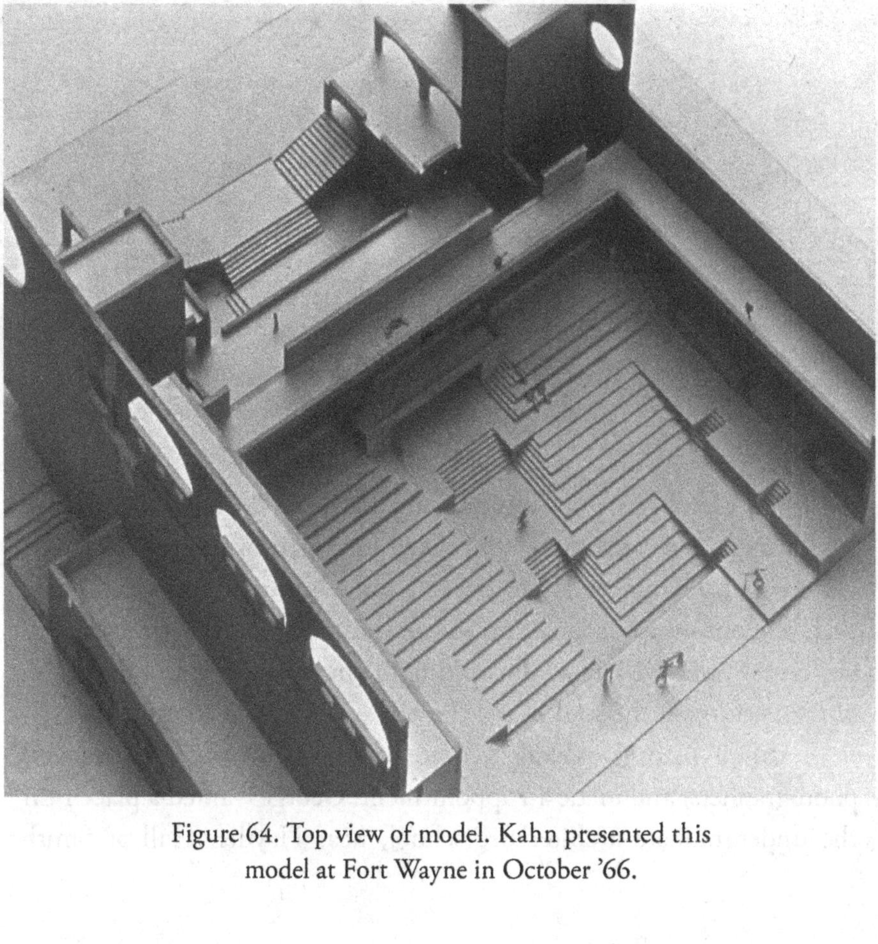

Figure 64. Top view of model. Kahn presented this model at Fort Wayne in October '66.

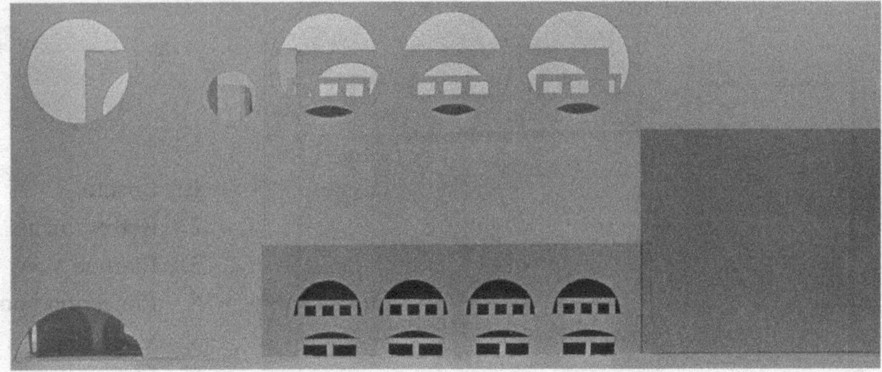

Figure 65. East facade of the theater; shows the elevation of the greenroom, rehearsal areas, and roof theater.

Figure 66. Kahn's hand-cut figures on the model.

It was October 1966. I was packing up the model for Kahn's trip to Fort Wayne. He came down and asked for a pair of scissors and some plain paper. He proceeded to cut out some human figures and glued each one onto various locations in the theater (fig. 66). I thought this was a very effective way of illustrating life in the theater and the realm of the performer, the soul of the theater.

I called George Alikakos (one of Lou's favorite architectural photographers) and made an appointment. George wanted a place near the undergraduate architecture school, near Hayden Hall at Smith

Walk. He took all the model photographs in the shade behind that building.

October Presentation

On October 1966, Kahn flew to Fort Wayne and presented this 1/8" scale model and the drawings to the Fort Wayne Fine Arts Committee.

On his return, he came down to the fourth floor and stood by my table. "They are strict in their view," he said. Obviously, the Fort Wayne Fine Arts Committee did not fall in love with what they had seen. "They did not like the central aisle. We'll simplify it, take out the central aisle and one of the tiers, and continue the seating from side to side. Do not change the scheme," he added. "We'll ask for their final approval and make a complete presentation the next time."

I did not like Fort Wayne's suggestion of removing the central aisle and limiting the side tiers. They were taking out its unique character. But the decision had already been made. I did not think it was my place to disagree. I kept my thoughts to myself.

It was almost November. I was also involved in the finals of the Exeter Library project, and later, the urban planning study projects in Kahn's class.

* * *

I started studying the revised scheme. I built a simple 1/16" (approximately 1/90 in metric) scale study model with no central aisle and one less side tier (fig. 67).

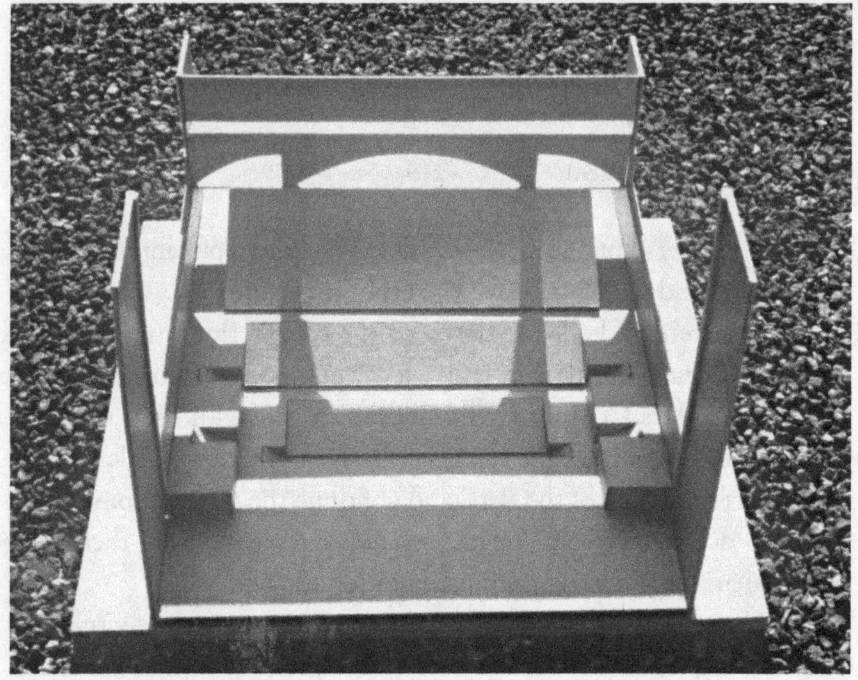

Figure 67.
Study maquette with no central aisle and one less side tier (1966).

I liked it. I realized the theater was reaching Trenton Baths–like simplicity. It had that minimal quality, the kind of "beginning" quality. Taking out one more component could make it lose its character. The elimination of the third tier greatly affected the sizes of the rehearsal rooms, dressing rooms, greenroom, and actors' lobby, and pushed them farther down under the audience hall. It made them not directly accessible to and from the stage. Relegating the performers to the basement, with no daylight, was hard to agree with and hard to accept.

Graduation

On December 1966, I completed my studies and graduated with a Master of Architecture degree from the University of Pennsylvania. There was no graduation ceremony for December graduates. There was no celebration, no party, and no cake for me. I just picked up my diploma from the post office window at the Thirtieth Street Station and happily became a full-time employee at the office of Louis Kahn.

In the middle of January, to my great surprise, I was offered a teaching position at the architectural school at the University of Pennsylvania. Three afternoons a week, I would be co-teaching architectural design studio with John Bower, a successful Philadelphia architect. I kept this teaching position until I returned to Turkey in June 1968. Teaching was a great source of joy, learning, creativity, and vision.

Job Captain

On February 7, 1967, a meeting was held on the fifth floor of Lou's office.[12] The purpose was to review the comments in the October meeting (figs. 60–65). Bud Latz, the chairman of the Fort Wayne Fine Arts Foundation; Edward Menerth, the Fort Wayne Fine Arts director; Tunc Yalman, the artistic director of Milwaukee Repertory (1966–1971); Dick Shoaff, a local Fort Wayne architect; David Wisdom; Kahn; and I were present.

At the start of the meeting, to my complete surprise, Kahn announced he was appointing me the permanent job captain for the Fort Wayne Theater project.[13]

Discussion followed. Fort Wayne insisted on the following:

- The central aisle and the third bank of tiers must be eliminated.
- Larger areas are needed for ballet, drama, and orchestra rehearsal rooms; dressing rooms; greenroom; and storage rooms.
- The number of seats must be fixed at eight hundred.

---

12 Kahn did not want to show the current study model I had made with the removed central aisle and fewer side tiers (fig. 67).

13 Minutes, February 6, 1967, Kahn Collection, University of Pennsylvania and Pennsylvania Historical and Museum Collection, Philadelphia (hereafter cited as Kahn Collection).

Kahn pointed out that eliminating the third bank of tiers would require that the dressing rooms be located deeper under the second and first tiers in the basement. Tunc Yalman added that the greenroom and dressing rooms must have direct and immediate access to the stage.

Kahn mentioned it was time for the office to receive the final list of requirements from Fort Wayne. A complete needs program had not yet been submitted. Lou also suggested there should be a meeting among all the user groups and participants, to list their requirements.

Discussion continued about ongoing uncertainties of the proposed site. Had this site been decided? Its purchase was still not clear. Earlier site plans had all been done from an approximate site dimension. A professional engineer's survey had not yet been received by the office, and it had recently been informed that the city of Fort Wayne had decided to widen Main Street, making the site limits even more uncertain. The next meeting was scheduled to take place in two weeks, in Fort Wayne. Kahn wanted me to attend that meeting.

Alone in Fort Wayne I

On February 20, 1967, I took a flight from Philadelphia to Indianapolis, where I transferred to a commuter plane to get to Fort Wayne. I had the October '66 model with me. I had never been to Fort Wayne. Richard Shoaff (the local architect for this project) met me at the airport and took me to his home, designed by Frank Lloyd Wright. Tunc Yalman was already there. The three of us went to the meeting together.

This was my first meeting with the extended members of the Fine Arts Foundation. I was surprised to see the meeting was being held in an auditorium. After introducing me to several individuals, they pointed me to the stage. This was very unusual. I remember thinking this was going to be a real performance.

I began by explaining the project in detail. I presented the October model and detailed drawings, then opened for questions. The questions started coming fast and furious. "Can we have such-and-such square feet area for such a place?" The side tiers and then the central aisle were questioned. Someone suggested a cut of five to ten feet on each side. Someone else spoke out against the open-air theater on the roof. The proscenium opening was too big, they complained. I pointed out that this would be made adjustable. It will not work, I was told. The typical opening must be fifty feet wide, twenty feet high, and a rectangle. They wanted less height for the stagehouse, more area for the scenery workshop, more space for the makeup room, more space for the rehearsal room. More and more questions and comments came. I believe there was not a single actor, dancer, ballerina, or performance artist in the meeting that evening whom I could receive some positive remark from.

The minutes of the meeting arrived from Fort Wayne a few days later and confirmed my suspicions. I guessed Lou was already aware of the challenging reaction to the design. Many new building areas were being requested. I thought it was best to wait patiently until the office received the formal letter for new detailed requirements from the Fort Wayne Fine Arts Foundation.

House of the Actor

Finally, the new requirements arrived from Fort Wayne. I made simple diagrammatic plans, then a sketch to compare sizes and positions for each of the newly requested areas. This was going to be a four-story, seventy-foot-wide square block. The fourth floor was for ballet rehearsals, a 55×55 ft room with a twenty-foot ceiling height, which was requested. The third and second floors were fifteen feet high, and they were for drama and music rehearsal rooms. They could be divided into two or four separate rooms. The ground floor had an artists' entrance, lobby, dressing rooms, showers, toilets, and greenroom, in addition to management offices. All floors were aboveground; all would receive full daylight.

I built a 1/16" scale maquette of the house of actors (fig. 68). This was at the same scale as the earlier audience hall maquette (fig. 67). Attaching this to the back of the stagehouse completed the theater.[14]

---

[14] Author's note: Years later, when I was researching the earlier studies of theater

Figure 68. The 1/16" scale model, view toward the stage (1967).

At the stage level, there were three large doors that allowed direct access to the stage. All levels had six-foot-wide balconies with large arched openings toward the stage. The proscenium remained wide yet with an adjustable opening, for differing productions of dramas, musicals, concerts, dances, or graduation ceremonies. My thinking continued to be that the proscenium should not create a barrier between the performer and the audience. The actual opening size could be decided by the play's director and the nature of the performance. The height of the stagehouse was reduced, as requested by Fort Wayne.

Kahn came down to the fourth floor for a review of the new plans and sketch model. I explained that everything on the model responded to Fort Wayne's new needs program. He was quiet for a while, and then

---

of performing arts projects in the Kahn archives, I realized the initial idea of putting the rehearsal rooms behind the stage was Kahn's.

In one of his models during 1963, there was a building called the philharmonic annex, located between the philharmonic hall and a theater of performing arts. This building contained all drama and music rehearsal rooms, offices, and greenrooms for both the philharmonic hall and the theater. Kahn had also talked about his belief of having this building where an actor crafts his art; it may be built elsewhere but must be rolled up to the stage before each performance.

slowly he raised his eyes, smiled, and nodded. "Good," he said, and he walked away.

The theater was finally becoming a complete statement. Now everything in the building was essential to make it a place for performing arts. Nothing more, nothing less. I thought it had reached its delicate balance.

The Fine Art of Performance

My love for the theater had begun in 1956, when I was in my last year in high school. That year, I moved from Adana to Ankara. State theaters were well established in Ankara. For a while, I even considered attending the state conservatory and majoring in theater arts for my college education. My family did not like the idea. Then in METU (1959–1964), I joined the METU drama club. We produced plays by Chekhov, Beckett, and Thornton Wilder, and we took those productions to various cities in Anatolia during our semester breaks. I didn't have much talent for acting. I was primarily involved in set design, setup, and construction. These early experiences played a significant role in my understanding of theaters and shaped my ideas about stage productions.

Actor's Porch

Stage plays are written to inspire us, to question our beliefs, and to sharpen our senses. An actor is not merely an entertainer. An actor shows us, informs us, and introduces us to life's games, joys, and fears. The audience in the theater is the guest of the actor.

The actor perfects his art at the actor's house. The actor's porch is the architectural expression of this house on the stage. The interaction created between the actors and the audience would be the essence of the theater architecture.

Theaters are art centers, meant for human expressions. They may be written in one language, but plain and simple, they are expressions of being human.

It seemed unfair to me that many theaters are designed and built solely for the paying customers. Everything is adorned, gilded, and ornamented on the audience's side; the hallways, stairs, and seats are all designed for the pleasure of the audience. The proscenium that fronts the audience is gilded and richly ornamented. The back of the house, the actors' zones, are narrow, dark, and grimy, which seems to discount the art and the artist. These thoughts were at the forefront of my mind as I began the hardline drawings and later the 1/8" scale model for the revised scheme.

A Hand Note

On March 17, 1967, the night before I left, as I was finishing the drawings and packing up, Kahn came down to the fourth floor. After reviewing the final model, he took a piece of paper and wrote something on it (fig. 69), then he handed it to me. "Give this to Bud [Latz]," he said.

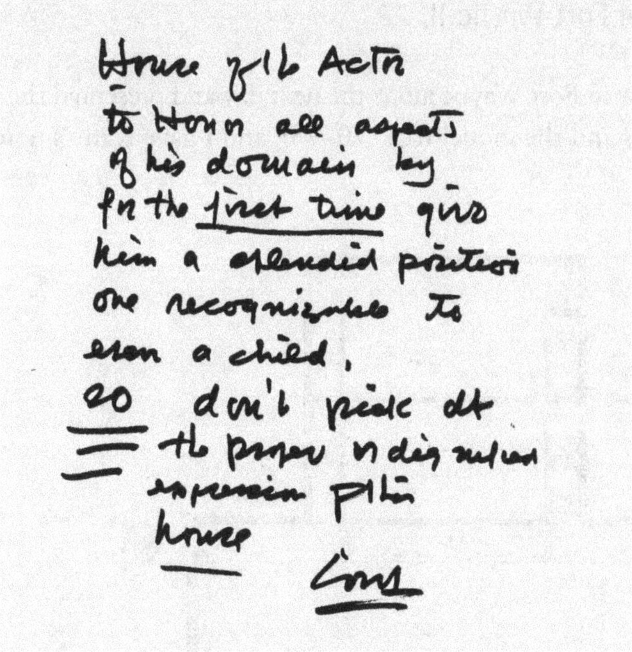

Figure 69

House of the Actor
to honor all aspects
of his domain by
for the *first time* give
him a splendid position
one recognizable to
even a child.
So don't pick at
    the proper or dignified
    expression of this
    house

Lou

Alone in Fort Wayne II

I flew to Fort Wayne alone the next day and presented the following drawings and the model (figs. 70–78), and I gave Kahn's note (fig. 69) to Bud.

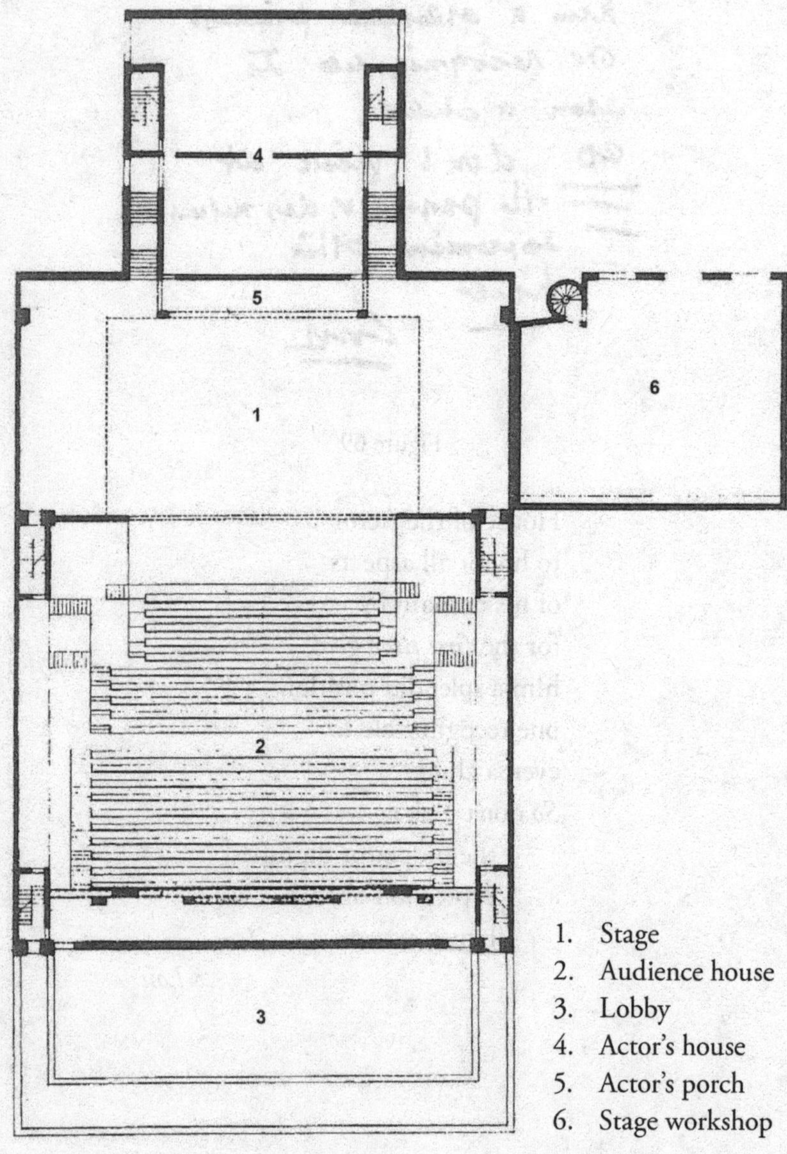

Figure 70. Plan (March 17, '67).

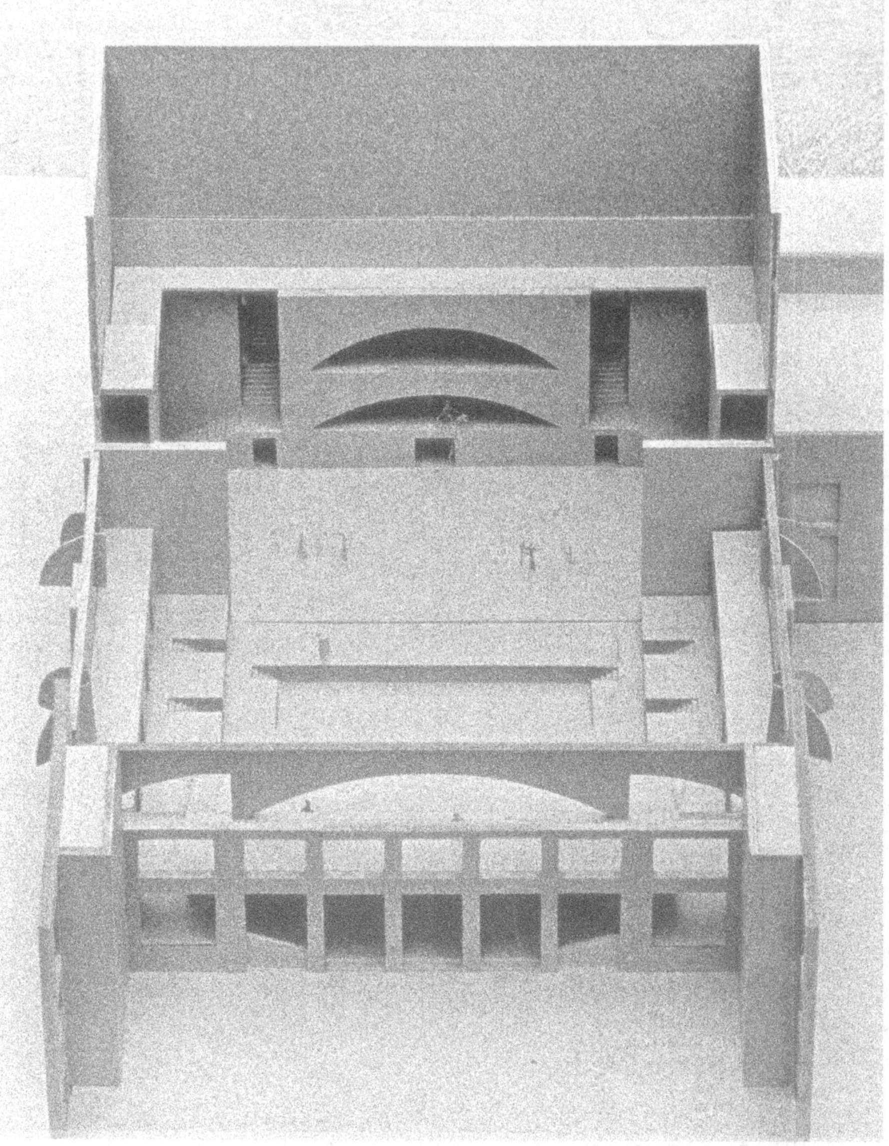

Figure 71. Presented on March 17, '67: 1/8" scale model by author, view toward the stage.

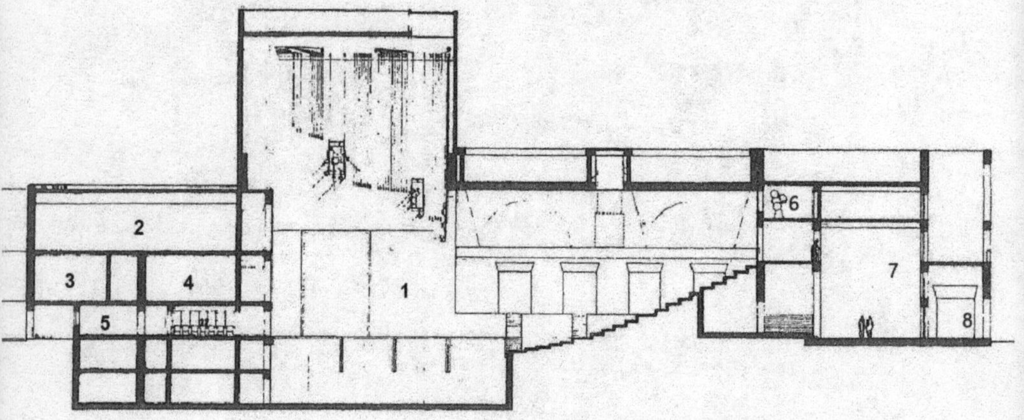

Figure 72.

1. Stage
2. Ballet rehearsal
3. Drama rehearsal I
4. Drama rehearsal II
5. Greenroom
6. Actors' entrance
7. Light gallery
8. Projection booths
9. Lobby
10. Main entrance

Figure 73. Exterior view of the actor's house.

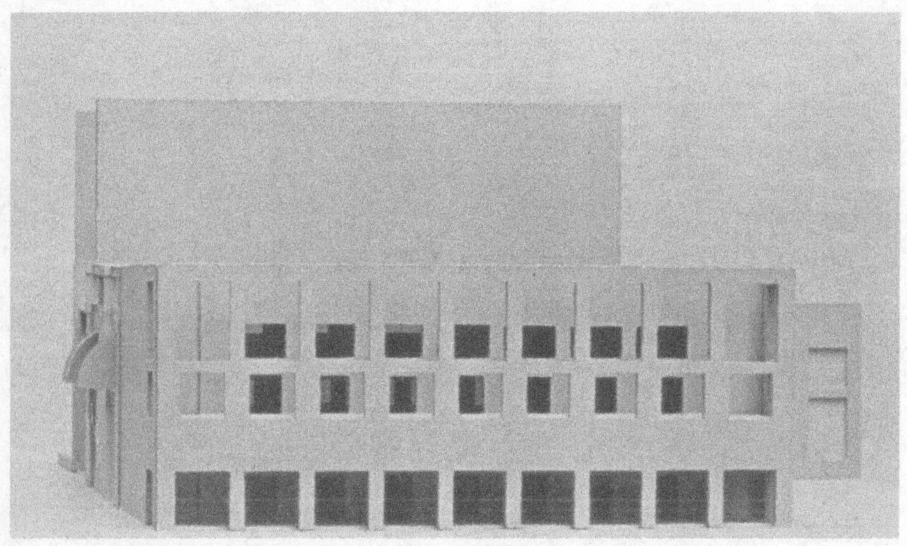

Figure 74. View from the main street.

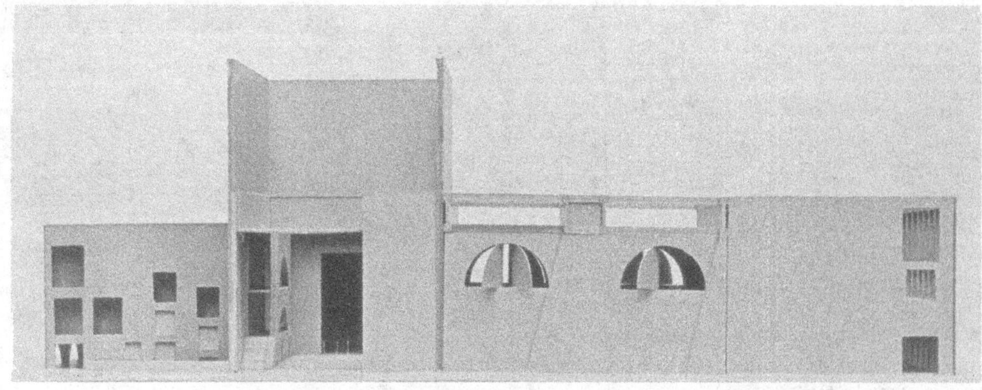

Figure 75. West elevation with stagehouse wall is left open. Notice the arched openings for the audience hall. High arched windows are meant to let the daylight stream in. This is essential for civic activities, like graduations, lectures, discussions, or debates.

Figure 76. March 17 scheme. View from stage toward the seating and the king's place. The last level in the audience hall was Kahn's favorite, and he called it "the king's place."

Figure 77. View toward the stage and actor's house from the king's place.

Figure 78. Like he did for the earlier model, he cut the scale figures and placed them carefully in their appropriate places before I took it away for photography.

The meeting was attended by a large group of people. I explained the revised scheme and pointed out the changes in the model. Most

of the questions were about the sizes and dimensions of some of the rooms. I answered the questions. It seemed to me the whole meeting went very well. I returned to Philadelphia the next day. Kahn was away, so I briefed David Wisdom about the meeting.

A few days later, the office received a letter from E. Menerth,[15] the executive director of the Fort Wayne Fine Arts Foundation. The first sentence of his letter was as follows:

> It is difficult to put into words how delightful [delighted] I personally feel about the Theater plans dated March 17, 1967.

---

15 Letter from Menerth (executive director) to Kahn, March 22, 1967, Box LIK 17, Kahn Collection.

The letter continued with comments about the difficulty of carrying furniture to the third-floor rehearsal rooms, and it ended with the following:

> It does seem a pity that the elaborate and [visually exciting] series of arches penetrating the face of the backstage wall will never be seen—blocked to the public … by drops, sets, etc., during all performances.

* * *

Kahn responded with the following letter on April 10.[16] This was the first time Kahn mentioned my name in relation to theater being a new beginning.

> Dear Mr. Menerth:
>
> The theater has developed, in my mind, as a new fundamental in attitudes "What is theater."
>
> The two termini—
>
> "House of the Stage" and the "Honorary Balcony Hhouse" to the rear of the auditorium.
>
> The auditorium—conceived as the place of gathering in the architecture of a "court."
>
> These developed elements are now an interplay for the play of the Proscenium, the play of the forestage, and the play of the theater in the round. The last brings the two termini into view as though the "court" has been extended. The inspiring element of a new beginning "theater" possesses Mr. Yetken's mind and mine. From

[16] Letter from Kahn to Menerth (executive director), April 10, 1967, Box LIK 17, Kahn Collection.

> indications of your letter, I sense the warm reception you give it. I am also sure that all questions which arise for practical reasons should not, and I believe cannot, destroy these now inseparable elements.

Kahn went on to explain some technical issues and finished with:

> In regard to the "House of the Stage"— the architectural configurations there are architecturally essential to the conveying of a new realization of the architecture of the theater. Imagine the stage traps provided with seats looking toward the forestage, as the stage of the theater in the round and beyond the terminus of the "Honorary Balcony" and those in the "court" looking across the theater in the round stage, toward a "pavilion" (stage house) in the distance.
>
> How complete the architecture of a place of the theater.
>
> Sincerely,
> Louis I. Kahn
>
> LIK: lmb
>
> Note: It is now a theater that evokes the writing of the play as well as the place where the play is played.

Alone in Fort Wayne III

The next meeting was scheduled for a month later, in Fort Wayne. On April 18, 1967, I traveled alone, taking the updated drawings of the March 17 presentation. A full-scale building committee was in attendance. They were prepared, with the list of required areas. I was grilled not with comments but with objections.

A few days after my return, the meeting minutes[17] from the Fort Wayne Fine Arts Foundation arrived. It included the following:

- o Reduce areas of makeup room, storage rooms, side aisles, size of stairs at the back stage.
- o Reduce proscenium height to 25 feet, reduce stagehouse height 15 or more feet, and reduce ballet rehearsal room ceiling height (from initial request of 20 feet) to 12 feet.
- o Move the third level of ballet rehearsal room to under the rear bank of auditorium seats.
  - o We don't want more "circulation space" than we need.
  - o Project has now entered the design development stage.
  - o Technical consultant is required.

The letter ended with a note:

> Intrinsic beauty of the arches in the backstage wall … is appreciated and acknowledged but there are very practical objections to it … the expense of such unseen decorative accent might be prohibitive.

(By this point, the project budget had neither been established nor requested by Fort Wayne.)

Budget $1 Million

In the next month (May), the Fort Wayne Fine Arts Foundation (I. Latz and E. Menerth) informed David Wisdom that the cost of the theater should be assumed to be 1 million dollars.[18]

* * *

17 Minutes, meeting in FW, April 18, 1967, Box LIK 17, Kahn Collection.

18 Phone memo, Latz to Wisdom (Kahn's office), April '67, Box LIK 17, Kahn Collection.

In mid-March, Louise brought me a folder with a smile on her face. She put it on my desk and left. I opened the folder and read the letter. I did not know what to think or say. I never thought about Kahn thinking of my work that way. The letter (fig. 79) had already been mailed to Dean Aptullah Kuran.

I did not mention this letter to anyone. I folder it and put it away. Then I remembered I had mentioned to Louise a month before that I was on a paid leave of absence from METU for two years, which would expire on June 1967, and I needed a letter from my US employer if I would be employed for another year, to extend my stay in the US until June 1968.

March 10, 1967

Dean Aptullah Kuran
School of Architecture
Middle East Technical University
Ankara, Turkey

Dear Dean Kuran:

I am aware that Cengiz Yetken has agreed to a two year leave of absence from the Middle East Technical University which terminates in September 1967.

During his work at the University he distinguished himself as a student most talented as a composer of architecture. His work went beyond mere design ability. Compositions of architectural elements, the stronger art, is a part of him.

His work in my office following his school is strengthening his practical knowledge which will prove important in teaching. He needs more of the art of practice and at present is working on several of my commissions which he started, contributed much to, and should complete. I urge you, in his interest and yours and mine to allow him to stay on in my office until June 1968.

My regards to my former students and other friends.

Sincerely yours,
Louis I. Kahn
LIK:bas

Figure 79. Louis's letter to Dean Aptullah Kuran.

PART 5

1501 Walnut Street

Many buildings are built without belief… built merely for profit, which I do not think you can include as belief… built to make things more convenient, more modern; they don't have in back of them the kind of belief that made the first monastery, the first school … that is the kind of belief which, when established, becomes an inseparable part of the way of life. An architect, when he is searching for belief, is not searching for his own belief after all, he is not a doctor when he makes a hospital. Through the way he expresses things he becomes a sort of custodian of the belief of those for whom he builds.[19]

—Louis Kahn

[19] Fort Wayne Theater Promotional Brochure, Author's Collection.

Office Life

Figure 80. View from Walnut and Fifteenth Street intersection, looking northwest. LIK office was at the top two floors of this building. (Photo by author, 1976)

A single manual elevator connected all five floors. The elevator was run by an African American man named Henry. He was a kind man and in charge of maintaining the whole building. The elevator opened to narrow landings on every floor. Kahn's office occupied the top two floors of the building (fig. 80).

On the landing on the fifth floor, a single door held a small sign: "Louis I. Kahn, Architect." The door opened to a reception area. This was where Louis Badgley worked. Kahn's office was on the right. This was the southeast corner of the fifth floor, with windows facing east and south. This small room appeared empty. There was a single table and three wooden chairs (figs. 81–82).

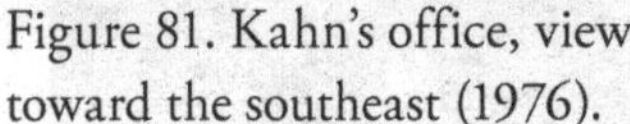

Figure 81. Kahn's office, view toward the southeast (1976).

Figure 82. Kahn's office, view toward the north (1976).

The reception room was where Louise Badgley (Kahn's personal secretary, the office secretary, and the receptionist) would work, and it opened to a large elongated room—the project studio (fig. 84). The four individuals who made up the permanent personnel had their work stations there. They were the full-time people: David Wisdom (fig. 83), the office manager; Henry Wilcotts (fig. 83); Galen Schlosser; and Reyhan Larimer. These four would primarily deal with construction documents, details, and specifications. And there was Vincent Rivera, a bright, talented young man who knew everything. There was a carpentry room and a lunchroom at the very end.

Figure 83. *From left:* Henry Wilcotts, Cengiz Yetken, and David Wisdom in 1977.

Figure 84. Fifth-floor studio, view toward the north (1977).

The other drafting tables on the fifth-floor studio (fig. 84) were occupied by Marshall Meyers and David Polk, and occasionally Marvin Verman, Tony Pellecchia, and Neil Thompson.

There was no specific space designated as a meeting room. Meetings took place either in Kahn's office or in the studio on the fifth floor. The fifth floor was the "presentable" floor of the office.

The fourth floor was quiet (and similar in setup and shape). There were four of us: Winton Scott, working on Exeter Dining Hall; Anant Raje, working on Interama; Hideki Shimizu, working on Exeter Library; and me, working on the Performing Arts Center. Occasionally, some others would come to work, like some students during charrettes. Sometimes Raje and I would strike up a conversation that would end up in laughter. We used to make jokes about the fourth floor being for exiled people, for non-Americans. Raje was a dear friend and always showed up to my final jury presentations at school. He was single at the time, like me. Hideki and Winton both had families.

Drafting tables on both floors were lined up along the east wall, along the windows. The tables were covered with green vinyl drafting sheets. Each table had a drafting lamp and an attached straightedge. The two rows of wood cabinets (wide, flat drawers for drawings) were lined up parallel to the drawing tables, back to back, at the center of this room, providing a large surface on which to review drawings at a height of thirty-six to forty inches. The top surfaces were always full of current sets, reference drawings, and study models. The drawers were designated for projects, with names tagged on the front. Original drawings were drawn on linen or on vellum with pencil. Original blueprints and sepia copies were also kept in these drawers. Every charcoal sketch by Kahn was marked with the letters *LIK*, dated, carefully sprayed with fixative, and placed in project drawers.

There were new projects in the office since my graduation. David Polk was working on the Dominican Motherhouse of St. Catherine de Ricci, Media, Pennsylvania. Fred Langford and Marshall Meyers were working on the Olivetti-Underwood Factory, Harrisburg, Pennsylvania.

In later years, I saw Marshall Meyers working on the Memorial to the Six Million Jewish Martyrs, New York City, New York, and later, Kimbell. Reyhan Larimer was on Eyub Han Hospital, Dhaka, Bangladesh. Henry Wilcotts continued working on Dacca, second capital of Pakistan, later renamed as Sher-e-Bangla Nagar, Capital of Bangladesh, Dhaka.

Throughout my work in the office, the following projects were being worked on there. In no particular order:

- Kimbell Art Museum, Fort Worth, Texas
- Indian Institute of Management, Ahmedabad, India
- President's Estate, Islamabad, Pakistan
- Family Planning Center, Kathmandu, Nepal
- Yale Center for British Art, New Haven, Connecticut
- Hurva Synagogue, Jerusalem, Israel
- Palazzo dei Congressi, Venice, Italy
- Kansas City Office Building, Kansas City, Missouri
- Dr. and Mrs. Norman Fisher's House, Hatboro, Pennsylvania
- Interama Center, Dade County, Florida
- Performing Arts Center, Fort Wayne, Indiana

- Library and Dining Hall, Phillips Exeter, New Hampshire
- Unitarian Church addition, Rochester, New York

* * *

There were no titles or ranks in the office. Everybody called Kahn by his first name, Lou. There were no principals, partners, associates, senior designers, junior designers, or architect 1, architect 2, and architect 3, as I was acquainted with in my later years in Chicago. There was no person titled as project manager, no TC (technical coordinator), no MSL (market sector leader), no green architect, and no sustainability specialist. There was no renderer, model builder, etc. When the time came, everyone did everything related to the project work.

I never heard Kahn or anyone else in the office utter the words *marketing*, *selling architecture*, or *selling design*. There was no publicity person for brochures or press releases for projects, office activities, or Kahn's activities, like his lectures, travels, or project dedications.

Toward Light

Kahn did a lot of thinking and a lot of sketching to carry an idea in his sketchbook. He carried a lot of conversations, with questions and explanations to carry his idea further. These could take place in his class, in his lectures, and in his office. He would talk about the beginning, the existence will, and in many poetic phrases that fascinated people. He would continue this until his concept clarified in his mind, until its connections were fully formed. He would then carry his conversations to the drafting table, with the associate architect he assigned for this work in his office. This exploration would continue all through the project.

Being a student in his class and working with him in his office, I noticed Kahn would introduce the project with a small story or a key sentence in class and would step into a project with a brilliant universal value. Then his questions would follow: What does it *want to be*?

What is its *nature*? What is the story of its *existence*? What is its *will of existence*? What kind of framework will the project have? What kind of human relations will it support, and what kind will it develop?

Kahn would start with a very thoughtful and abstract idea in his class, which would inspire students into deeper thought, and would relate stories with complex ideas for projects' essential meanings. This indicated that the *concept stage* or *realization phase* requires deeper thoughts than when a project moves into the *production* or *development* stages, as in the difference between the questions of *what* and of *how*.

I did not think Kahn had any personal agenda. He just worked with determination to do his absolute best. Through his hard work, Kahn demonstrated that artistic endeavor cannot be just a part-time activity, but a lifetime involvement. The involvement must be based on belief, knowledge, insight, and love. Kahn had a strong sense of purpose, excitement, and passion that was backed up by endless energy.

I did not think his initial sketches were particularly earthshaking. Those were just ideas drawn in grease pencil diagrams that showed a kind of creativity. His objective did not seem to be making an iconic or merely *interesting* building. The major thrust of his work was to discover the most suitable life experience in such setting.

The intention was to expand that sense of wonder, to create a warm place to live, work, or learn, so that one may not even notice the hard setup (the enclosure, the construction, and the built-up walls, ceilings, and floors) but simply carry on and be delighted with the life found in and around it.

I never thought Kahn worked for money or fame. I did not think money was of value to him. I never thought he was seeking to make a name for himself. Architecture was his destiny, and he was born to be an architect.

* * *

I always thought and believed Kahn saw architecture as a service to humanity—to inspire, to elevate and to honor life - like an artist would, like Picasso, like Van Gogh and like Mozart did. -.

For Kahn, architecture was like fine art—like a piece of classical music, a fine sculpture, a great painting, a work of literature. He saw architecture as one of the essential arts to sustain advancement in society.

I could imagine that every single line on a plan, on elevation, was a struggle for his creative mind. It must have been hard for him to choose one out of so many other options in his mind. How was he able to pick the final scheme out of so many good ones he could have made? And how was he able to be consistent over time and still get better with the next one?

Charcoal

During regular office times, on an ordinary day, Kahn would stop in front of your table or sit down with you. Or if he saw something he liked or disliked, or if he had time to spend on his favorite project (even if you are not there at the time), he would ask for a piece of charcoal and yellow tracing paper. Then he would start sketching and talking about the project to the person who gave him the paper or charcoal. After he would finish and leave the table, the person would carefully write the date and add *LIK* on the bottom right, spray a fixative on his sketch, wait until it dried, obtain a blueprint copy for future work, and carefully lay the yellow trace in its project drawer.

Translating these charcoal sketches into a hardline drawing was not easy. The people working on these had to be in tune with Kahn's ideas; one had to know how to read his sketches and his references, and know about his way of thinking or doing things. After the person who was working on that project completed the hardline drawing, Kahn would come back to see if it had to be corrected. He would look at it, and he might say, "No. No. No, this is not what I meant here." He would explain and sketch again. "There is a separation joint here, you see. Look at my sketch." He would be pointing to a dot on the charcoal line. "There is a joint here."

He would periodically check the progress or eye it while passing by your table. This could be late at night or even when you were not there. When he saw something unclear or interpreted wrongly, or if he had a new discovery or saw anything that was not quite consistent in your drawing, he would sketch over it and leave a note. These would mostly become his unsophisticated drawings/sketches—informative, quick, and sometimes even quite tough to understand.

Between teaching, lecturing, and traveling, Kahn spent his life in the office.

Charrettes

Almost once in every two weeks, a charrette would take place in the office for project presentations. The night before a meeting, everyone would be in the office, helping in the charrette. Drawings and models would be prepared for the meeting. Kahn would visit everyone and check the progress and design consistency. If everything held up well, as he would like to see it, he would be out of the door with rolls of drawings and a maquette early in the morning, off to the Philadelphia airport. Or as in some sad and disillusioning occasions, Kahn would not like the progress, cancel the meeting, and call everyone to stop and go home, usually around three a.m. He would take a roll of blank yellow trace and a box of charcoal sticks, and leave for the airport.

* * *

I usually arrived to work late in the morning and worked until 10:00 p.m. or midnight. I did not think there was a fixed time to arrive or to leave the office. I do not remember anyone complaining about late nights or weekend work. People were there when work needed to be done.

Everyone in the office was very talented, experienced, and well educated. Everyone seemed to be doing their best. Each one held the belief that they were doing special work in architecture. And Kahn was above us all. His confident enthusiasm and creativity were infectious.

The work was exhilarating. Witnessing his love for architecture, his constant energy, his complex thinking, and his continuous challenge to himself was a unique experience that would sustain and guide us for the rest of our lives.

Colloquium in Montreal

In the early days of June '67, David Wisdom informed me that Kahn wanted me to attend a theater colloquium in Montreal, Canada, June 19 to 25.

The colloquium was taking place during Expo 67. The formal title was "The Design of Theaters: A Colloquium on Architecture and Technology of the Theater in Relation to Its Artistic Aims." I traveled to Montreal and attended all the sessions. Most presentations were about the promotion of certain materials, in the audience hall, lighting, and sound equipment, as improvements in the theater. There were a few about the needs for defining a new theater. I remember talking to some people about Kahn's new theater that would address these concerns.

The trip was also a perfect opportunity to experience Expo 67 buildings: Fuller's geodesic dome and Moshe Safdie's Habitat 67 housing complex. I classified them as "architecture for entertainment."

The Lawn

In the middle of summer, David Wisdom told me I had two weeks of paid vacation. Friends in the office suggested I go south to see Jefferson's university in Charlottesville, Virginia.

I drove to Chesapeake Bay, then to the Blue Ridge Mountains, down to Charlottesville to Jefferson's university, and then to the house he called Monticello.

Jefferson's Lawn was masterly. Here was another lesson in architecture. What a wonderful, confident, and solid way to make a setting for higher learning. I saw a strong connection between Jefferson and Kahn in site organization, in crisp planning, and in identifying and locating the major components of composition.

* * *

The following sections show Lou's keen sense of awareness and unrelenting observation of his surroundings.

The Enemy

It was late in the day. Hideki was preparing to return to Japan. He had just finished the drawings and wood model of the Exeter Library (fig. 170). Kahn and Hideki were discussing the final model of the Exeter Library just behind me. The model was sitting on top of the central flat files, between Hideki's table and mine.

For a brief second, I turned back and looked at it. From the sound of their comments, I understood that they were looking at the top terrace openings. From his tone, I could hear that Kahn was not very comfortable about something. I turned back again and looked at it a few more seconds. Suddenly, he raised his eyes from the model and looked at me. "What do you think, Cengiz?" he asked. This was not a question. He was getting me involved in the discussion.

I stood quietly for a while, looked at the model, and shrugged and murmured, "It is OK." I immediately realized this was a stupid reaction on my part, a careless one.

"You are becoming my enemy," Kahn shot back. He wasn't looking at me.

This was a good lesson. *Think before you talk,* I told myself.

Unlearning

I was working on the Salk Institute Housing project. There were ten residential units southeast of Salk Institute, located along a most beautiful curve.

I was at the beginning of my study. In any of my design studies, I would start from the simplest and go toward the most complex. My charcoal sketch in front of me at that time showed housing units arranged along a simple straight line.

Kahn suddenly showed up at my table. Looking at my sketches with a smile, he said, "It is hard to unlearn architecture, isn't it, Cengiz?" This was not a question to be answered. He smiled and left my table.

Taxicab

Taxicabs in Philadelphia had taximeters with a loud ticking noise that indicated fares (in ten-cent increments). These units were located at the far right of the driver, near the windshield in front of the passenger seat. It had a long arm that the driver would pull down when a passenger would get into the cab. Kahn would always take the passenger seat going to the airport. He once pointed out how this simple ticking sound created unnecessary tension between the driver and the passenger paying for the accumulating cost of the trip. I remember the same feeling in my own experience in taxicabs. Even when I was speaking to the driver, I could hear this mechanical sound softly affecting our genuine human relationship.

Beethoven's Fifth

I had this nervous habit of whistling Beethoven's Fifth Symphony in the office during my work. "Cengiz, please. You cannot whistle Beethoven." It was sudden, unexpected. He had just walked into the fourth floor. Kahn continued: "You can't whistle classical music. You can hum if you like. But you cannot whistle classical music."

Kitchen

Kahn wanted me to work on Indian Institute of Management. He patiently explained its kitchen as a large square room with a cone-shaped roof. He described to me the popular Indian dishes. In the area at the center, there were cooking grills, and the perimeter was for preparing food. There were large openings at the base that provided fresh air, which allowed the heated air and smoke to leave at the top. He defined an Indian kitchen to me as a working chimney.

Happy Hour

Almost every Friday, on the fourth floor, Hideki, Raje, and Winton would tease me. Knowing well that I did not drink alcohol, they would say, "Let's go for a drink this Friday. This time, Cengiz will drink." The rest of the group, including Neil, would always agree and say, "Yeah, we should celebrate."

We would all leave together around five o'clock and walk to a bar a few blocks east of the office. They would order their drinks, enjoy their beer, and watch me order ginger ale. "Ginger ale," they would all laughingly say. "That's not good for you."

We enjoyed a good fellowship beyond the office atmosphere. I later learned this was a tradition in America called happy hour.

A Friendly Trust

Owning a car in America had never been a dream of mine. Hideki had a white '66 VW Beetle that was a few months old. During one casual conversation, he mentioned he was planning to leave for Tokyo, and he asked if I would be interested in buying his car. "Well, yes," I said. Hideki would leave the car for $1,350. "Pay whenever you can," he added. He left a few days later. There was no signed agreement, no advance cash, nothing. I was astonished he trusted me. The only reason for his trust was that we both worked for Kahn. A few months later, I sent the total amount to him in Tokyo. Years later, in 2006, when I met him in Tokyo, we had a very nice evening and dinner together, and we laughed at this reminiscence.

DD Phase

Finally, in April '67, Fort Wayne approved the schematic design. We moved into the design development phase, and change requests became very intense. Put this in, take that out, larger area for this, smaller area for that.

Catwalks

My next focus was to study the ceiling of the audience hall, to integrate the sound and light components into the hall (fig. 85). It is customary in the industry to mount the required lights and speakers on open trusses above the audience hall. These trusses are also used as walkways for light and sound technicians. The trusses or walkways are often referred to as "catwalks." Technicians would be able to walk, adjust, move, or change these instruments for performances. This may take place even during performances, so they must be very quiet, without falling or dropping things on the audience below. I was sure Louwould not want open trusses in this theater, and neither did I.

I think the ceiling of an audience hall is the most complex design problem. It must respond to numerous design objectives:

- To carry the whole weight of the ceiling across the width of the audience hall
- To carry the sound from the stage to the back of the auditorium and not create reverberation
- To accommodate all sound and light equipment focused toward the performance

- To allow a safe and secure work space for the light technician / soundman, away from the eyes and ears of the audience
- To be aesthetically and architecturally pleasing

I built the ceiling study model (figs. 86–88).

Figure 85. Violin ceiling study. Charcoal sketch by Yetken (1967).

Budget $1.2 Million

In August 1967, a letter from E. Menerth, the executive director of the Fort Wayne Fine Arts Foundation, informed us that the expected budget for the building should not exceed 1.2 million dollars. This was the very first time a budget was mentioned for the project.

I continued building study models for the ceiling of the theater.

Figure 86. Ceiling study model, view from the top. Notice daylight openings in the side walls. (Photo by Yetken, 1967)

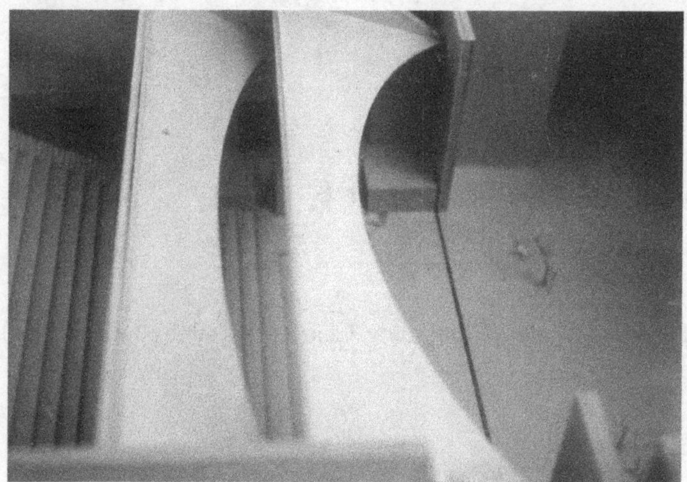

Figure 87 (Photo by author, 1967)

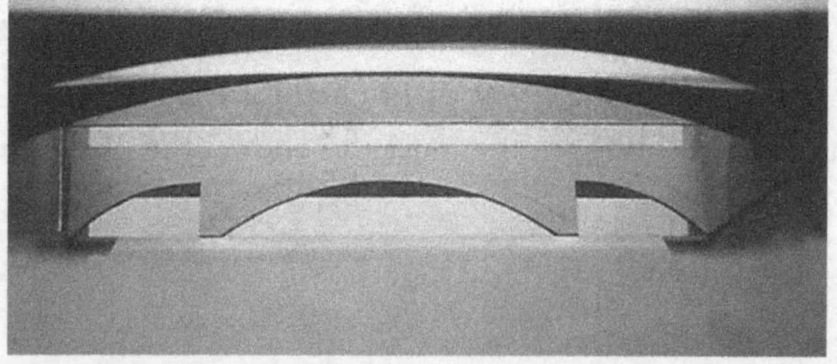

Figure 88. 1/8" scale study model for ceiling study, view from the stage toward the king's place. (Photo by author, 1967)

On September 1967, upon Kahn's approval, the Fort Wayne Fine Arts Foundation appointed George Izenour as the theater engineering consultant. Izenour had a consulting business as a theater, stage, and lighting designer. He was also teaching theater design and technology labs at the Yale School of Drama.

Izenour Visits Kahn

A few weeks later, Kahn and I had a meeting with Izenour in Kahn's office in Philadelphia. The meeting was also attended by Bud Latz and E. Menerth from Fort Wayne. Kahn explained the theater. Izenour commented the following:

- Izenour liked the side tiers. "This is the only theater I know," he said, "where the king takes out his sword and shouts 'Forward!' and his army doesn't turn back and exit backstage. They can go forward here."
- He suggested a curved surface at each side of the proscenium to extend the sound toward the audience. Putting his hands around his mouth, he demonstrated this effect (fig. 89).
- He recommended a similar surface at the upper edge of the proscenium opening that would curve up to project the actor's voice toward the audience. Lou immediately called this the "upper lip" (fig. 90).
- Izenour pointed out that the overall volume should expand toward the back of the audience hall (figs. 90–92), like a megaphone, in order to carry clear, crisp sound.
- The theater had to be protected from outside noise, like the sounds from the railroad tracks located to the north of it.

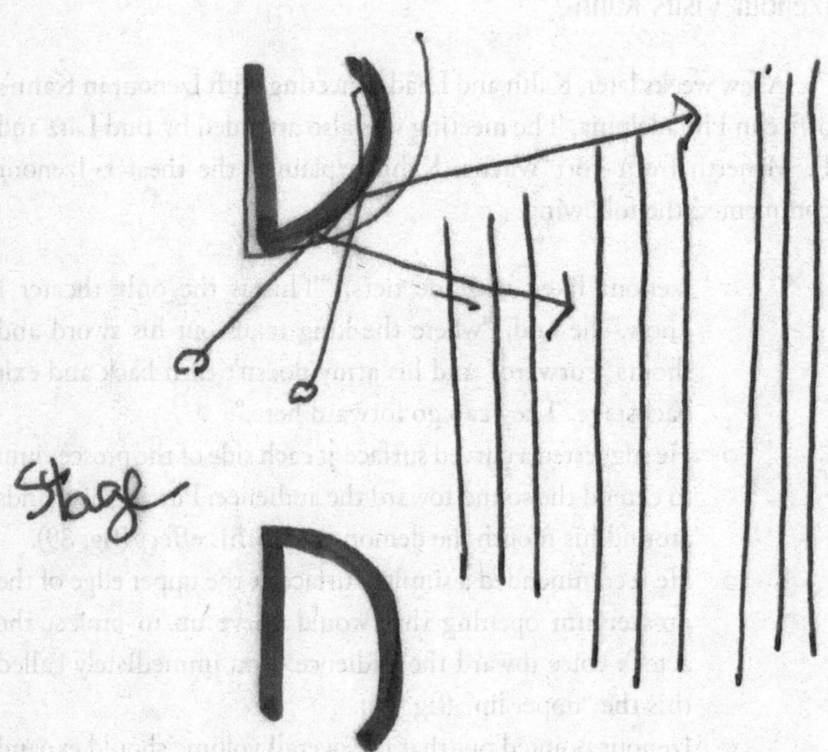

Figure 89. Yetken's sketch for Izenour's comments. Kahn called it the "mouth."

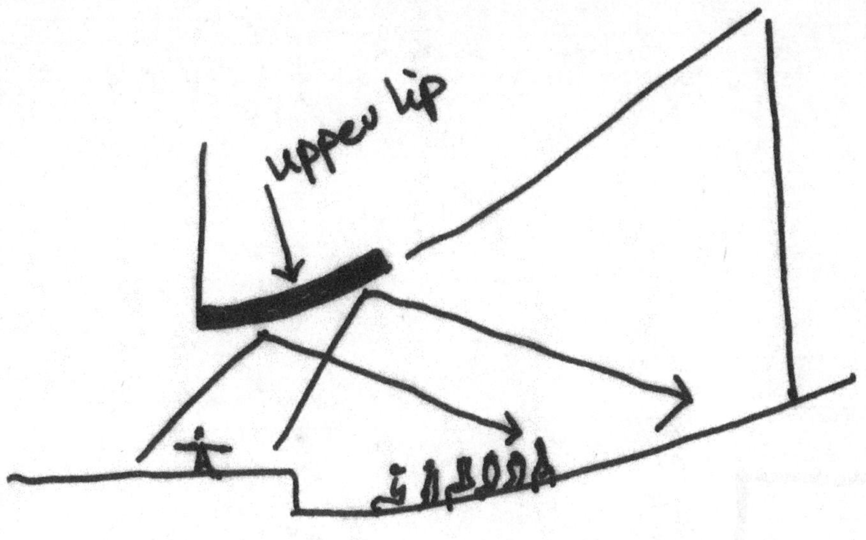

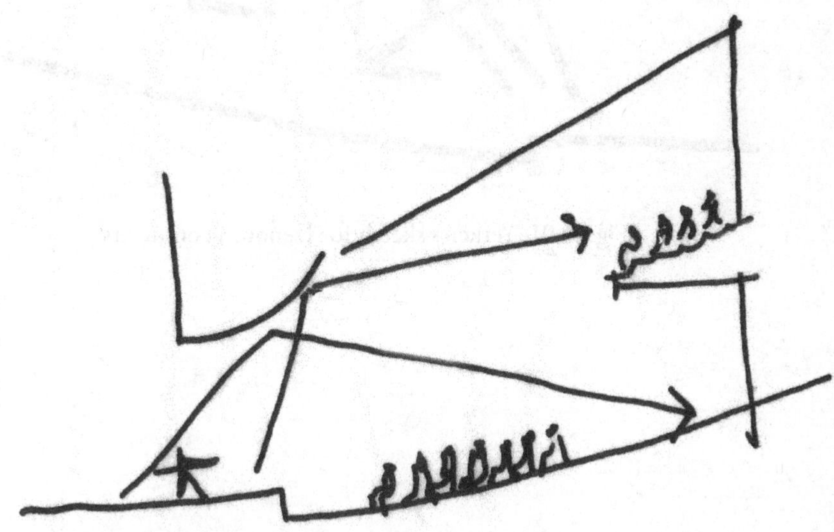

Figure 90. Yetken's sketch for Izenour's comments. Kahn called it the "upper lip."

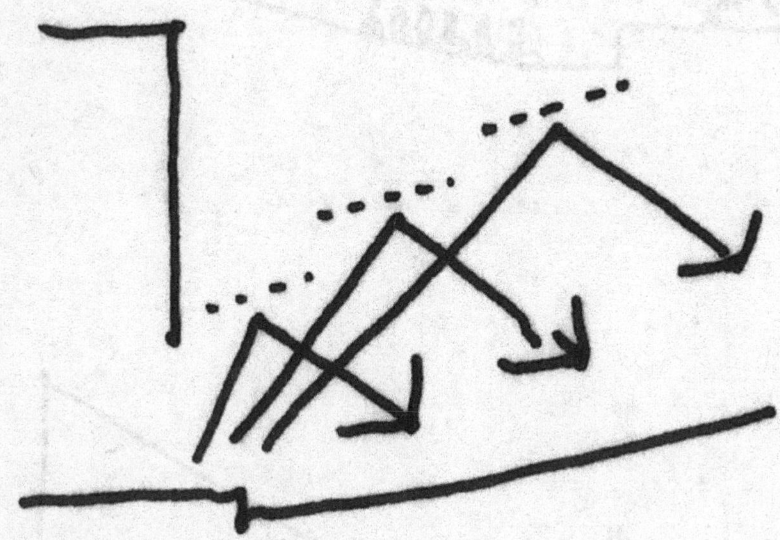

Figure 91. Yetken's sketch for Izenour's comments.

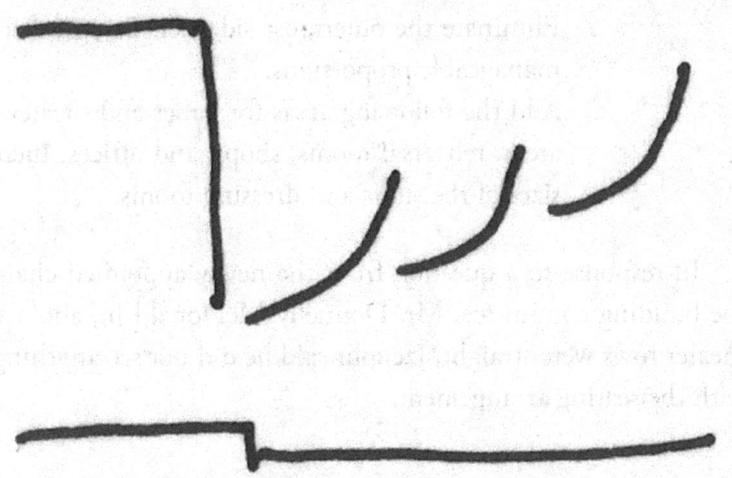

Figure 92. Yetken's sketch for Izenour's comments.

After the meeting, Izenour, upon learning I was from Turkey, talked about his upcoming trip there. He was anxious to visit the theater in Pergamum, the one in Ephesus, and the one in Aspendos.

Visiting Izenour with Kahn

On October '67, Kahn and I took a flight to New Haven, to Yale University, to talk with Izenour. Kahn explained the updated theater plans and sections. The meeting was cordial and collaborative.

Izenour Visits Fort Wayne

A month later, Izenour traveled and met with the Fort Wayne building committee. A week later, the office received the minutes/ letter[20] of this meeting. Izenour had summarized his meeting with Kahn

---

20 Minutes, November 17, 1967, LIK Box 17, Fort Wayne Corres. 2.1.67 to 12 '68, Louis I. Kahn Collection, University of Pennsylvania and Pennsylvania

in Philadelphia and mentioned he had recommended the following to Kahn.

- Eliminate the outermost side tier. Bring other tiers to manageable proportions.
- Add the following areas for ballet and theater: storage areas, rehearsal rooms, shops, and offices. Increase the sizes of the stairs and dressing rooms.

In response to a question from the newly appointed chairman of the building committee, Mr. Donnelly McDonald Jr., about why the theater rows were straight, Izenour said he did not see anything wrong with the seating arrangement.

Visiting Fort Wayne with Kahn

The next month, on December 12, 1967, I traveled with Kahn to Fort Wayne for a meeting with the civic and ballet building committee members and George Izenour.[21]

The newly appointed acting chairman of the building committee, Milford Miller, opened the meeting. To my shock, George Izenour started to talk about his reduction of the building area from 90,904 to 72,334 square feet and saving of half a million dollars (from the current estimate of $2,672,000 to $2,198,350). This was a cut from the approved schematic design (20% of the building area and 25% of the building cost). Then, of course, there came a discussion about eliminating the actor's house and stuffing the required spaces into the basement under the auditorium, using rehearsal rooms as multipurpose rooms, narrowing the lobby, and reducing the greenroom area.

Historical and Museum Collection, Philadelphia (hereafter cited as Kahn Collection).

21 Minutes, December 12, 1967, LIK Box 17, Kahn Collection.

Izenour went on to suggest that Cyril Harris of Columbia University be hired as an acoustical consultant for the project. His suggestion was seconded and approved by the members.

Kahn took the floor and first mentioned George Izenour's positive contribution to the project and pointed out that any extensive reduction would have a big impact on the design of the building and would ruin the building's character. He suggested cutting cubic footage, not square footage. The final product, Kahn said, would be judged as much on beauty, grace, proportions, and the essential detail of how well it worked. He said that to take more away would result in nothing but a box. He noted that the visibility, sightlines, and atmosphere were all excellent now. The auditorium, despite its reduction in overall size, would retain his concept of providing an environment where people come together, as in a plaza, to participate in the give-and-take of a theatrical experience. Also, he pointed out that the stage area would retain enough flexibility to help allow various styles of productions.

Harris Hired as Acoustical Consultant

A few days later, Cyril Harris was hired by the Fort Wayne Fine Arts Foundation as an acoustical consultant. I did not know what to expect from Cyril Harris, but it eventually became clear his participation would turn out to be explosive for the project. He insisted everything be changed to the way he wanted it to be.

Budget $2.2 Million

After a few days, on December 18, a letter arrived from the executive director of the Fine Arts Foundation. Ed Menerth informed Kahn that the "absolute ceiling limit … for the theater is $2.2 million for a turnkey job, including all fees."[22]

---

22 Letter from E. Menerth to Kahn, December 18, 1967, LIK Box 17, Kahn Collection.

Harris Visits Kahn

A month later, in January 1968, a meeting with Cyril Harris, Kahn, David Wisdom, and me took place in Kahn's office in Philadelphia. Cyril Harris suggested the following.[23]

- Keep the volume small. It makes the acoustical materials unnecessary.
- Do not use "clouds" on the ceiling. It creates all kinds of problems. [There were none.]
- A nonstructural interior surface solves all kinds of sound problems.
- Theater (speech) needs a quiet interior. Watch for background noise.
- Noise control measures made on structural work are expensive.
- Using acoustical materials means "you are throwing away sound."
- Avoid traps in the ceiling (to avoid reverberation).
- Convex curve is OK.
- Avoid concrete surfaces. Use carpet, wood, or plaster.
- Beams and columns are helpful in an auditorium.

Cyril Harris said nothing about the "mouth," "upper lip," or bullhorn shape for the audience hall that Izenour had suggested in an earlier meeting. I thought his comments were too general and did not address the current scheme, and most did not apply to the building. He did not say anything about the opening at the back wall of the audience hall arched openings or the actor's porch on the stage, which he would oppose vehemently in later stages.

---

23 Minutes, January 16, 1968, LIK Box 17, Kahn Collection.

Harris Visits Fort Wayne

After the Christmas and New Year break, on February 5, 1968, Kahn received a copy of a letter[24] detailing Cyril Harris's meeting with the Fort Wayne Fine Arts Foundation. The letter mentioned that Cyril Harris had made the following recommendations to Louis Kahn in his office in Philadelphia.

- From the standpoint of acoustics, the present volume of the house is excessive and should be reduced.
- There must not be any large unbroken concave surfaces in the theater.
- All niches must be eliminated.
- Interior surfaces must use wood, not concrete.
- The auxiliary structure at the rear of the stage presents a potential noise problem.
- Noise insulation for the train tracks behind the theater will be costly.

Kahn's Charcoal Sketches

A week later, on February 12, 1968, Kahn was at my table. I had a 1/8" hardline floor plan laid out. He sat down and asked for yellow tracing paper and a piece of charcoal stick. His sketches, comments, notes, and the way he thought of things are indicated in the following pages.

He first sketched the overall outline of the plan. Then he moved to the proscenium opening. Talking to me, he made a round chamber on the west end of the proscenium (fig. 93). He described how this would direct the actor's voice, from the stage to the audience. The proscenium was now analogous to the mouth, and he said this would project a human whisper to the depth of the auditorium (figs. 94–95).

---

24 Letter from Harris (acoustical consultant) to E. Menerth (executive director), February 7, 1968, LIK Box 17, Kahn Collection.

He indicated the walls of this round chamber with thick charcoal lines. He sketched the outline of the violin with thick lines, and the violin case with rolling lines. Then he started describing what else could be inside and around this curved chamber. He added a stair inside, and while explaining to me, he wrote "little stair." Then he added "could be watch place for the actor" (fig. 94) and "also a place for stage lighting." He indicated a small box to receive the curtain, and a joint that separated the violin from its case. He calmly defined the activities in and around that chamber, and wrote "the case" and "violin." He carefully wrote "space violin from case" to indicate the separation between the exterior walls of the stagehouse and the audience hall. Exceptional moments were developing in front of me. He made another small round enclosure at the landing of this stair, indicating that is has to be dark. Then he added a similar round chamber on the other side.

Kahn then started another small sketch just to the left of the round chamber, describing how this would look to the audience (figs. 95 and 100). He sketched the free-form openings for the stage lights. He showed how this would combine with the upper lip, and wrote "lips of the mouth." He continued with the irregular waving for the vertical cut in that wall for stage lighting. Under this, he wrote "the violin concrete, the case brick" and added at the bottom of this sketch (fig. 93) "the walls of the violin are all concrete—the brick openings only as the openings permit." Then he extended to the upper-right side of this large sketch, made a longitudinal section, and described how the ceiling would shape up with the lights pointed toward the stage (fig. 96). Then he sketched the view from the stage toward the audience hall (fig. 100). This sketch also showed how a free and sculptural form could be made, how the interior could be shaped and molded like a violin (figs. 96–97, 100).

"The place of invitation," Kahn wrote. "The free shape of the concrete is contrasted with the more rigid of the house." He moved to the upper-left side. "The place of invitation has now the place of concrete … the rear wall is of brick."

While writing his ideas on yellow trace, Kahn was also repeating them to me: "The concrete violin is the structure of the hall [fig. 96]. The working of brick is separated from it, as in the case of a *violin*." He pointed to the ceiling of the violin. "These shapes will be adjusted to be better streamlined and formatted as light bridges."

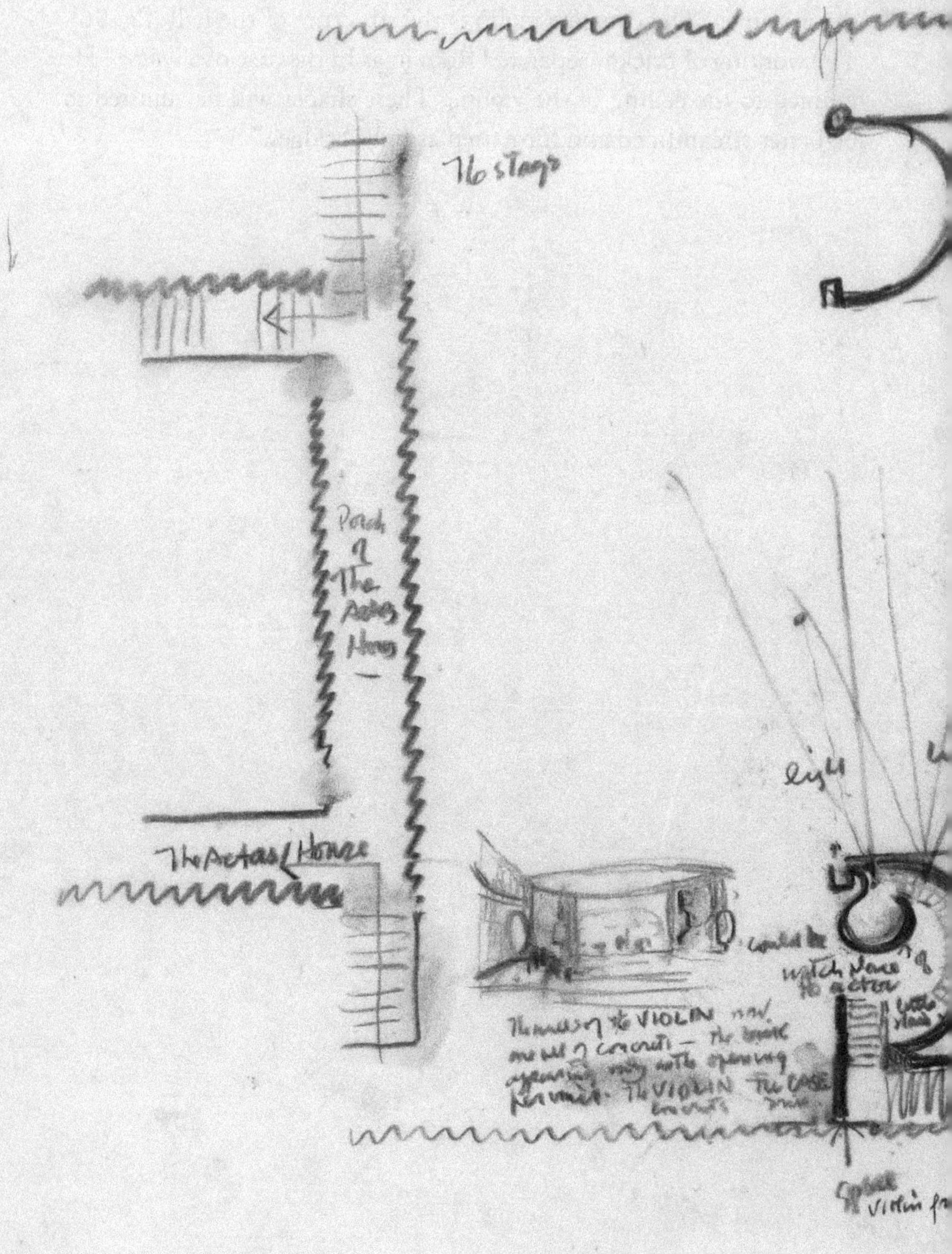

76 steps

Porch of The Actors House

The Actors House

light

VIOLIN

watch place the actors

Violin

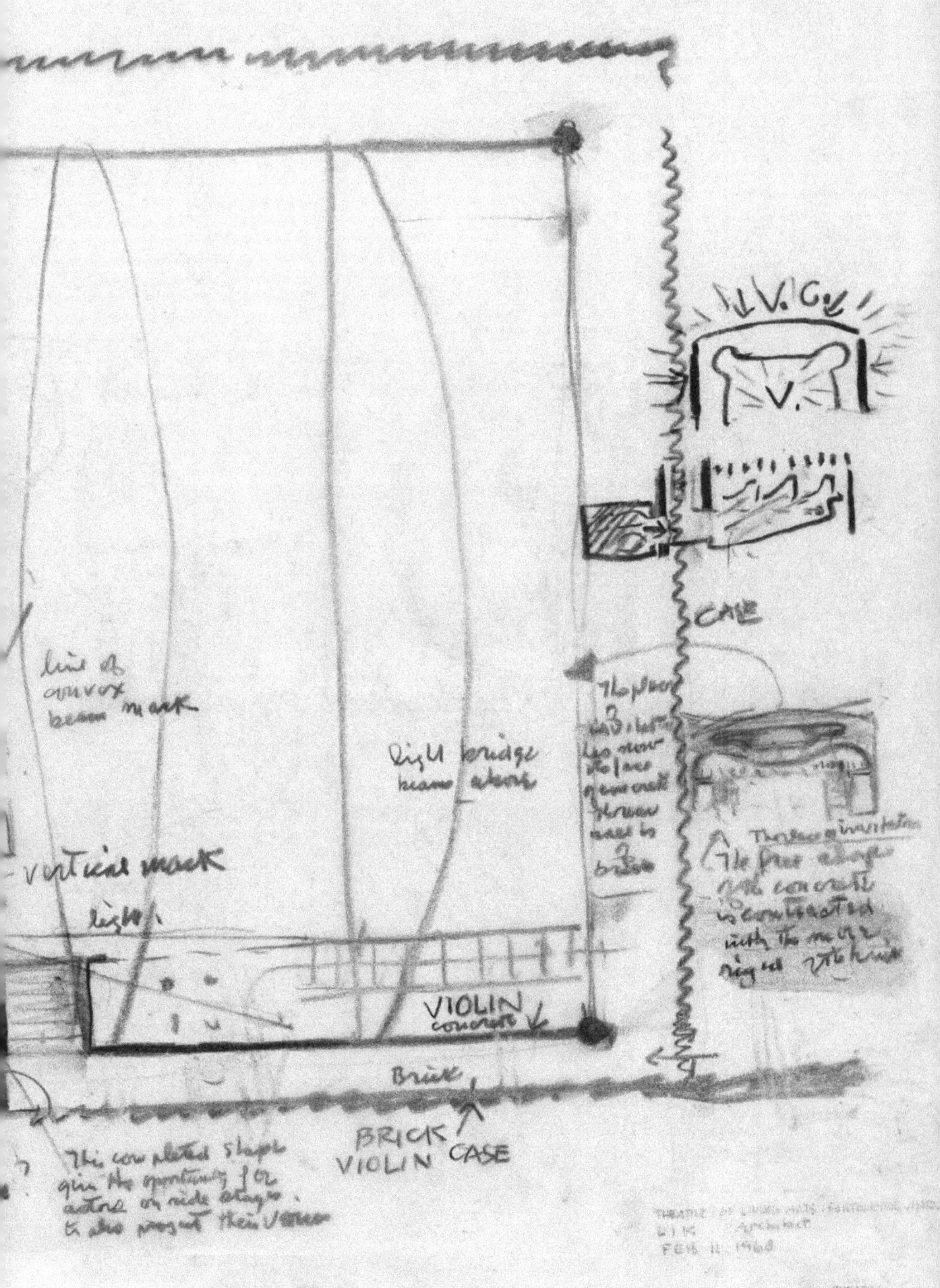

Figure 93. Kahn's sketch of the violin.

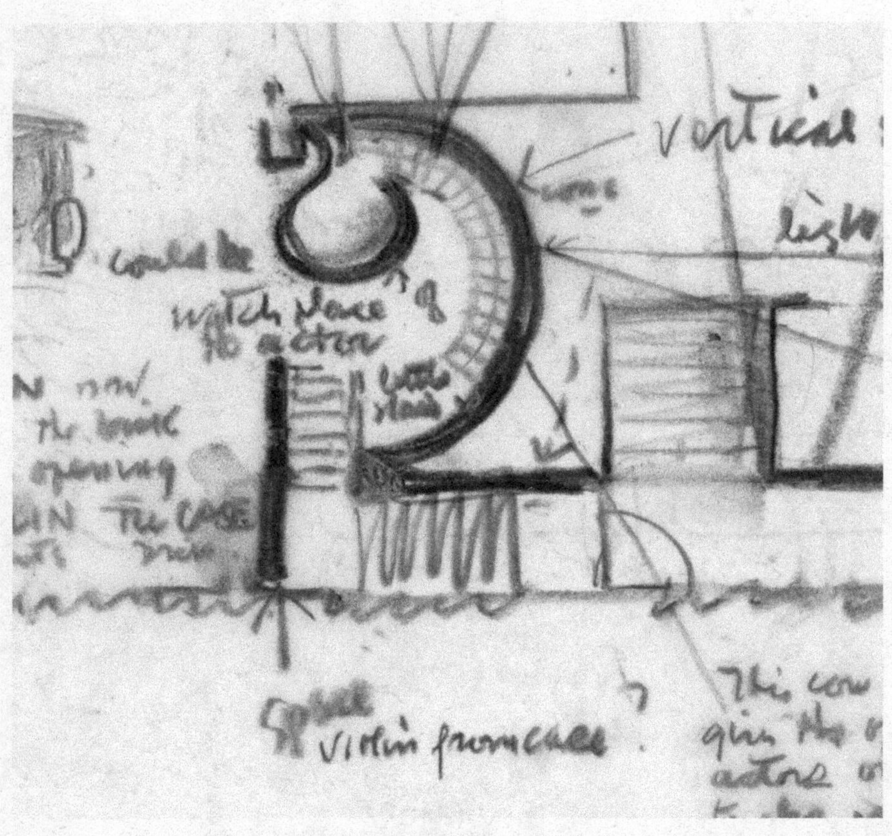

Figure 94

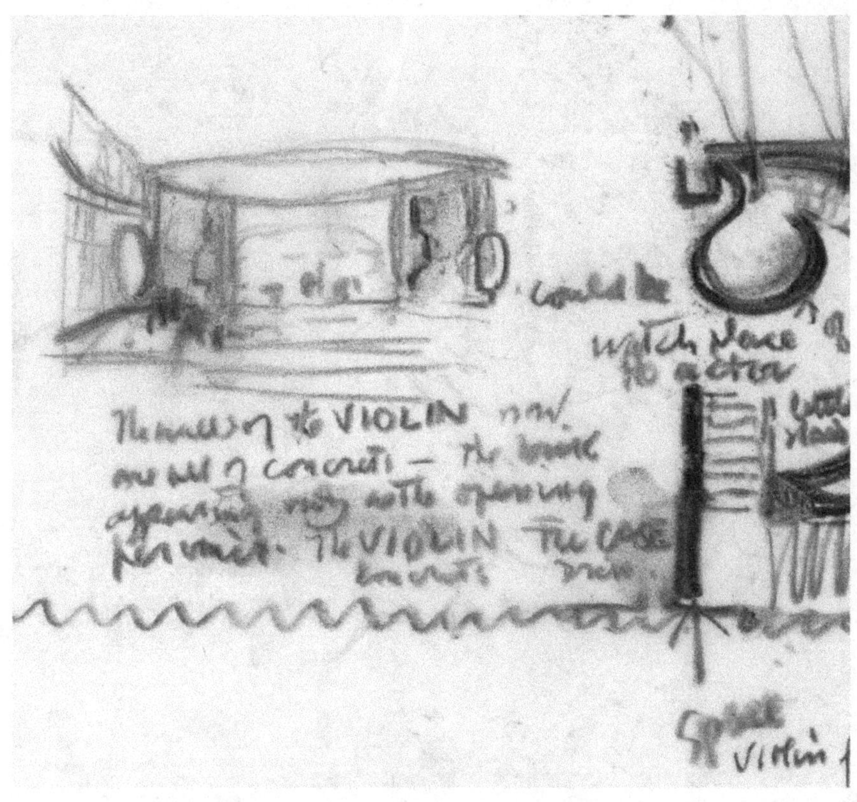

Figure 95. "The walls of the violin are all concrete—
the brick openings only as the openings permit."

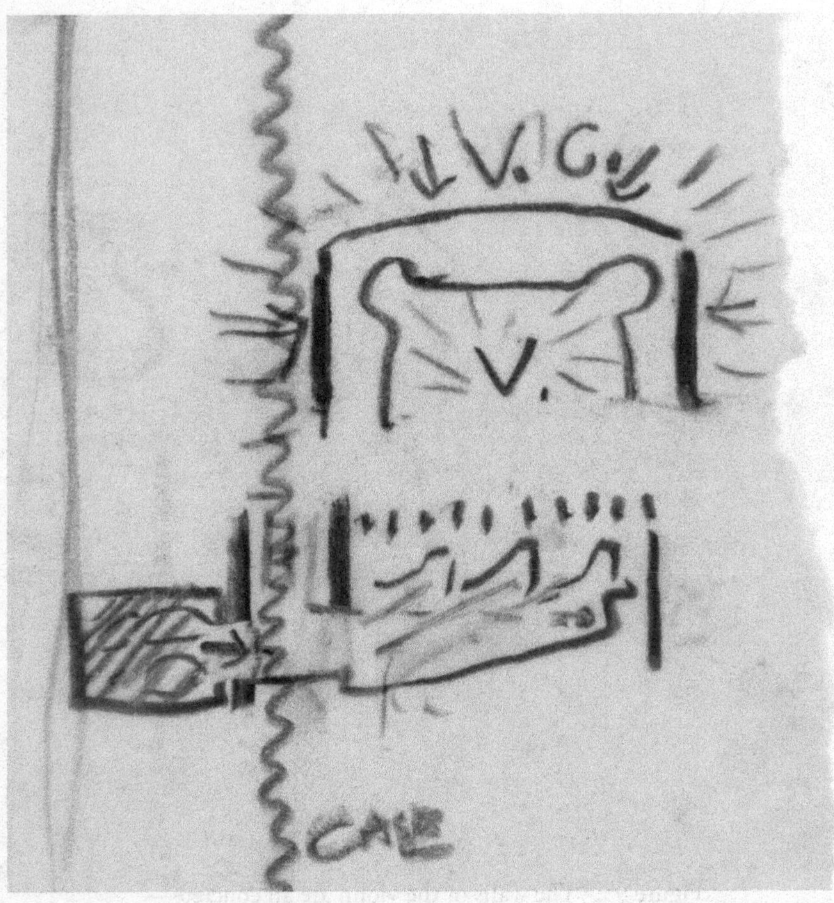

Figure 96. This summarizes and simplifies the conversation. The outside noise is to be kept away. The violin has its own unique shape. In the long section, the light bridges are set below the violin case.

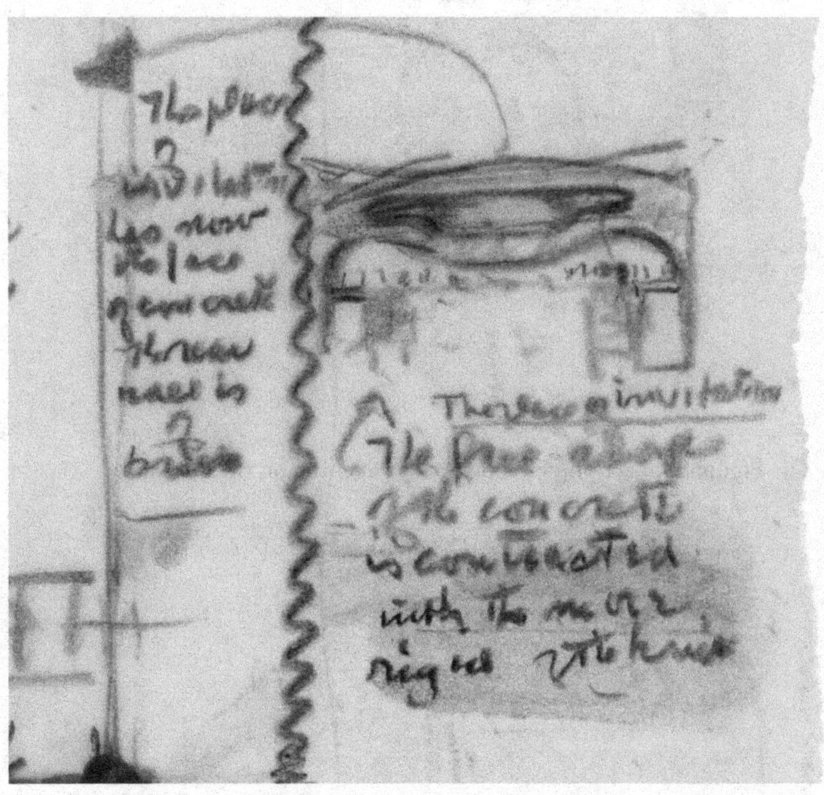

Figure 97. "The completed shape gives the opportunity for actors on the side stage to also project their versions."

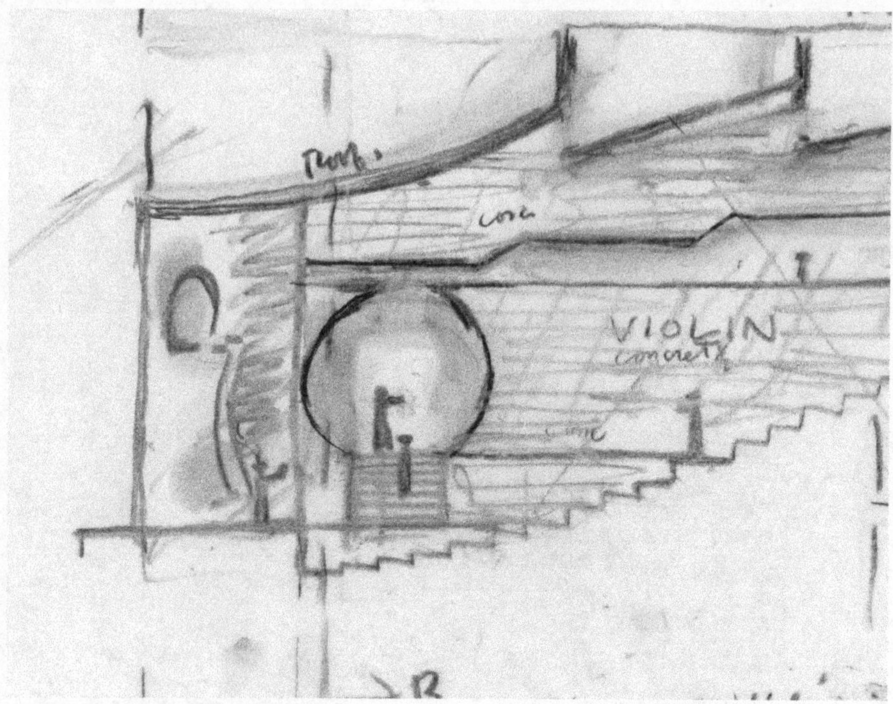

Figure 98. Section/detail of circular opening on the side wall.

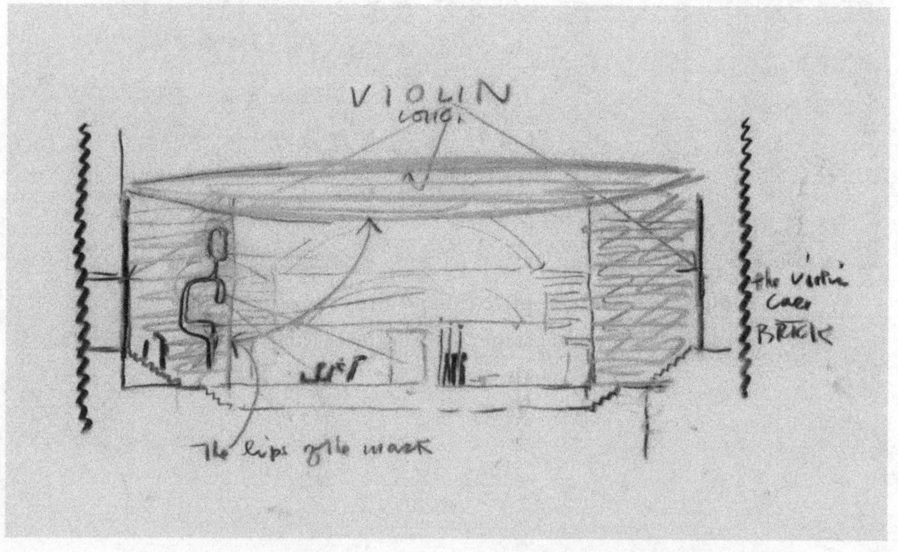

Figure 99. Detail of the sketch showing the opening for the "lips in the mask" at the side of the proscenium.

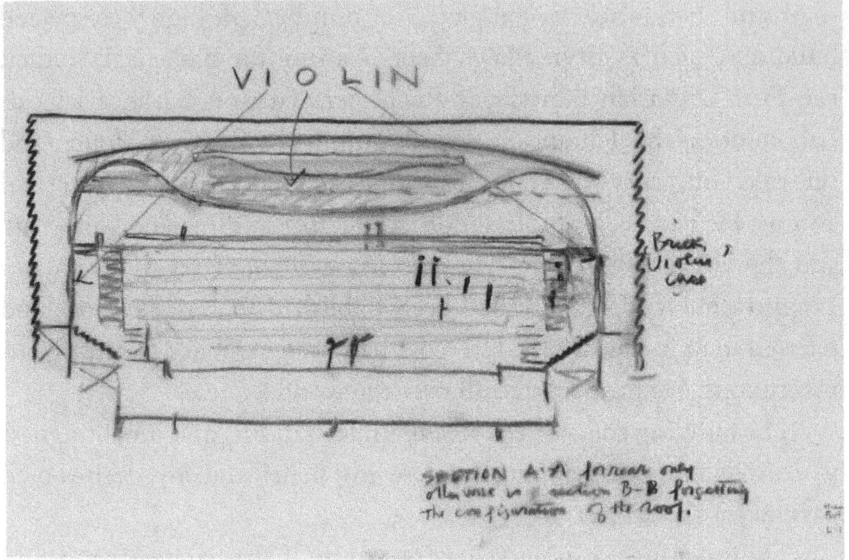

Figure 100. View toward the seating from the stage.

A few days later, David Wisdom informed Fort Wayne that Cyril Harris's comments required further study and that this would add two months to the project schedule. David also added a comment from Kahn: "Lou says we are not going to have an ideal theater ... We are trying, however … to come close … as close as our means will allow."

A Call from Fort Wayne

In March, David Wisdom received a call[25] from Bud Latz, now the chairman of the Fort Wayne Fine Arts Foundation building committee's lack: "The committee will not approve any design which is not approved by both Izenour and Harris." A subnote in David's phone memo continued with the note "Latz recommends that the whole contract be terminated."

I could not believe my eyes. This was beyond unbelievable. How could Fort Wayne say they could terminate the contract with Kahn?

---

25 Phone memo, Latz to Wisdom (Kahn's office), May 24, 1968, LIK Box 17, Kahn Collection.

Kahn had already completed a number of highly respected buildings, such as Bryn Mawr, Salk Institute for Biological Studies, the First Unitarian Church of Rochester, Trenton Baths, Richards Laboratories, the Tribune Review Building, the Esherick House, and the Yale University Art Gallery. He had received various architectural awards. He had been a professor of architecture at Princeton University and the University of Pennsylvania on a graduate level (both are Ivy League schools). His work had been published in various books and referred to in many articles. His work had been exhibited at prestigious institutions. He had lectured all over the world.

The building committee's lack of understanding and unwillingness to trust Kahn were making me lose my belief and my deep-rooted passion for the project.

Things were not progressing positively. I was disappointed and began to think there was no chance for this project to arrive at its reality. I couldn't figure out how it had happened that Fort Wayne had lost their trust and belief in Kahn. The Fort Wayne Fine Arts Foundation was insisting on things Kahn would not accept, and he was talking about things the Fine Arts Foundation would never understand. They were getting further and further apart. And I could not do anything to change that. Slowly, I was realizing there was no possibility of completing this theater. And worse, Fort Wayne did not have the funds to complete it.

I started thinking about my future. I wasn't going to be an architect in the US. I was going to go back to teaching and designing buildings in Turkey. I missed my friends, my family, and my school.

It was May, and there was less than a month until my J-1 (academic visitor) visa expired. I was warned by knowledgeable friends that the INS (Immigration and Naturalization Service, currently called Homeland Security) would never extend this kind of visa over three years.

In June of 1968, I would have been in the United States for exactly three years. My Turkish passport was also about to expire. The Turkish Consulate in New York would not extend my passport, because I needed to complete my compulsory military service. I had to return to Turkey.

Adding to my worries, my mother and my uncle were writing painful and passionate letters asking me to return home, saying that everyone missed me and that I had responsibilities to my mother. There was some drama added about how she was now alone and how she had long cared for me and sacrificed her life for me. It was typical of Turkish families to use this type of pressure to induce the younger generation to do their bidding. And, of course, it usually worked for the family structure.

The year 1968 was not a good year for America. There were war protests at Penn campus every day. There was the Tet Offensive, Walter Cronkite's comments, the unending Vietnam War, the execution of a Viet Cong prisoner in front of TV cameras, the assassination of Martin Luther King Jr., and later, the assassination of Robert Kennedy. All these events served to tarnish my admiration for America. So much so that I didn't think I would ever come back. I had no idea that the twists and turns of my life would not only bring me back to America; it would even bring me back to Fort Wayne.

Farewell to America

I informed David Wisdom that I would be leaving. I took my VW Beetle to New York City and put it on a cargo ship to Istanbul and started packing. In mid-June, I boarded a Pan Am flight to take me back to Ankara.

On the way back home, I spent a lot of time thinking about how fortunate I was to have been a student of Kahn's and to have worked in his office, learning from the master architect himself, and to have taught architecture at Penn, his school. I had witnessed his brilliant, creative mind and had been part of his architectural practice. It was amazing how he could distill complex ideas and concepts into smaller and simpler components so that others could also see them. Kahn understood how architecture brings light into life. He could see how a way of life could be expressed in architecture, in a structure, in a place. He could even express, sometimes through a cryptic phrase, the essential characteristics of living life through essential architectural values. How lucky I was to have been his student and to have worked in his office. I would carry this experience into the rest of my life.

PART 6

Way of Life

When you make a building, you make a life. It comes out of life ... When you have only the comprehension of the function of a building, it would not become an environment of a life.[26]

—Louis Kahn

[26] Cook and Klotz, *Conversations with Architects*, 1973, pp. 215–217.

Way of Life

The years 1968 to 1971 were special all over the Western world, and it was quite reactionary at Middle East Technical University (METU), where I returned to teach architecture. Students were highly political. The military police occupied the university frequently. Students fought back, and classes were canceled regularly. I was assigned to teach the masters class, but after a while, with so much confusion and disorder, I decided this was a good time to start and complete my compulsory military service. I joined the army in September 1969 and moved east to my military post, to the Turkish Third Army headquarters on the Russian border.

In May 1971, I returned to teaching. This time, it was for a second-year architecture class that had taken one year of a basic design course in their freshmen year. I thought teaching the core issues of architecture to students who were beginning their architectural design would be a good challenge for me. I had good students. They were smart, responsive, and enthusiastic. There is nothing like a bright student asking a challenging question that forces a teacher to review his own thoughts and beliefs on an issue. Teaching is a wonderful way to unlearn.

I did not talk about Kahn. I did not use Kahn's poetic sentences or refer to my years with him. Those were all gone. They belonged to the past. This was a time to find out my own architectural character.

At the beginning of each academic year, our teaching team[27] would discuss how we would direct students toward memorable architectural/spatial experiences, away from customary spatial expectations, and introduce them to unique and extraordinary characteristics of place-making.

Cappadocia, in Central Turkey (three hours' drive from Ankara), is such a place where habitable spaces were created by carving away the rock (fig. 102), an unusual process of creating places. This is also a place to observe the poetry of daylight, created by the variety of curved surfaces indoors and outdoors (fig. 101).

---

27 Team teaching with Esber Yolal and Suha Ozkan

This was an ideal start to learn *how to make a place*. Students examine their own *way of life* and learn about their *own desires* to make their own place for *living*, *sleeping*, and *studying* activities on their own, with *limited knowledge* of construction and technology.

Figure 102. Landforms in Cappadocia.

Figure 101. Carved rock dwellings.

For their first project, we thought students must be encouraged to think about the art of architecture, the art of place-making.

We traveled to the carved-out cities of Cappadocia and walked through spongelike spaces, where doors were secured with large circular wheel-like rocks. We observed rooms with three different openings: one for daylight, one for fresh air, and one to admire the view. There were no corners; the floors, walls, and ceilings were all carved smoothly out of curvilinear forms.

Carve Your Room

After returning from Cappadocia, each student was given a 30×30 cm cube of lightweight, easily carved material available in Europe and Turkey called YTONG (fig. 103), and they were asked to *carve* their room for three activities: studying, sleeping, and living (accepting visitors).

They were not given a needs program. They were asked to examine their own desires and needs and priorities for their own understanding of architectural responses for the three activities.

Once their carving was completed (fig. 103), they were asked to make a drawing of it (fig._104). They were to explain their own living scenario and its character verbally and graphically to their classmates and invited jury members, as would be the case in their professional work in the future.

Figure 103. Carved rooms done by students.

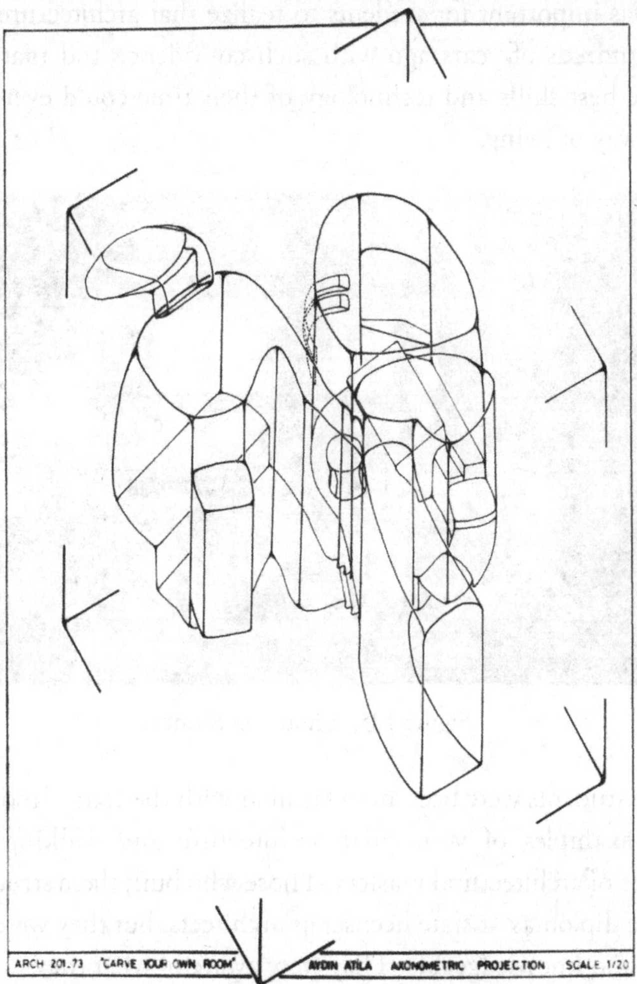

Figure 104. Drawings by students.

During the spring semester, we traveled to the distant regions of Turkey, visiting beautiful Anatolian villages with mud-brick houses, fruit gardens, spacious homes, spectacular views, and picturesque streets. Vernacular architecture teaches modesty and simplicity, as well as efficiency, availability of materials, and reflection of way of life. Students produced a multiscreen visual presentation and shared it with the whole school.

It was important for students to realize that architecture that was done hundreds of years ago with such confidence and maturity and with the best skills and technology of their time could even adapt to today's way of living.

Figure 105. A house in Sirince.

The students were becoming familiar with the clarity and crispness of the examples of vernacular architecture and walking through examples of architectural mastery. Those who built these structures did not have diplomas or state licenses as architects, but they were creative, skilled, and knowledgeable. They were aware of what they were doing, and clearly guided by love and respect for their work (fig. 105).

Figure 106. Priene.

Priene

The class visited many antique sites. The students admired the boldness of their expressions and were able to read their way of life thousands of years ago. They were stunned that they did not have any hesitation for building in marble (fig. 106), that they did it with such confidence and with such hope for the future. What a source of pride and inspiration they must have had to project their future. Architects of earlier centuries were teaching us architecture beyond centuries.

It expanded our knowledge that the design of a place indicated how life took place in such settings, how it was valued, and how lives were lived. It expressed cultural and social values, and brought up the desires and aspirations that enforced it.

Students were not simply reading about architecture or listening and looking at a slide in a dark classroom. They were recording essential personal experiences and storing them in the wrinkles of their brains.

* * *

The years 1971 and 1972 were very busy for me. Besides teaching regular classes in METU, I attended the Salzburg Seminar in American Studies in Austria. Also, that academic year, I produced a 16 mm documentary film on the theme of *architecture and leisure* (the assigned theme for UIA Congress in Varna, Bulgaria). My sculpture *Nineteen* and a painting titled *When and Where* were both exhibited in the National Gallery of Art in Ankara.

That same year, I started working on my PhD, but deep down I felt that PhD was not what I wanted. METU did not allow the faculty to engage in professional practice, yet that was exactly what I wanted. I was not sure teaching was an architectural pursuit for me. I did not learn to be an architect to teach class or to publish an article about it. I wanted to be an architect. With these thoughts on my mind, I wrote a letter to Kahn describing METU's faculty limitation for professional practice, and I inquired if I could come and work in his office. A few weeks later, I received Kahn's letter. His response was positive (fig. 107).

LOUIS I KAHN ARCHITECT FAIA

14 April 1973

Mr. Cengiz Yetken
8 Sokak 4/12
Nese Apartments
Bahcelievler
Ankara, Turkey

Dear Cengiz:

It was a delight to read your letter. I feel very much the frustration you must feel of not getting the work you so fully deserve in your own country.

I am anxious to tell you that you are most welcome here. There is work to do. Please advise me what you want me to do to prepare the way and let me know when you are able to come.

Sincerely yours,

Louis I. Kahn

LIK/kac

1501 WALNUT STREET PHILADELPHIA 2 PENNSYLVANIA LOCUST 3-9844

Figure 107

I started communicating with Louise and sent the required documents. I received copies of many letters that were sent from Lou to the American Office of Immigration and Naturalization.

Jerusalem

1974 started out busy. I traveled to Israel for my pilgrimage to the Baha'i Faith Holy Places in early February, in Haifa and Akko. The last few days of that visit, I was in the ancient city of Jerusalem. I called the mayor's office in Jerusalem and asked if I could visit the construction site of Hurva Synagogue (fig. 108). Hurva Synagogue was being designed in Kahn's office when I was there seven years ago. I was hoping to see the completed or maybe in-progress construction of the synagogue. I got a nondescript answer from the mayor's office; it seemed no one in Jerusalem knew what I was talking about. In fact, Hurva was never built. I returned to Istanbul on February 17, 1974.

Figure 108. Photo of Hurva Synagogue model.

Shortly after my return, I learned my uncle had passed away. I traveled to Istanbul for the memorial gathering. Then I traveled to Baymus Village to visit my Baha'i friends near Cappadocia, and I again returned to Ankara late on Sunday night, March 17.

Sadness

March 18 was Monday. I arrived at school and continued teaching my regular classes. There seemed to be nothing out of the ordinary. On March 21, Thursday, I learned the sad and shocking news of Kahn's passing in New York City on Sunday, March 17, 1974 (fig. 109). Kahn had been returning from a work trip in India. His funeral was Friday, March 22, in Philadelphia. I was terribly saddened by the loss of my mentor and wished I could attend his funeral to pay my respects to this man, whom I had admired and respected.

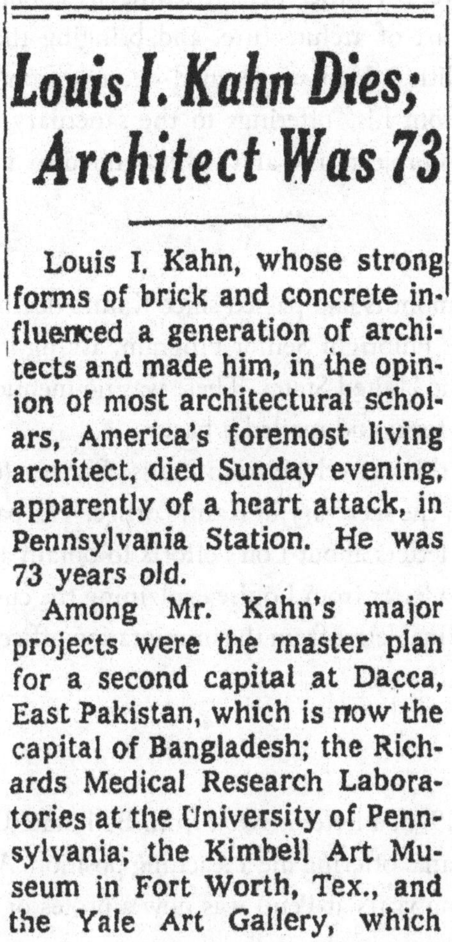

Louis I. Kahn Dies; Architect Was 73

Louis I. Kahn, whose strong forms of brick and concrete influenced a generation of architects and made him, in the opinion of most architectural scholars, America's foremost living architect, died Sunday evening, apparently of a heart attack, in Pennsylvania Station. He was 73 years old.

Among Mr. Kahn's major projects were the master plan for a second capital at Dacca, East Pakistan, which is now the capital of Bangladesh; the Richards Medical Research Laboratories at the University of Pennsylvania; the Kimbell Art Museum in Fort Worth, Tex., and the Yale Art Gallery, which

Figure 109. Obituary in the *New York Times*.

A great teacher of architecture was gone. I remember that sense of awe I felt in his class and in his office, trying to understand and decipher his words and the sense and feelings behind it all. A constant search for clues that were all around me, so close that I could touch. That glimmer of light on the path of the act of design and that sense of architecture.

Kahn was the master of finding and expressing the primary characteristics of a place—its relatedness, its emotional base, its inherent character, and its social and cultural presence. Architecture was not just making buildings but expressing its existence with life to represent its being.

Will we have any other person telling us about that elusive art of design, that art of architecture, and bringing that magical sense into spatial realities? Had we learned enough from his talks, from his buildings, from his "offerings to the sanctuary of art"? Had he completed all his projects and all that he wanted to do?

* * *

Nearly five months had passed since Kahn's death when I received a letter from the Fulbright Senior Program, asking if I was interested in teaching in the United States. There was no mention of any school. I completed the form and mailed it back.

I received a thick envelope from Louise Warner (married name of Louise Badgley), the secretary in Kahn's office. The package contained documents and letters about Lou's efforts to obtain a US visa for me. It also included a letter from Louise explaining the current situation in the office and a final letter from the immigration office, refusing Kahn's request for my US visa.

* * *

In January 1975, a letter arrived from Ball State University (BSU) in Muncie, Indiana, offering me a teaching position. A student of mine from my teaching years at Penn was now a professor at BSU. He had recognized my name in the Fulbright announcement and provided a positive reference on my behalf, which led them to offer a teaching position there. This time, the university could somehow get a US visa for me.

* * *

I left Ankara in August 1975 and once again headed for the United States. I flew to New York and then to Philadelphia to meet old friends. Having been gone for seven years, I felt like I was walking in a dream. I called each of my old friends one by one and was pleasantly surprised to learn that they remembered me and even pronounced my first name correctly. After a few days, I traveled to my new post at Ball State University.

The Midwest

At my first faculty lecture at the College of Architecture, I was introduced as an architect who had worked with Louis Kahn on the Fort Wayne Theater of Performing Arts. I heard some low booing sounds coming from the upper balcony. Later, my friends explained to me that there had been a huge controversy during the construction of the theater—about the brick arches. The contractors had wanted to use face brick, and Kahn had insisted they use structural brick arches. Apparently, this conflict was front-page news in Fort Wayne. The theater had been completed and dedicated in October 1973, just two years earlier.

I had good students at the school in their last year. I noticed some students were uncertain in defining prime design objectives. I challenged them to think about the character of a place before they think of the architect's liabilities, before building codes, before its shape, before the coordination of complex requirements. I challenged them to think about the living that goes in and around the building first, to think about the art distinct from the physical act of construction. I encouraged them to experiment with charcoal sketching techniques and explained its positive effects on the fluidity and the freedom in architectural realization. We traveled to Chicago, a four-hour drive, to

Figure 110. Fort Wayne Theater of Performing Arts, view from the west. (Photo credit: C. Kuhner)

experience good examples. We visited the works of Louis Sullivan, Frank Lloyd Wright, Ludwig Mies van der Rohe, and Skidmore, Owings, and Merrill, and discussed their primary characteristics and their influence on their surroundings.

Return to Fort Wayne

When I left the United States seven years before, I believed the theater project was never going to be built. I had no idea that it had proceeded and that it had been completed. In one of those ironic twists of fate, I found myself living only an hour's drive from Fort Wayne. Of course, I had to go and see the completed building.

The first time I saw it, it looked to me like the cardboard model I had made many years before (fig. 110). This was the same simple building composed of attached rectangular volumes. There was the actor's house, the stagehouse, and the audience hall. All three types of performance experiences (rehearsing, performing, and observing), "people seeing people," were integrated. The purity of its composition, its proportions, and its directness were undeniable (fig. 111).

I detected efflorescence on the front wall (fig. 112). *A sloppy contractor,* I told myself. The building looked lonely. The park next to the theater (Freimann Park) was not yet matured; the trees looked like they had just been planted (fig. 113).

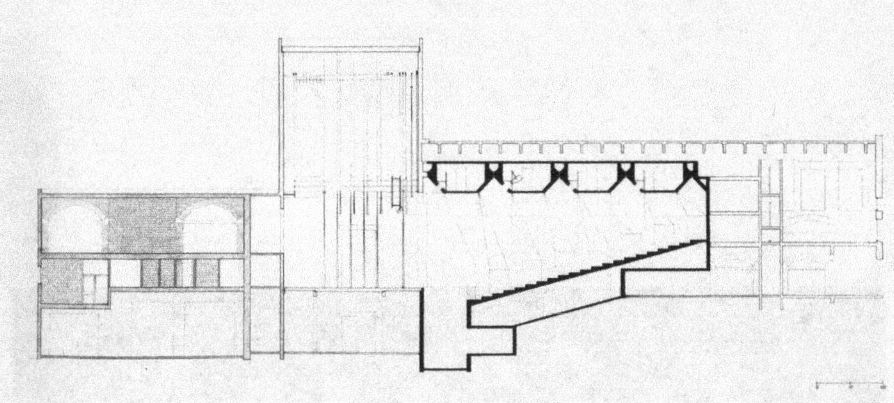

Figure 111. Section.

I visited this building with students many times. It was a great opportunity for me to illustrate architectural concepts related to the completed building. I was able to reconstruct the process step by step and explain several stages that were developed.

On one of our visits, our tour guide told us a story: After a lively talk on one of Kahn's visits to Fort Wayne, an older lady approached Kahn and said, "I like your work, Mr. Kahn, but I like colonial architecture. Do you know any good colonial architect to recommend to me?" With a kind smile, Kahn answered, "Yes, ma'am. Thomas Jefferson."

Figure 112. View from the main street.

The mask. Simple palette of materials used. Concrete and brick are expressed in this entry facade. (Photo credit: C. Kuhner)

Figure 113. View from Freimann Park.

Figure 114. Mask detail. (Photo credit: C. Yetken)

Figure 115. Mask at night. View from the main street.

The Mask

The theater introduced itself to the city through its "mask." It conveyed its identity as a place for the art of performance. This abstraction was beautifully expressed with architectural elements in the simple brick and concrete formats. The mask (fig. 114) also recalled the art of makeup, costumes, stage sets, lights, and other essentials in the art of performance.

At night, the theater looked even lovelier (fig. 115). Light shining through these openings from the activities of the banquet hall created the most contemporary public performance for the city.

Figure 116. Stairs from the ground to the second-floor reception area. (Photo credit: C. Kuhner)

The audience would use open stairs to enter or exit the audience hall. The stairs offered a good view of people leaving the theater, creating opportunities for people watching.

Daylight from the east and west windows gave these stairs a sculptural appearance (fig. 116). The windows framed the daylight and created an elegant effect. To me, it looked like a stage set. Someone should produce a play there. Walking down the stairs felt like moving within a cutout massive block. This was an architectural gift to sculpture.

On one of our visits, the tour guide told us a story. "Young schoolkids visit us here, and they almost always ask about the arches," she said. "I say to them, the architect, Mr. Kahn, says if you ask a brick what it wants to be, the brick says it wants to be an arch. These kids, with wide eyes, move their heads up and down as if they agree and understand. However, when I say the same thing to a group of adults, I see eyes roll up to the ceiling with an expression of what nonsense it is." She smiled, indicating that she thought young people were often much more insightful than adults.

The audience hall was very simple (fig. 117). The house lights were elegantly masked in the folding ribs of the side walls. The ceiling and walls were all exposed concrete. The entrance and exit doors were well hidden from direct sight. These doors were located at both sides of the rows, and they opened directly to spacious side galleries.

The audience hall was designed with the inherent characteristic of a musical instrument. The outer structure absorbed external sound and kept it from disturbing the performance. The interior of the theater was ready to be tuned to human voice. I heard the theater had exceptionally good acoustics.

Figure 117. The wide proscenium opened to the audience hall. Every row of seats exited comfortably to a fire-safe zone. The latecomer doors did not create a disturbing glare for the audience.

This was a minimal setup. Everything existed to make this a place of performance—nothing less, nothing more. This showed me a most delicate balance. (Photo credit: C. Kuhner)

Figure 118. Catwalk, light galleries, structural box beams.
(Photo credit: C. Kuhner)

The interior was clean and dedicated to the event itself. It was not cluttered with draperies, dangling lights, or acoustic panels. There were light galleries (fig. 118), but no catwalks.

The light galleries were contained in structural box beams spanning the whole width of the audience hall (fig. 117). The light technicians and soundmen could comfortably and securely adjust worklights and sound for the performances.

The proscenium was wide open to the audience hall (fig. 117). There was a direct relationship between the performer and the audience. This wide-open proscenium conveyed a suitability to civic quality for activities like graduations, debates, and conferences.

Figure 119. Stage during dress rehearsal, with actor's porch at the rear.

There was a dress rehearsal on my visiting day (fig. 119). The proscenium was fully open, and I could see the triangular opening of the actor's porch. The "House of the Actor received its proper place in the architecture of this theater. The greenroom (fig. 120) and rehearsal rooms (fig. 121) were removed from their usual placement in the basement and were brought up to daylight in the House of the ctor. This reflected the recognition of the actor's importance in this place of performing arts.

Figure 120. Entrance lobby and greenroom. (Photo credit: C. Kuhner)

Figure 121. Rehearsal room on the second floor. (Photo credit: C. Kuhner)

In my explanation to the students, I pointed out five distinct characteristics they should note for a theater archetype.

1. A theater is an actor's domain (figs. 119–124).
2. The backstage area, rehearsal rooms, and greenroom must be dignified spaces with daylight and a view (figs. 120–121).
3. The proscenium must allow a variety of performances and presentations (figs. 117, 119, and 122).
4. The interiors should stay spartan, indicating that the art of performance is what brings color, life, and joy to this place (fig. 117).
5. Light galleries must be discreet, safe, secure, and comfortable to work in (figs. 117–118).

Figure 122. Photo by Cemal Endem

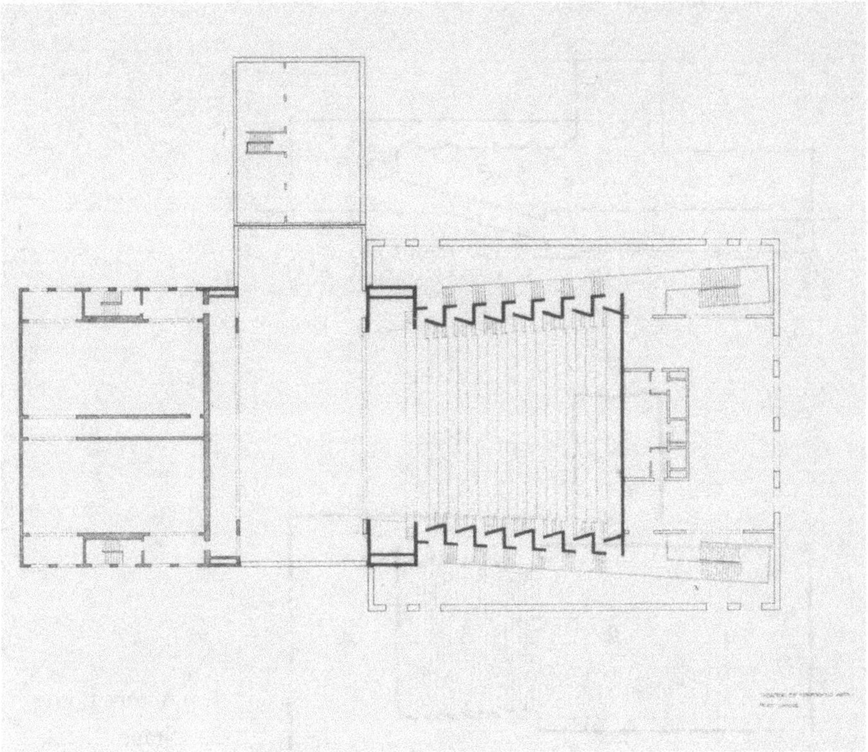

Figure 123. Theater plan.

Architecture reveals itself in layers, like a piece of music or a good book would. Each layer points to another. Slowly, one begins to see and understand how layer on layer builds up, until the end, when space reveals its ultimate clarity. It is only then that one would be able to realize, appreciate, and absorb its overall character, importance, and worth.

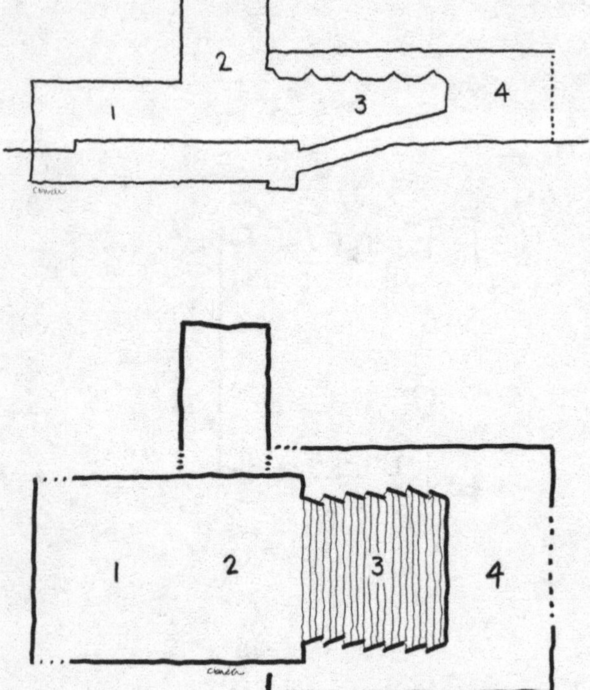

Figure 124. Author's sketch section.

1. Actor's house
2. Stage
3. Audience hall
4. Entrance/lobby

Virginia

In the spring of 1977, after teaching architectural design for two years at Ball State (1975–1976 and 1976–1977), I accepted an invitation to join the architecture faculty of the University of Virginia (UVA) in Charlottesville. I had started a family and moved there with my young wife. Walking across Jefferson's Lawn, I thought of how like-minded Kahn and Jefferson were in their architectural beliefs. I remembered how Kahn once spoke about the Lawn and mentioned how wrong it was for the architect, Stanford White (1853–1906), to locate Old Cabell Hall at the south end of Jefferson's Lawn.

Jefferson's plan for engaging gardens and pavilions with the land was masterful. That same touch can also be seen in the house he built in Monticello. Never mind the technical aspects of architecture; just gazing across Jefferson's Lawn brings out a sense of spirituality. One couldn't just talk to students about this concept; the students had to be there and see it for themselves. I needed to bring them there to experience it, body and soul, and to record it for themselves.

The architecture students at UVA were intelligent and industrious. Architecture had a special place in the hearts of all UVA students, maybe in all Virginians. I believe this was mainly because Thomas Jefferson is still identified as an architect. The students took pride in their work and showed high self-respect by working hard.

Because I had been Kahn's student and had practiced in his office, everyone was expecting miracles from my teaching. Yet I felt I was not trained to be a teacher of architecture. As a matter of fact, none of those who teach architecture are. I had a strong belief that a student of architecture must start learning architecture from architecture itself. They must think of living in the buildings/places they design—intuitively, mentally, spiritually. They must develop a conscious awareness of their design, of the life they shape and relationships they form. Their designs should not be a mixture of partial responses to made-up circumstances.

Fallingwater

At the beginning of the design class, I proposed a trip to my students to visit Frank Lloyd Wright's Fallingwater House (1935–1937) in Bear Run, Pennsylvania. The purpose was to create an opportunity to gain spatial memories, to start thinking outside the box of accustomed frames of references, and to understand the potentials of architectural connections.

Figure 125. Fallingwater. Its sculptural completeness is admirable. Its parts and pieces represent a coherent whole.

There are many credible lessons of architecture to be learned on the site of Fallingwater (fig. 125). Selection of the site, its complex spatial relationships, its selection of materials, its proportions, its expressive placement on a waterfall, and its anticipated lifestyle all indicated Wright's creative mindset. Its beauty is easily understood and acknowledged, and it is not hidden in architectural theories or an obscure interpretation of architectural scholars.

Other field trips followed, comparing different sites around the East Coast, such as James River Valley, Charleston, Savannah, and nearby Washington, DC. Lessons were learned in rich architectural environs.

I introduced design exercises without sites, to guide the students to expand their understanding of the inner workings of architectural spaces, and gave a project to make a room for the most efficient use of daylight and energy. To me, the most important objective in class was the students' development of their own sense of accomplishment.

I was at UVA for four academic years. By spring of 1981, an opportunity showed itself in an unexpected way. It was a good time to make the break; my wife had just finished her master's degree in landscape architecture from UVA. By early summer, my family, with our two-year-old son, moved to Chicago to follow a job offered by Bruce Graham, the senior partner at Skidmore, Owings, and Merrill (SOM). *Here is my opportunity,* I thought. *Go and find out how good you are. Climb the mountain and search for your long-lost love. Go on and be an architect.*

BOOK 3

Transition to Practice

Instead of saying "the one who," let's say "the way of life that gives you the commission." Forget about who it is, whether it is a king or a simple man. You don't take a commission from a person. You take it from the way of life. That means that when you are designing a house, you are designing it for the person, but you are designing it also for the person who will take it after this person. Otherwise, you don't serve architecture at all.

You can't make terrific castles which no one can afford, because the way of life won't let you; it tells you that you can't do it. There are no kings anymore ... Now, this is the way of life telling the architect this ... The expression of an era can come only from architecture, which has the way of life as its commissioner.[28]

---

[28] Kahn, Louis I., 1973, *Conversations with Architects*, eds. John Wesley Cook and Heinrich Klotz, Praeger Publishers, Connecticut, p. 190.

PART 7

Architect's Job

Selectors of Tasteful Finishes

Some architect friends in Philadelphia were puzzled about my accepting a job at SOM, Chicago, but I was determined to learn current technologies and be able to make buildings like Salk, Yale, and Mellon.

Our arrival in Chicago reminded me of my student days, especially that one particular cold winter day sixteen years before when I made my declaration that I would never return to Chicago. Yet here I was again, arriving on a beautiful summer day, being reminded that life takes unexpected turns.

Chicago Center City is impressive. Just walking through well-designed public plazas, streets, buildings, museums, art galleries, and sculptures in parks and gardens, and being around the civility can affect one's sense of beauty and self-respect. It educates us on art, on architecture, and on life.

Tall buildings were icons in the city, but I always felt peculiar about them. I couldn't help but think they were made-up places for a life of their own, attractive to those who were either working within corporate lifestyles or aspiring to be in such environments. Being so high above a beautiful city and not partaking in its life makes one merely an observer—not a citizen, not a real participant, but an inspector.

I needed to learn what a tower wanted to be, where corridors and elevators would take the places of streets full of life, plazas, parkways, sidewalk cafés, shops, and taverns.

The quintessential beauty of tower building—its elegance, its simplicity, its soul—lies in Mies's work. I began to understand how great a match of Mies and Chicago were. And I thought Chicago had copied Mies without true understanding.

Skidmore, Owings, and Merrill (SOM) was a good place to see the workings of large projects in large teams. The firm had 960 people working in their Chicago office when I started; architectural design grew out of the accumulated knowledge of tenant standards, building codes, zoning laws, and liability/contractual issues. The firm had successfully captured the market of high-rise buildings and was renowned internationally. Architecture was business. The architect served the market. The client was the boss. "If you don't have a client, you don't have architecture" was what I heard frequently. A good friend reminded me recently that "You'll have a client but not architecture" is a more appropriate saying if you look at the city overall.

I had to forget what I learned from Kahn. Architecture was good if it made profit for the partners and the firm. But how could it be that the understanding of architecture was so different?

The speculative mixed-use tower was a typical project at SOM. The people who were financing the project were "investment builders." SOM had become capable of producing technically perfect but also specimens repeatedly, reminding me of Kahn's description of "designers of exteriors and selectors of tasteful finish materials."[29]

Every single note, every scrap of paper related to a project study, was being recorded, dated, and kept to eliminate potential liabilities.

[29] *Louis Kahn: Essential Texts*, p. 32.

The desire to maximize profits did not allow time to develop concept studies. Each project started as if it was in the DD (design development) stage. This was a whole new experience for me. The office felt like a production floor. I remember being told by a managing principal not to waste my time making freehand sketches. "Draw it hardline on Mylar sheets. It's OK if you throw it away. It is just the cost of a Mylar sheet." Or they would say, "Don't work hard. Work smart." I still do not know what that meant.

Everyone was aware and protective of their own place on the totem pole, and they were very assertive of their position in the decision-making process. Every decision was confronted with code and cost issues. There were complicated technical requirements, time constraints, and rigid requirements. This wasn't a place to talk about the relevance of Kahn; Mies had already occupied that place.

Our Daughter Was Born

I worked hard through long hours and cold weekends to be good on this side of professional work. I took the professional architect exams and became a licensed architect and a member of the American Institute of Architects (AIA). In 1982, I became a proud father of a beautiful baby girl.

After five years of SOM Chicago work, I resigned from my position to start my own professional practice in Oak Park.

Oak Park

Oak Park is the first of the suburbs to the west of Chicago, six miles from the Loop. There is better-than-average knowledge and experience of architecture among fellow Oak Parkers, being the heart of Frank Lloyd Wright's early work, where his home and studio are located. Unity Temple and many great examples of Prairie School buildings are just around the corner. Of course, Chicago is also the place of Wright's

Robie House; works of Louis Sullivan; the Loop, with its rich heritage of commercial buildings; and the Lakefront, with its signature open space, all merging together as a vibrant urban statement. I gave frequent Chicago and Oak Park tours for visiting friends. One of the tours most admired was Wright's Johnson Wax building in Racine, Wisconsin, two hours' drive north of Chicago. One should visit this building to reaffirm Wright's genius and understand the feeling of joy in architecture.

There is a term used in OP, having many FLW-, E. E. Roberts–, George Maher–, and Tallmadge and Watson–designed residences. They call them "architect-designed houses." And they are willing to indicate a higher value in buying or selling these houses.

Private practice was a challenge for me. With the encouragement of friends, I started in furniture design (figs. 126–127). *Tacha* is the name of the chair (*ta* and *cha* were combined from the first syllables of the words *table* and *chair*). The idea came from the need to have a large horizontal surface at elbow level. I produced this chair and exhibited it in Merchandise Mart. There was not much interest.

I continued my involvement with product design and produced a tabletop soccer game called Kick-a-Shay (figs. 128–129), for which I received a US patent. I started promoting it at youth soccer games.

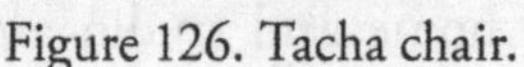

Figure 126. Tacha chair.

Figure 127

Figure 128 Figure 129

I worked on some house additions and alterations, and on some commercial interiors. My work later expanded into master planning studies for the WLGI Baha'i radio station in South Carolina and included the space planning of the Second Baha'i World Congress at the Jacob Javits Convention Center in New York City for thirty thousand attendees.

Life was good. I had my young family and my work close to home. My wife opened her landscape architecture professional practice, CYLA (Carol Yetken, Landscape Architect), in Oak Park, and it was a successful practice. We enjoyed raising our two children and spent many hours at their school, with friends, and attending their dance and theater performances. We continued our travels to London, Rome, Paris, Haifa, Spain, Italy, and Turkey.

Farnsworth

My landscape architect wife asked me to join her and a group of landscape architects on a visit to the Farnsworth House. Built between 1946 and 1951 (fig. 130), it was a weekend retreat designed by Mies van der Rohe (1886–1969) for Dr. Edith Farnsworth. A raised rectangular glass box appeared to be floating on relatively flat open land along the Fox River in Plano, Illinois. It represented the modernist style; it was minimal, and it was the simplest place to live.

The town of Plano is about an hour's drive from Chicago. I was very curious to see this glass box in its setting. There was an essential discomfort in my mind with its transparency.

What I saw was not a work of a formalist architect. This was a pure, genuine, and magnificent work of architecture—an architectural expression of a *desire to live within nature.* Nature could be scary; it could be untamable. It could be hot, cold, wet, dry, or wild, and life there is vulnerable, exposed, uncomfortable, and precious. I saw Farnsworth as a friend of nature, sitting near the river, amid trees, secure and confident.

Figure 130. Farnsworth.

In the car, going back to Chicago from Plano, my mind was busy with Mies. Everything was masterfully done. The front porch, living room, dining area, roof, ceiling, doors, windows, garden, floor, nature, the river—all were showing new definitions for me. Suddenly, Frank Lloyd Wright's Fallingwater climbed into my mind. This was a very peculiar similarity. These two, Fallingwater and Farnsworth, came out of almost the same human desire—to live within nature.

I started comparing Farnsworth to Fallingwater (fig. 130). Weren't they both masterful, dramatic architectural expressions? And how different they were. This was a magical discovery for me. Two architects at the peak of their profession had started with the same human desire and ended up so far away from each other.

Conceived ten years apart, each was a part of different circumstances and created a different cycle of life for different individuals. It was as if these two giants, Mies and Wright, had arrived from another planet to point out what architecture is capable of and how to give a soul to a built place.

I thought of Mies's IBM building in Chicago (1973). It was an expression of the cutthroat realism of a corporate business. It was efficient, strict, hierarchical, and machinelike, and it was elegant, even noble, and beautiful. IBM was a complete statement; it had nothing extra—nothing to add, nothing to subtract. It could not have just been a technical decision, but a product of exceptional understanding of aesthetic.

There was Mies's Crown Hall (1950–1956). It was an expression of the spartan life of an artist and the desirable purity of an architectural composition. The art of design creates the excitement of color, passion, imagination, and love. There was also Mies's 900–910 Lake Shore Drive towers on Chicago's Lakefront (1949–1951), an expression of the life of an urban dweller and the imposed constrictions to an occupant's life.

Architecture is a complex art. It has potential to express the complete range of human emotions and endeavor. Every architect has contributed, one way or another, to this collective array of art.

Another Large Firm

In mid-1989, I was offered a position at Perkins & Will, another large and prestigious architectural firm in Chicago. Work in P&W was enjoyable and rewarding. There were many different project types, which included airports, cultural facilities, universities, libraries, leisure facilities, public buildings, institutions, offices, corporate buildings, convention centers, research centers, and multifamily residential towers. The firm marketed itself primarily as a design firm. Designers were respected and supported by the whole firm.

There were no rigid lines of ranks among working people. It was heartwarming to see new young architecture graduates from faraway places like China, Japan, Romania, Taiwan, Korea, India, Turkey, Greece, Iran, and Canada, working alongside more seasoned architects. The talents of the designers were diverse and varied. The most enjoyable aspect of working at P&W was the cooperative spirit of the work. Everyone understood formal priorities and could acknowledge and carry out architectural concepts all the way through to the end. A highlight was the opportunity to work closely with the firm's most talented and internationally recognized architect, Ralph Johnson, with whom I shared a compatible design language. I worked on many local, national, and international projects, and I traveled extensively to Seoul, Shanghai, Beirut, Dubai, London, Bahrain, Ankara, and Dusseldorf. I continued to work at Perkins & Will until my full retirement in 2009.

Ever a learning environment, I gave several talks and slide presentations at P&W, and I organized series of talks to demonstrate or pose questions about the architectural experience and the importance of concept development.

Selected Works

The work on a large project goes through a series of conditions and circumstances involving many individuals, each person adding their contribution to the outcome. There are many professionals who share their effort and talent in the development of the buildings we see on our streets. Every individual on the team brings their best, their own quality and contribution, something very special to the project's character. The following images are of some of the projects I was involved with from 1989 to 2009.

Dubai International Airport. Terminal 3

Dubai International Airport. Terminal 3

Dubai International Airport. Terminal 3

Dubai International Airport. Terminal 2

Dubai International Terminal 2

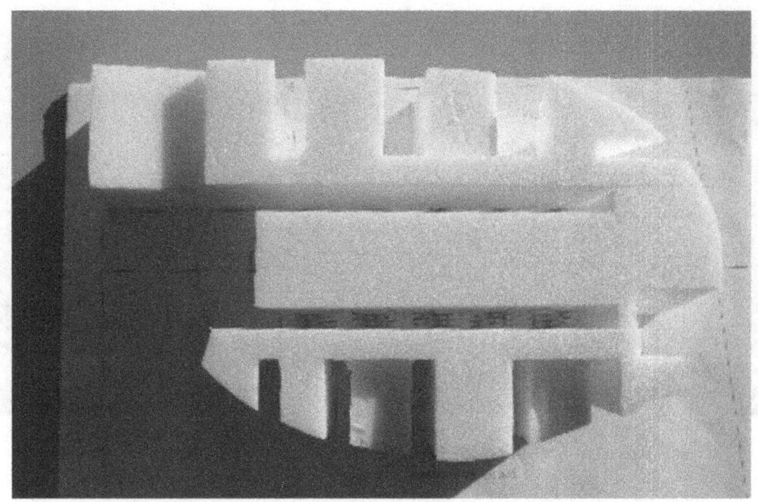

Shanghai, PRC Pudong Central Library concept model

Shanghai, PRC Pudong Central Library rendering

Thomson Consumer Electronic Center, Indianapolis, IN

Thomson Consumer Electronic Center, Indianapolis, IN

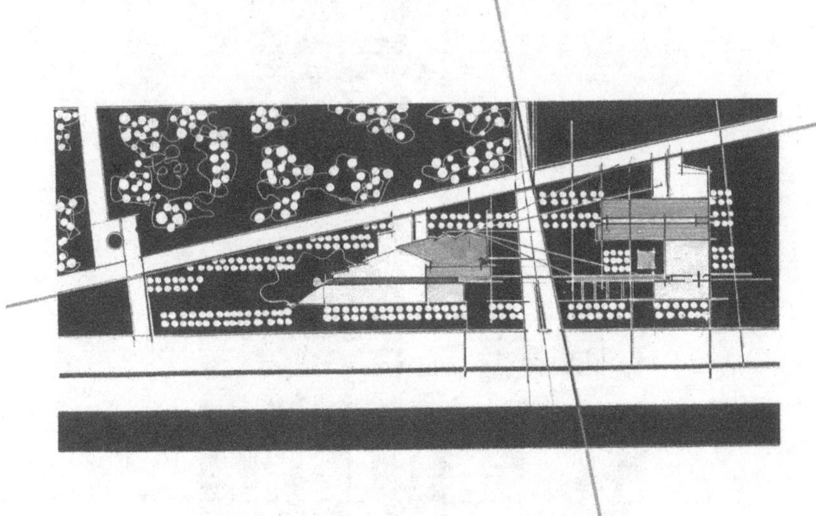

Sogutozu Office and Commercial Center, Ankara, Turkey

Sogutozu Office and Commercial Center, Ankara, Turkey

Sogutozu Office and Commercial Center, Ankara, Turkey

Interdisciplinary Science and Technology Center, ASU, Phoenix, Arizona

Interdisciplinary Science and Technology Center, ASU, Phoenix, Arizona

Peninsula (Signature) Mix use development, st. Petersburgh, Florida

Peninsula (Signature) Mix use development, st. Petersburgh, Florida

PART 8

A Good Building

A good building does not impress you at first sight. It comes back to you as a recollection, when you say, "That was a good building."[30]

—Louis Kahn

[30] In-class statement.

I first realized the meaning of Lou's "good building" statement after visiting the Trenton Baths. I was able to discover its life in its interrelated spaces and its spatial structure. One must walk through its spaces and observe the life it nurtures and its overall structure before deciding its true architectural value.

Visiting Kahn's buildings taught me a lot. Each one was noble in its simplicity and powerful in its existence. Each one possessed a silent uniqueness. There was nothing flashy about them. His designs allowed for the intrinsic luminosity of the life to shine through. One may not see any earthshaking statement in Kahn's work at once, but if you look carefully, you will find the works to be of great integrity. Kahn's buildings are modest, full of humble architectural statements, truehearted, well-defined, and original.

Throughout the years, I visited Trenton, Bryn Mawr, Mellon, Kimbell, Exeter, and the parliament building in Dhaka, and I found that each was a testament to Kahn's beliefs and his architectural talent, with uncompromising clarity and consistency. These were great testimonies to his admirable talent. His contribution to the field of architecture is entirely unique and very different from his peers. In my mind, Kahn brought an original perspective to the art of architecture that will endure long into the future.

In order to understand its power, we must learn to look at spaces between walls and observe how they and their relationships support activities, inspire actions, and evoke feelings that every human can relate to. A building should not be understood by its exterior walls or through its photo-realistic renderings. The aesthetic statement of it is often misleading about its life.

A good building creates an impression that stays with me. It wraps me up in warm, friendly, and familiar feelings and tells me stories of how it was made. It displays the energies of its nature. It tells me about the weather and its life throughout the seasons and years, and it sings me the songs of daylight.

Baths of Trenton

For a long while, I wondered how it was that the Baths of Trenton, such a simple building, could be considered worth putting in an architectural publication. What made it so important? And why was I so affected by it?

"I wish I knew how to make the first barn." Kahn's sentence in class was a puzzle in my mind. I did not know what a barn was. I was unable to figure out how this idea related to our work in class. My questions were resolved after a weekend trip to the Amish countryside near Philadelphia, where I saw many barns and understood them to be the most efficient and most unassuming minimal structures that enclosed a large volume of space. I could see the barn's beauty, structural simplicity, and suitability for its life.

The Trenton Baths (1955–1957) project reminded me of Kahn's barn reference. I find the Trenton Baths (figs. 5 and 147) spectacular in its conception and ingenious in its execution. It is a most confident spatial setup, a perfect architectural lesson in its simplicity and pure beauty.

Figure 147

It was over fifty years ago that I first saw the Trenton plans. The purity of it had excited me. Its directness and honesty fascinated me. It displayed a positive engagement with its environment and indicated a unique courage in showing how it was built. It was made of simple economical materials expressed in a straightforward composition.

It had just four squares connected at corners. The plan looked to me like an abstract painting at first, where life's richness had reason to shine. Its life was the only reason for its existence.

Trenton is minimal. It is nothing more than a place for a community gathering around an outdoor swimming pool. Nothing is exaggerated; nothing is glorified. A special talent brought it into architectural reality and made it worthwhile to build. It is such an agonizingly simple response to a community's desire to have a swimming pool and changing rooms. It may not even be appropriate to call it a building. It is a place—nothing less, nothing more.

Years ago, during one of my visits, a man approached me. “You must be an architect,” he said.

“Yes, I am,” I responded. He was one of the locals, I thought, enjoying the sun and the pool that day.

“Many architects come here, take pictures, and admire this place. I guess they like it,” he continued.

“Yes,” I murmured, nodding in agreement. “It is worth visiting.”

“Could you tell me,” he asked, “why you think this is so good?”

I looked at the building again. It needed repairs[31] and some good maintenance, I thought. But even if it were maintained well and even when it was brand-new, I guessed people would have asked the same question. Its simplicity confused people. Perhaps they thought there was nothing architectural in it. I remember thinking, *This man is not an architect, so I shouldn’t use my design vocabulary in my comments.* Yet after every sentence I said, I could hear myself thinking, *You make no sense, no sense at all.* I could see from his eyes that he was trying to understand what I was saying, but it was obvious I was not making any sense to him. Occasionally, he shook his head. “Balance, totality, clarity, new aesthetics,” I continued, but my mind kept whispering to me, *Not a chance. You are making this up. It doesn’t even make sense to* yourself.

At the end, he looked at the building again and said “Thank you” and politely moved away. I was embarrassed. *Think about this very seriously,* I warned myself. I fully realized I was unable to talk about architecture and explain the value and sense of the life that surrounds it.

Rooms of Bryn Mawr

The first time I visited the Bryn Mawr dormitories (1960–1964)[32] was in fall of 1965. The building was not yet occupied, and I was unable to get inside. The slates covering the exterior wall were an unusual very bright green. A few months later, when I was Kahn’s student, I heard him say in class that the sun was a great painter, referring to the fading of the slate color.

---

31 This happened years before the most successful restoration in 2010.

32 Currently named Erdman Hall.

This three-story structure had a plan with three square blocks connected at the corners. The sizes of the squares were the same in each pod (fig. 148).

Figure 148. Plan sketch diagram.

Figure 149. View from the west Bryn Mawr dormitory (Erdman Hall).

To the romantic eye, the Bryn Mawr dormitories may look like a chateau from the Middle Ages, where beautiful princesses were kept away from disreputable Casanovas (fig. 149). During the early 1960s, my guess is that there were strict rules governing the social lives of the young women living in this women's liberal arts college. The plan demonstrated a balance between private and public areas using simple responsive geometry. Kahn had gone through a long process of design development.[33]

I read this building almost as a stage set where an individual will be eased into living in groups.

The spatial context gives the student a degree of choice to be inside or outside the subgroup. The rooms are located around the perimeter, each with a view of the outside. Each room has an entry niche distinct from the gallery. This is not a typical dormitory with corridors and straight walls. There is no double-loaded corridor. The large central spaces are for common activities. These include a dining hall, the living room, and the entry hall. Service rooms, such as showers, bathrooms, and laundry, are located between the private rooms and visually separate the individual rooms from the large halls.

As a place to learn to live together, it is spatial poetry. Life here can be as private or as personal as one wants it to be. Students can be alone, choose to join others, or only partake of a certain set of activities. I sensed a unique spatial/architectural character there. There is a delicate sense of privacy one would not typically see in dormitories. I felt Lou found those essential characteristics of a way of life in a dormitory and reflected that in this design solution.

Bryn Mawr is a good example of two of Kahn's statements.[34]

- "Architecture is the thoughtful making of rooms."
- "A plan is a society of rooms."

I liked this building. It is a good lesson for architects to see how a life setting is defined in architecture. A building also invites the interplay of the natural sequences of daylight and seasons (fig. 150). One student, referring to the light scoops, described her experience to me: "We were having our Christmas dinner, and it was a delight to see the moon from my seat in the dining hall."

---

[33] These design studies can be seen in Louis I. Kahn Complete Work 1935-1974 by Heinz Ronner, Sharad Jhaveri, Birkhauser (1977 first edition – 1987 second edition), p. 162.

[34] In-class statement. Also published in *D'aujourd'hui*, p. 1.

Figure 150. Common spaces have cutouts for daylight.

Order at Connecticut

Kahn's Mellon Center for British Art (1969–1974) is in New Haven, Connecticut, on the Yale University campus, just across from Kahn's earlier building, the Yale Art Gallery (1950–1953). When one passes by the modest exterior of Mellon or Kahn's Yale Gallery or even the Kimbell Art Museum, one does not realize the artistic brilliance until they step inside. The life, the lived experience, is inside, and that is where the spark is.

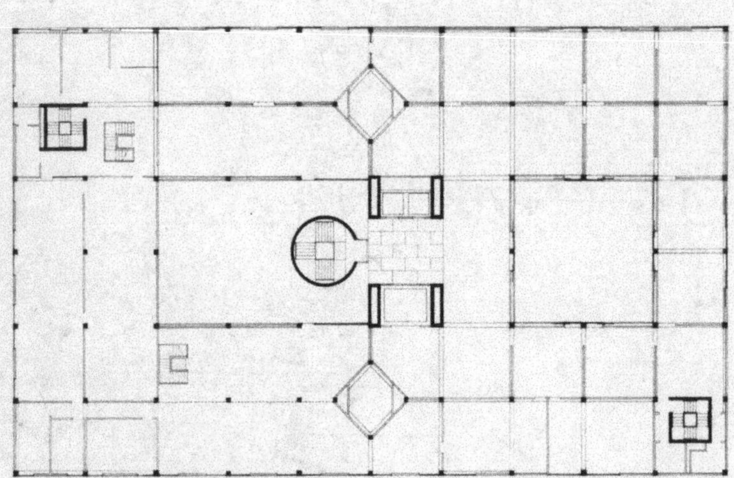

Figure 151. Plan, Mellon Center for British Art.

It has wide, spacious galleries that can be opened or closed to one another with massive wood panels within a simple concrete structural grid (fig. 151). It has a sensible, agreeable, and understandable character in the composition of spaces. Decisions are not in conflict but complement one another. This is a place to witness strong architectural order; simplicity and clarity abound in this sophisticated and attractive building. There is unexpected simplicity and perfect proportions—nothing more, nothing less.

Galleries are flexible. There are almost limitless wall surfaces on which to hang artwork. This accentuates the richness of the collection. Interconnected galleries emphasize the experience of being in an art center. Openings into the interior square courtyards further expand this experience. Well-placed windows on the exterior wall relate the art to the outside. Is the weather changing in New Haven today? Is it sunny still, or raining outside?

I liked the stark interior (fig. 152); it shows a genuine indication that art weaves color, joy, and life around this naked state. Whatever *sense of order* means in architecture, I found it there in Mellon. And if I understand the meaning of *simplicity* in architecture, it was made clear to me there.

Figure 152. Cutout spaces.

Books in Exeter

I was a passenger in the car, and my wife was driving. We were moving northwest. We had passed Pine Street, and now Elliot. On my right, above the trees, I could see the tops of brick buildings. Then suddenly, the Exeter Library (1965–1972) came into full view, and I mumbled its name in awe.

We were in front of the library at the Phillips Exeter Academy, in Exeter, New Hampshire. It was nicely settled among the tall trees and a well-manicured lawn (fig. 153). We parked along the street and walked toward the building. I could smell barbecue coming from one of the buildings on my left. This was a pleasant campus. It felt like a peaceful and friendly place, where people enjoyed their lives. They were happy; they were young, safe, and secure. It must provide a great opportunity to live and to learn together in peace and harmony.

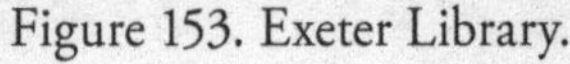

Figure 153. Exeter Library.

Figure 154. Wood model.

I first noticed the overall height of the building and the many openings along its sides. It looked like the wood model that had been sitting on Hideki's desk (fig. 154), and here was the real one, in full view. And brick, brick, brick.

Figure 155. Brick arcade as cuts from the massive brick.

I spotted the roof of a dining hall in the distance. That one also looked so much like the scale model in the office. Both buildings looked new. Bravo, they took good care of them.

I brought my sight back to the ground level and noticed the flat arches (fig. 155). An arcade was all around the base, with a relatively low ceiling. How would I find the main entry? Was this the place "where everybody meets everyone else in the campus," as Louis had said to us in class? It was a beautiful space to walk through, and led to a series of glass doors on the left. I walked in. I climbed the curving marble stairs to the second floor. The spatial richness captured my breath.

Like all of Kahn's buildings, this one also addressed universal human characters. One could have this building anywhere in the world to be used as a university library, primarily designed for and built on the relationship of books and man.

Figure 156. Cutouts at the center.

There was a large volume in front of me, above me, and all around me (fig. 156). It gave me that warm feeling of being important. Yes, this was a temple of knowledge, a treasury of books, a wellspring of collected knowledge.

The central space showed one where the books were and how to get to them. This is the reason to build libraries. The circle openings in the concrete were impressive, true to their structural and material character. This was the aesthetic of poured-in-place concrete. Concrete carried the heavy stuff, books and book stacks, around the tall central space. This central space received daylight from the top, which created a clear sense of direction, essential in a library.

The perimeter held the reading rooms and carrels (fig. 157), brick with wood, warmed by strips of natural light and connecting with the outside world. Work and study translated well into architecture. This was not a complex building; the most attractive part of the Exeter Library was its spatial simplicity. Dead corners were occupied with services, stairs (fig. 158), and toilets, where they should be.

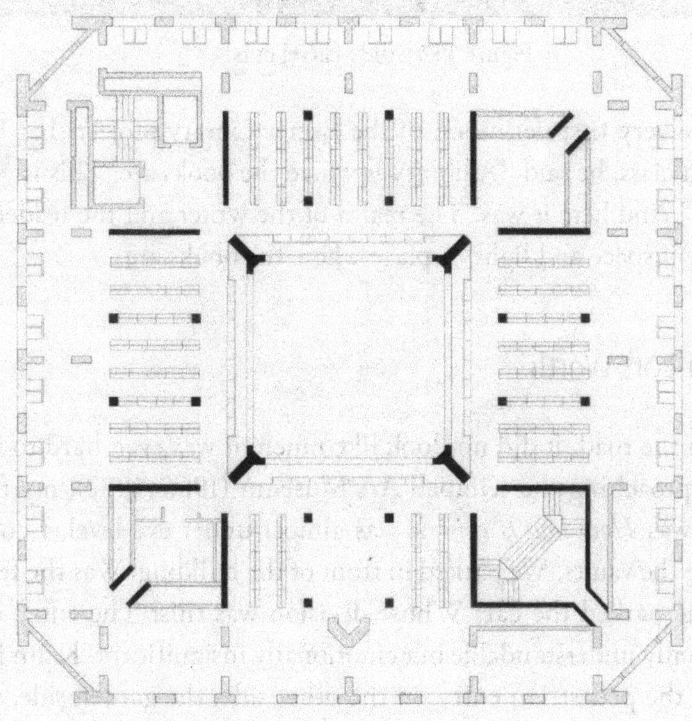

Figure 158. Plan of Exeter.

Figure 157. Study carrel cuts.

In the very first definition of the Exeter Library project that Lou gave us in class, he said, "A library is where the books are. This is your program." And here it was. The realm of the writer and the reader. A structure of space and light. A place where the books are.

Lights of Fort Worth

From the road, it did not look like much; it was even hard to see. Upon approaching the Kimbell Art Museum (1966–1972), my first thought was *How low is this?* It was almost under eye level. I could barely see the vaults. We parked in front of the building. Was the front where one parked the car? Whose decision was this? The entry was intellectually understandable but emotionally insignificant. Kahn had designed the pedestrian entry on the other side, the garden side. On this side, the entry hall was small, and the ceiling was lower. Then I saw the ticket booth and a group heading up the narrow steps. I followed and felt like I was being invited upstairs. I told myself, *This is good.*

The building opened when I reached the main floor. This was where the gift shop was. Suddenly, I realized its totality. The garden was in front of me; the courtyard was on my right (fig. 159). I turned and walked toward the courtyard. A little rain was coming in, and the stone terrace was wet.

Figure 159. View of the courtyard.

Courtyards are where nature is, where the plants are, the water, the sunlight, the shadow. I remembered Kahn's words: "Nature does not make art. She works by circumstance and law. Only man makes art."[35] I heard a whisper: *Good architecture is important for a civilized society.* I sensed crispness here, clarity.

This was a good building. Kimbell did not look like one that was designed by a star architect. It was not an iconic building, nor were Exeter or Mellon. They just felt right to me, like something well-done. Kahn knew how to craft his art. Kimbell was polite and kind and delicate; partaking in its life brought out a warm and noble feeling (figs. 160–162).

Inside, natural light poured into the galleries. This was a great way to experience art. Long galleries stretched out. I touched the travertine wall, although I was not sure if this was allowed.

---

35 In-class statement.

Figure 161. Carved-out ceiling.

Kahn's "Structure is the maker of light"[36] was clear to me now. I had complete comprehension of its architectural representation, its meaning, and its reflection. Kimbell was a maker of light. I believe now that the purpose of a room is to catch and enclose daylight. No, not only daylight, but also the other, what Kahn called "made light." *In here, the light dissolves in architecture, in the hands of an architect,* I told myself. Kahn's "A vault or a dome is a choice of the character of light"[37] was clear to me now (fig. 161). This simple structure sat in its own silence, holding its light.

Kimbell enclosed daylight in strips of light. Kimbell captured daylight to honor art. Daylight was available to all galleries. I felt Kimbell was made for light, and light only. "Light, the giver of all presences …"[38]

Wow. Nothing was out of place. Was I home?

---

[36] In-class statement.

[37] In-class statement.

[38] In-class statement.

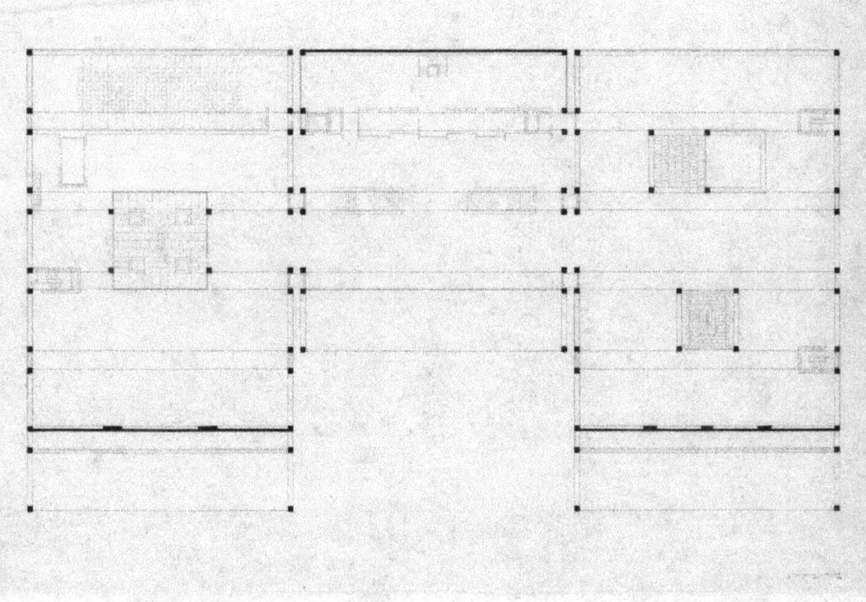

Figure 160.

The plan was a simple rectangle of light, no light, and light.

Figure 162

Figure 163

I remember once in class, Kahn referred to Wallace Stevens's "What slice of sun does your building have?" (figs. 162–163) statement and added "What slice of sun enters your room? As if to say that the sun never knew how great it was until it struck the side of a building." (See also Wurman, 1986, p. 128.)

I found a book in the gift shop that described this building: *Light Is the Theme* (reference cited). At the end of that book, Kahn is quoted:

> I like this building; it feels as though I had nothing to do with it, as if someone else had done it.

This is another great lesson for architects. When a building is completed and occupied, then the architect leaves, and life begins to own it.

Halls of Dhaka

Only a special permission allowed me to visit the Bangladesh parliament building (1962–1974). The building was completed in 1983, nine years after Kahn died. My guide drove me around the building first (fig. 164).

The experience, the spatial character, and the qualities of this building are a grand statement. Being there is not describable in words or in still or moving pictures.

Figure 164. View from the ring road.

Figure 165. View around the building

Kahn created a grand stage for his actors. The plan diagram was simple. Eight separate segments were brought together from different directions to discuss, negotiate, debate, and reach a decision at the core center, in order to run the affairs of a country for the good of their citizens (fig. 168).

There were many lessons for architects here: how to curve walls, how to meet curves with straight lines, how to join large volumes, how to cut out openings (figs. 165–166). It was full of mastery and excitement. Here Kahn was in his element. He knew this territory well, and he was there with full confidence. He created new cuts, shapes, and joints (fig. 166). This was indeed a sculpted, carved-out space on a grand scale. Kahn must have felt great pride challenging himself with this project. It was created from a thought, out of nothing.

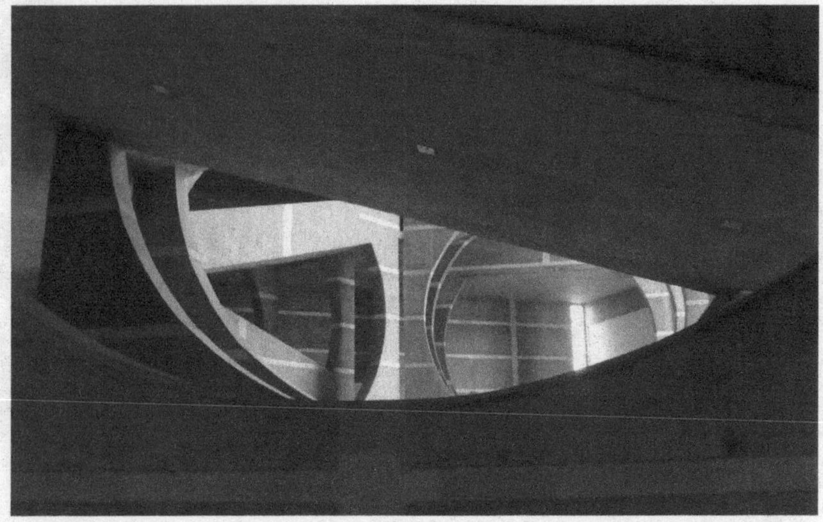

Figure 166. The whole building was full of carved-out/cutout spaces.

Figure 167. Straight and curved exterior wall

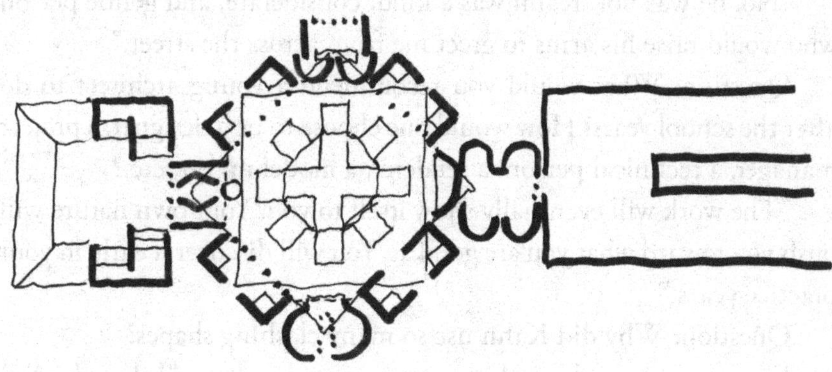

Figure 168. Sketch plan.

Addressing Students

I was invited to speak to a group of architecture students in Dhaka. The students could express themselves well in English. I made a brief introduction and went on to give them two simple introductory comments for their future as architects.

- Learn to read places as sets of human experiences.
- Observe and identify places as expressions of human desires.

I also mentioned they should examine a building with an eye toward its connecting spaces. The students were very attentive. I opened the discussion. The first question came.

Question: What was Kahn's attitude toward project deadlines for him or for his students?

A curious question, I thought. "*Deadline* is an awful term. *Due date* is better," I said. "If due dates are set by different people with different assumptions and priorities than the artist, they are bound to create conflicts, disagreements, and misalignments. In the professional area, priorities and assumptions must be agreed on to avoid conflicts. For class projects, we kept all the due dates that we were assigned."

Question: Was he an arrogant or temperamental person?

"No, he was not. Kahn was a kind, considerate, and gentle person who would raise his arms to greet me from across the street."

Question: What would you recommend a young architect to do after the school years? How would one choose to be a designer, a project manager, a technical person, a renderer, a model maker, etc.?

"The work will eventually show itself to you. Your own nature will push you toward what you are good at. You will discover it early in your practice years."

Question: Why did Kahn use so many clashing shapes?

I was not sure where this question was heading. "Like what?" I asked.

"Like triangles, arches, circles, some big, some small," the student answered, referring to the parliament building.

"To me, they are not clashing," I said. "They are curves and straight lines, circles and triangles. They are all great complements to one another. One empowers the other, gives life, and defines clear identities to the other. We must know dark to recognize light. Look at it this way. There are narrower vertical triangles outside, and then wider horizontal triangles inside. Complete circles outside, half circles [arches] inside. Maybe some in the execution of concrete are not carefully poured, and some formwork is not done well. In some areas, the joint between the ramp and the wall was not matched properly. But the essential architectural statement is strong and powerful.

"Look how particular this building is. Whatever picture you see of this building, one immediately recognizes that it is in Dhaka and that it is the work of Louis Kahn. There is no other building like it. Does it look like any other grand-scale building? Does it look like a convention hall, a shopping mall, an Olympic sport center? Well, of course not. This is a parliament building for the Republic of Bangladesh. It is in the capital city of a brand-new nation. The size and scale and all the cuts and joints indicate that it is."

Figure 169. Simple openings along exterior wall

Question: Why did Lou use concrete?

"Look how durable it is," I said. "Kahn used to say 'Concrete is a fluid stone.' Concrete is stone that we can pour." I was remembering things I had never talked about before. It felt good to revisit these memories. I continued, "Remember the process of pouring out concrete. Circles and triangles are suitable as openings in solid monolithic surfaces. They are also suitable shapes to pour. And concrete is so durable, they are still all in perfect shape on Salk, on Mellon, on Yale, on most of his projects. Brick and brickwork require more detailed skills. Also, concrete has a scale to it. It is different than brick. It is much more grandiose. Don't you think it is more suitable for a parliament building of this scale? By the way, I am sure you have heard of Lou's phrase 'Ask brick.' This expression was his way of pointing out the importance of searching the depths, widths, and breadths of a task one is about to begin. Ask this question not only for various materials but also for the character of a place.

"Every material, every place, every shape has its own nature and its own constitution, so to speak. A circle, square, and triangle each have a unique quality and characteristics. For example, wood has a structural aesthetic suitable for certain applications, like shaping, bending, joining. Steel, plastic, and concrete—each of these also lend themselves to unique configurations and applications."

Question: Do you remember any occasion when you were scared or nervous before your jury?

"Yes, of course, I do. Whenever you are opening yourself up to criticism, you are vulnerable and therefore scared and nervous. The key is to be able to explain your work, your vision, and your understanding completely, with drawings or with models, at that time."

Question: Did Kahn have any favorite project?

"Well, I don't know of any one. My guess is that Kahn was excited by every new project. The most challenging time for him was at the beginning of a project. Kahn excelled at developing concepts, new ways of looking at space and how best to achieve the results for the life to take place within it. This is similar for any architect, isn't it? It is a challenge of discovery, a chance to go further and to better oneself. But I will tell you what my least favorite aspect of any project would be. The least favorite aspect of any project for me was the outright rejection, or one that suddenly cuts off the project budget or shortens the schedule without any consideration or acknowledgment of the effects on the project. Kahn's favorite project may have been when he could fully communicate with the person or the committee that selected him for the project, like Dr. Salk. And out of this came the Salk Institute in La Jolla, California. This must be one of the great buildings in architecture."

Question: What buildings or which architect in Bangladesh inspired him most while designing the assembly hall?

I knew where this question was coming from. Their design teacher had lectured extensively in the US, pointing out various historical buildings in Dhaka and drawing connections between some in Dhaka and Louis's work. "I'm not aware of any architect," I said. "But I'm sure Kahn, with his talent, could instantaneously grasp many of the cultural cues inherent in people's words, sentences, songs, attitudes, in their arts and architecture. One thing to remember, as Kahn wrote once, 'A dish that has fallen in Mozart's kitchen is a beginning of a symphony.' Kahn was like the Mozart of architecture." I pointed to a wall and continued, "Kahn was so creative that he could get inspiration or discover something new from these two nails and apply a certain meaning of their spatial relations to a new condition."

Question: Can one repeat building the Dhaka parliament building anywhere else?

This question puzzled me. Was this coming from a deep understanding of form, or was it just an innocent question regarding the size, volume, and shape of this building? I explained that this depended on the student's definition of the term *building*. If he meant the actual design, the completed building, the volume, shape, material, openings, levels, etc., then no, the same building would not be built anywhere as it was built in Dhaka. The circumstances (or availabilities) would be different in other places.

"Kahn used two separate terms for the realization of a building: *form* and *design*. *Form* does not mean 'shape.' *Form* is the essence of its being. Think of it as a verb, as in 'to form,' 'to establish.' The design is to a place and to its time. The design cannot be repeated anywhere else. It belongs to Dhaka.

"The form of Dhaka, as a set of relationships, as a sense of connections, in its most pure existence, as a primary spatial chart, may be repeated if the nature of another place complies with the same particular lifestyle or way of living."

Question: When you were working there [at Kahn's office], did you feel that you were maturing professionally or getting better?

Gosh. These are good questions, I thought. "Not really," I said. "First of all, I was too young to worry about such things. Secondly, you don't realize that need when you are doing the day-to-day work. It comes afterward, when you look back. I know now that being with Louis helped me greatly. It helped structure my thoughts and refine my beliefs. He helped me understand certain frames of references, certain views and values, and how they related to procedures in design and in architecture."

Question: Did Kahn have any favorite architect?

"I don't believe any person of Kahn's standing would admit that to anyone," I said. "But I do remember hearing him once say that he learned nothing from Le Corbusier. That was probably a moment that came out of his sense of his own uniqueness. But if you ask me, Kahn could learn from anything, from anybody." Pointing to a few nails sticking out of the whiteboard behind me, I continued, "Kahn could get inspiration from their relationships."

On my way back to the hotel, I was thinking what a great opportunity it was that these students could study this building in their city. Then I remembered that they were not allowed to visit it, because of security issues sweeping through our world and their city.

* * *

That night, I was still answering questions in my head and wondering if I had more to say about form. These questions were teaching me something I never thought about. I should have said this: In its spatial being (as its *form*), the Exeter Library could be repeated on any campus, as well as the Salk Labs in any country. Form rises from a way of life and not from a location. Form needs to be figured out and brought into an architectural realm. I also see a commitment to design, or what Kahn called "availabilities," the circumstances surrounding a project, like how much money is available and what materials, skills, or knowledge are available. Form is clear of circumstances, the specific conditions of the site, a particular culture, or any physical or historical context or character in the neighborhood.

I believe Kahn's buildings to be part of the world's culture. Their form is their nature, their beginning. It is their spatial character, their spatial structure, their inner working. The exterior appearance is partly the available light in that location, partly the expression of form, and partly the availabilities.

All of Kahn's buildings address the universal characters of man. They do not address the regional, local, or circumstantial characters of man.

Kahn's buildings, writings, drawings, lectures, and teachings all address the universal character of man. Visiting a Kahn building teaches you what architecture is. Do not expect to learn architecture from talks, discussions, lectures, or books.

In large-scale plans, I see individual buildings as their participation in their placement. The Bangladesh Master Plan and the India Ahmedabad Master Plan are two good examples (fig. 170). Units are given shapes to integrate with one another. The overall sense of coming together becomes their context. Their design and arrangement are adjusted for their immediate surroundings, to relate to their gardens, to their streets, and to their neighborhood. I should have ended my talk with this advice: Observe, think, analyze, and design places as as expressions of life, of culture, of time, of sets of human desires and aspirations. Read every room, every place, every building, and every street as a lesson of architecture. Make your design part of the life of the community. And your design will be worthwhile to build.

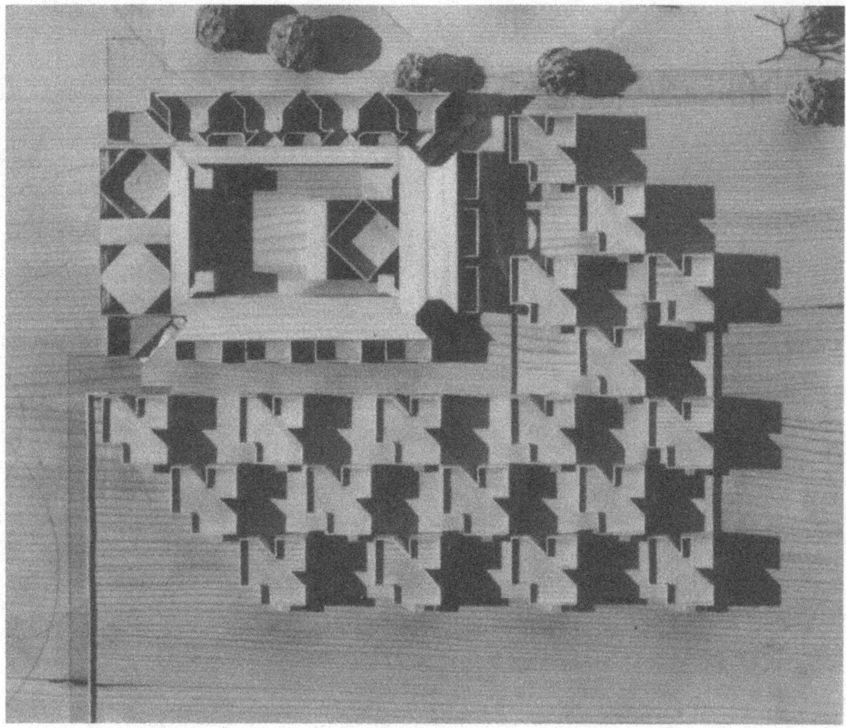

Figure 170. Outdoor spaces that were carved out.

PART 9

Whisper in Fort Wayne

> *A whisper on the stage must be heard by everyone in the audience. This motivated the thought of the "violin" and the "violin case." The place of the voice is the "violin"—the stage and the people. The "case" is the entrance, the lobby, and all other outside services.*[39]
>
> —Louis Kahn

[39] From the dedication letter Kahn sent to Fort Wayne in September 20, 1973.

In 1985, the Art Institute of Chicago was preparing a show called *Kahn in the Midwest* (February 15 to June 26, 1989). I was invited to authenticate some twenty-two sketches they had recently bought from Philadelphia.[40]

I was also asked to give a lecture at the Graham Foundation during the exhibition. This prompted me to conduct some research about the project. I took some time off from my work at SOM, and traveled to the Kahn Archives in Philadelphia to learn the history of the Fort Wayne Theater project before and after I had worked on it in Kahn's office.

This part of the book outlines the Fort Wayne project from start to finish in order to enable a better understanding of the architectural work in the proper context. Initial design through building fruition is typically a long and winding process between a building committee (trustees in charge of financing the project) and the provider of architectural service, the architect. It starts with huge enthusiasm by both, overshooting the financial and aesthetic realities as the project progresses.

This chapter describes the Fort Wayne Theater of Performing Arts in two parts: the conceptual phase in the first five years (1961–1966) and the last phase (1969–1974), during the construction.

First Five Years (1961–1966)

The Fort Wayne Fine Arts Foundation (FWFAF), formed a building committee (BC) and began a search for an architect for their Fine Arts Center (FAC) in late 1959. They considered architects Edward D. Stone; Minoru Yamasaki; Philip Johnson; Eero Saarinen; Harry Weese; Skidmore, Owings, and Merrill (Chicago); Marcel Breuer; and Mies

---

40 Author's note: Many of the sketches were from the time of my tenure in the office and were of the Fort Wayne project (including two sketches that were mine). I was told that these sketches were purchased for $220,000 or $10,000 per sketch. *How ironic,* I thought with a bitter smile, remembering all those drawers in the office full of Kahn's sketches (over 6300) and remembering his critics, those who talked about money before looking at his great talent. When he died, it became known that the office owed almost $ 460,000 to engineers and office staff. Here was the value of almost half that debt in twenty-two sketches.

van der Rohe. As Bud Latz (chairman of the committee selecting the architect) explained, Kahn was not known by the committee at the time. It was only after Philip Johnson's suggestion that Louis Kahn would be the best choice that Kahn was included in the list of possible architects.[41]

* * *

Kahn visited Fort Wayne for an interview on March 22, 1960,[42] and stayed for two days, having meetings and discussing the project. He was awarded the commission by January 1961.[43]

The project included a fine arts school for music and dance, a community center, a reception center, a philharmonic hall, a museum of history, a civic theater, a fine arts foundation, an art alliance, dormitories, and parking facilities. As Kahn initially described Fort Wayne, a town of 180,000 population, as desiring a small Lincoln Center in his early talks.[44]

Site Selection

Site selection, programming, and urban planning issues seemed to have taken the rest of 1961 and the first half of 1962. Kahn recommended a downtown location rather than the initial proposed site near the university.[45] Long discussions were carried out about the site,

---

41 Wurman, Richard Saul, *What Will Be Has Always Been: The Words of Louis I. Kahn*, New York, 1986.

42 Letter from Gibeau (president, Fort Wayne Fine Arts Foundation) to Kahn, March 7, 1960, Box LIK 17, Louis I.Kahn Collection, University of Pennsylvania and Pennsylvania Historical and Museum Collection, Philadelphia (hereafter cited as Kahn Collection).

43 Brownlee, David B., and David G. Delong, eds., *Louis I. Kahn: In the Realm of Architecture*, New York, 1991, p. 461.

44 Tyng, Alexandra, *Beginnings*, John Wiley & Sons, New York, 1984, p. 115.

45 Wurman, 1986.

utilities placement, and difficulties of clearing the area, and continued throughout negotiations with the city's redevelopment commission.

In March 1961, the Fine Arts Foundation (FAF) sent a letter to its members describing Kahn's request about the needs program. Kahn cautioned them, "All organizations submit building needs solely in terms of their own current program, without regard for combined or joint use of facilities with any other group. I urge you not to need too much, because nobody can pay for it. Unless you state your needs, you will never know what is possible."[46] He reminded them of the complexity and largeness of the project and warned them that their undertaking was an enormous financial responsibility.

Kahn subsequently made studies of the master plan that explored composition of the desired elements. Various schemes prompted discussions that continued over the next year. Kahn had a belief that the city is to be the ultimate work of human art and he He continued to study the civic design issues that were presented to the City Planning Council (fig. 171).

In a letter to Latz in April 1962,[47] Kahn suggested the formation of an urban development group in Fort Wayne, "enlisting the enthusiasm of Fort Wayne's responsible and interested citizens" He also mentioned "last week, in our presentation of the clay model" to be used as the primary base. In the same letter, he also explained the details of the site planning issues. The model which he mentioned may have been the model shown in Figure 171.

In May 1962, Fort Wayne informed Kahn of their decision to select the downtown site for the project: "Louis Kahn is to work on the exact

---

46 Memo to FAF members, March 1961, Box 17, Kahn Collection.

47 Letter from Kahn to Latz (chairman of the building committee), April 25, 1962, Kahn Collection. This letter indicates that in April 1962, Kahn presented a clay model to the Fine Arts Committee to discuss his preference for the site development presented in figure 171 was not necessarily the one illustrated on April 25, 1962. The development in figure 188 indicates a site development after autumn 1963 (as also noted by Brownlee, 1991).

location for the Fine Arts Center within the rough rectangle bounded by Main Street, Lafayette Street, the railroad, and Clinton Street."[48]

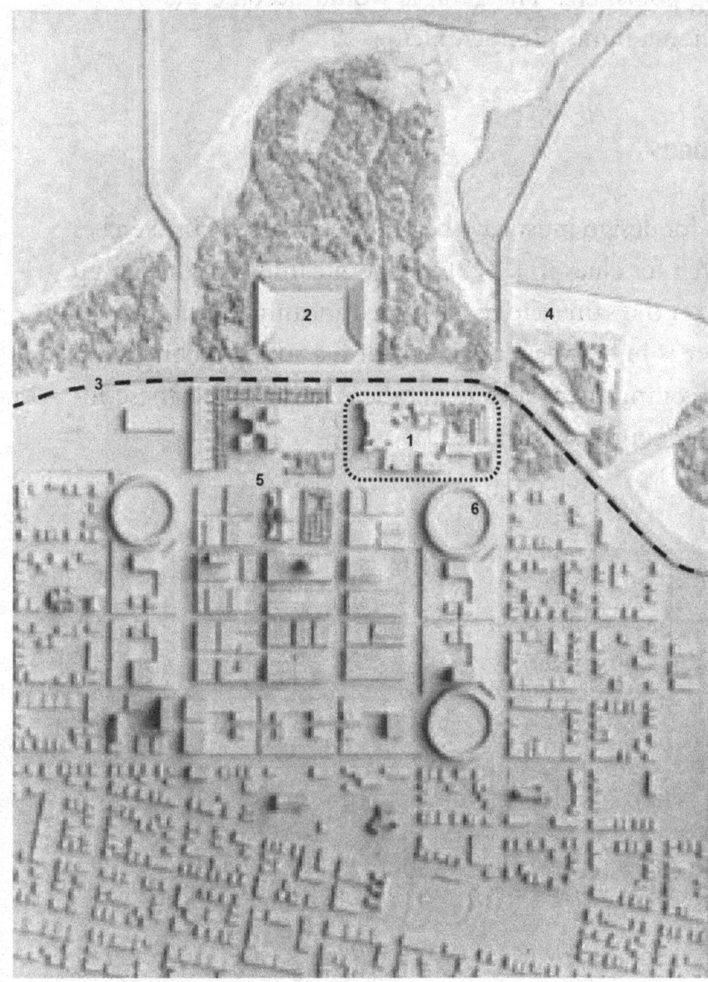

Legend

1. Fine arts center site
2. Sports center/ stadium
3. Railroad
4. St. Marys River
5. Main Street
6. Reservoirs/ terminals

Figure 171

This model shows Kahn's city planning and civic design concerns, as he had done in his earlier study for the Market Street East (Philadelphia) project.

[48] Letter from Kahn to Latz (chairman of the building committee), May 3, 1962, Box LIK 17, Kahn Collection.

> Below the stadium: the new institutions of sports, health, or recreation centers. On the roof: garden facilities, swimming pools, etc. The garages would become the walls of the stadium. (Ronner, Heinz, 1987)

Courts of Entrances

Kahn's search for design must have begun shortly after. His sketches indicated the search for clues (fig. 172) to find meaning for this group of facilities to be on the same site. Each added meaning to the whole, as well as to the areas in between, all to establish a strong architectural identity for their commitment to one another. Kahn called these in-between spaces the "courts of entrances."

Figure 172

Different architectural models (later exhibited at MoMA and other galleries) were presented to the Fort Wayne Fine Arts Foundation during these early years.

Figure 173

1. Parking structures
2. Entrance court
3. Civic theater
4. Philharmonic hall
5. Historical museum
6. Art gallery
7. Reception center and art alliance
8. School of art, music, and dance
9. Dormitories

The scheme in figures 173 and 174 reminded me of Kahn's early sketches shown in figure 172. The civic theater and the philharmonic hall with a long parking structure were located on the north edge, along the service road. Main Street, on the south, was shared by the art gallery, historical museum, reception center, and art alliance buildings.

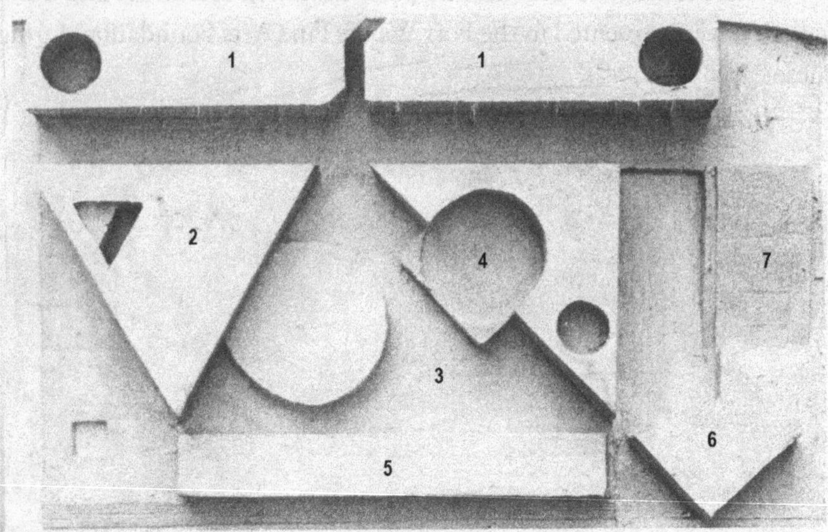

Figure 174

1. Parking structures
2. Philharmonic hall
3. Entrance court
4. Civic theater
5. Reception center, art alliance, and historical museum
6. Art gallery
7. Open-air theater

The philharmonic hall at the northwest corner of the site was indicated in Kahn's earlier sketch (fig. 174). The large triangular buildings with large stage areas also included rehearsal areas and workshops. The circular building was the audience hall for the philharmonic hall. Kahn's effort to move away from the accustomed building shapes was obvious.

I chuckle when I think of the conversations between the building committee members after presentations. What did they say to one another about Kahn's words? What did they think about these shapes for the buildings? What was Kahn's architectural language? It was obvious to me that Kahn was wiping out his client's preconceptions, misunderstandings, long-held notions, and expectations of architecture. These were not shaped for any condition. What purpose could one attach to these shapes? What sense could they evoke, except expanding thought and forcing everyone to question and rethink their idea and understanding of architecture?

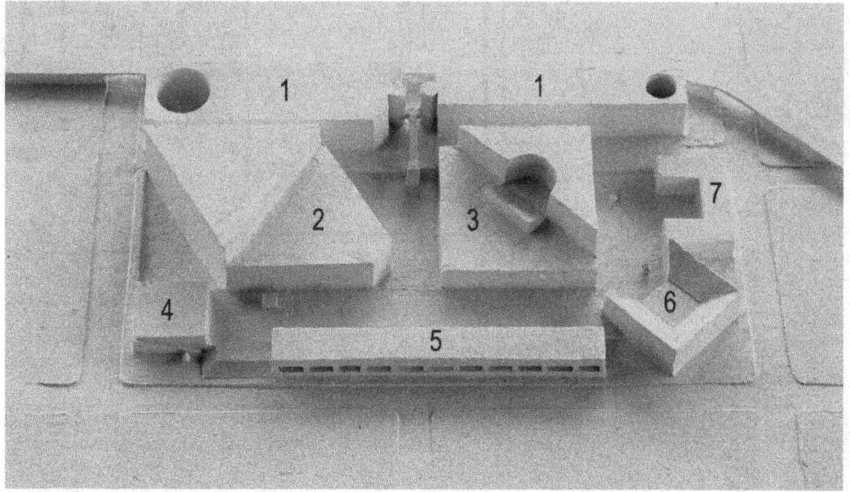

Figure 175

1. Parking
2. Philharmonic hall
3. Theater of performance art
4. Historical museum
5. School of art
6. Reception center dormitories

A more developed scheme as shown in figure 175, and another in figure 176. The philharmonic hall was being transformed into a parallelogram. The audience hall was floating within this mass. The ample amount of space around the auditorium was for other civic events. This plaster model had created a force for new discoveries and Kahn's way of shedding the client's architectural and spatial biases with brand-new shapes was continuing.

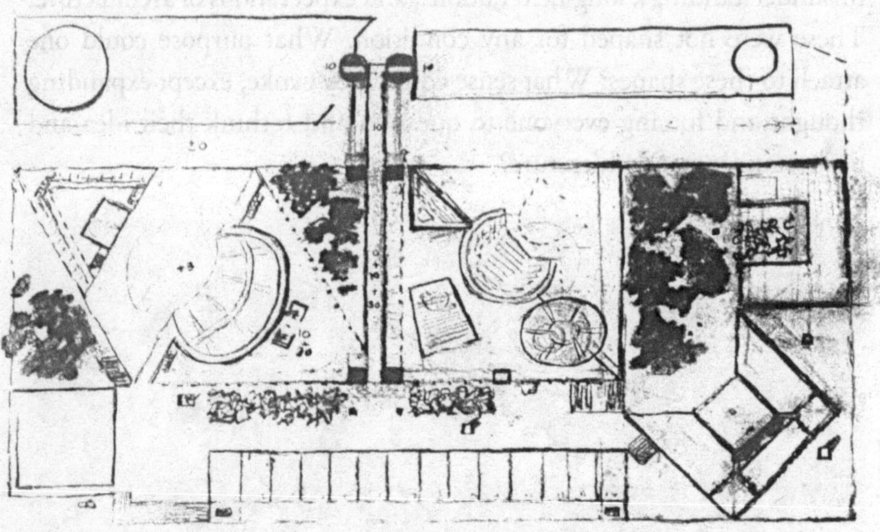

Figure 176

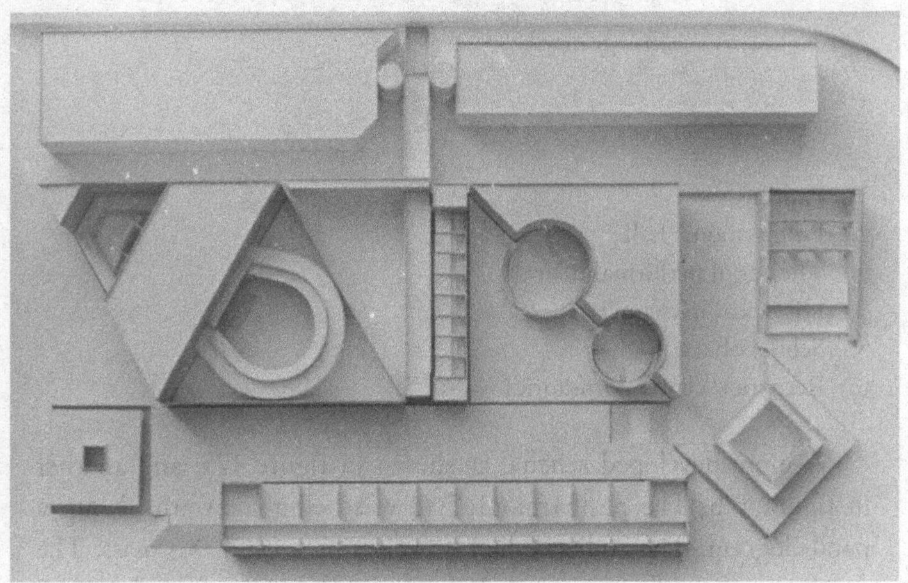

Figure 177

The relationships between masses were being investigated. The location of the parking building at the north edge of the site would block the noise generated by elevated freight trains (figs. 175–176). The two parking buildings in the north were different widths. I mused that Kahn had made one building narrower, with a smaller circle ramp for smaller, more modest cars, for the civic theater audience, and the wider building, with the larger, wider ramp, was for the philharmonic hall customers, who generally drove larger cars.

A cardboard lift-off model (fig. 177) opened to show the interior workings of the facilities.

After the July 1963 presentations, the garage buildings were taken out of the program due to cost concerns.

At this early stage, the project was received enthusiastically by the Fine Arts Foundation and the people of Fort Wayne. Many fundraising events, lectures, exhibitions, and activities began to take place. Models and sketches, such as those shown in figures 178-179. were exhibited.

On August 9, 1963, another model was presented to representatives of the FAF at Kahn's office. A reduced scope was noted in the meeting minutes which [49] indicated the following:

> Kahn discusses the overall program, emphasizing the idea and image of the center ... Parking garages, dormitories and the service tunnel were eliminated from the project. The philharmonic hall and civic theatre are connected by a common gala lobby. The ticket and administrative offices opened to a controlled garden area. All services were from the street.

---

49 Minutes, August 9, 1963, Box 17, ibid.

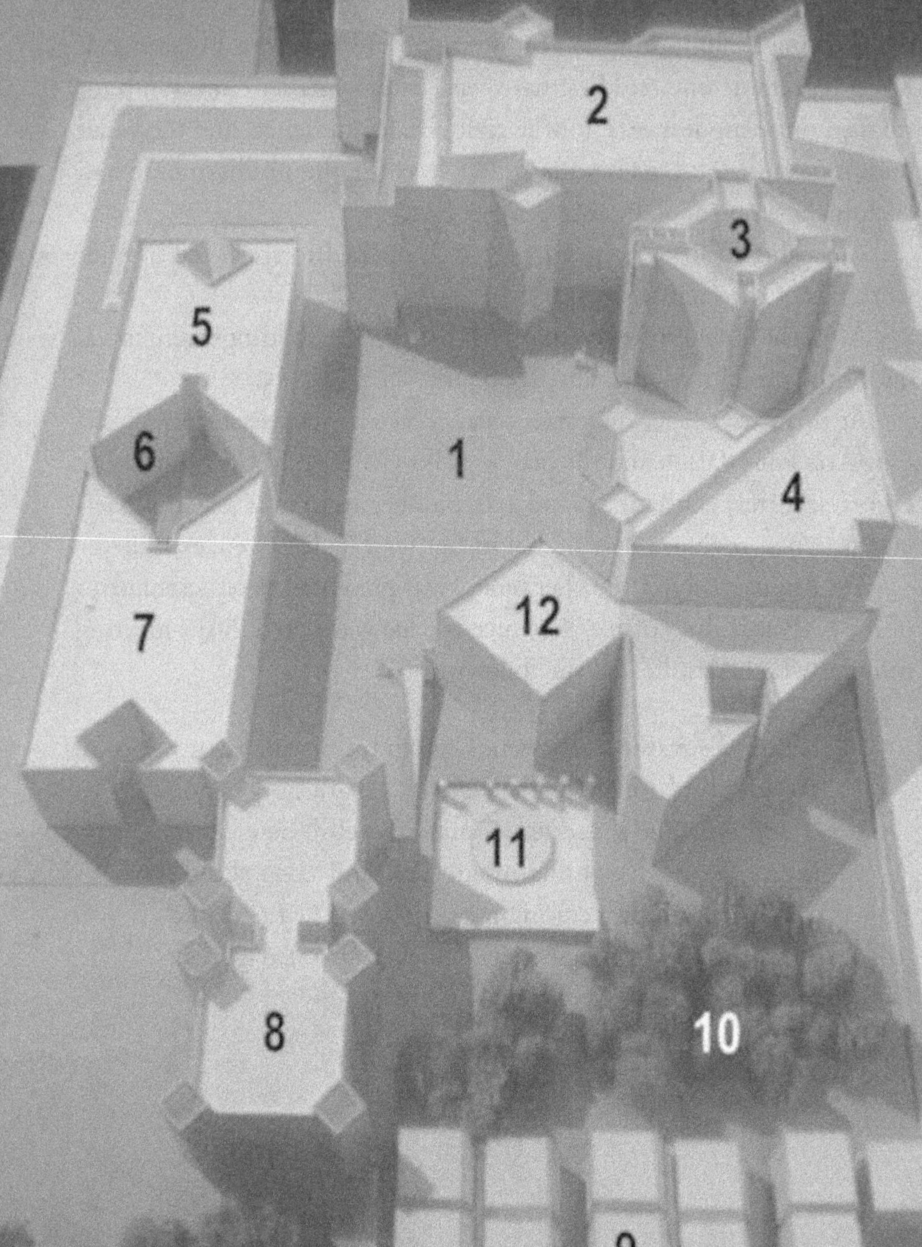

Figure 178

1. Court of entrances
2. Philharmonic hall
3. Philharmonic annex
4. Theater of performing arts
5. Historical museum
6. Museum garden
7. Art gallery
8. Reception center
9. School of art
10. Garden
11. Open-air theater
12. Experimental theater

Hind Legs

Two weeks later, on August 23, 1963, another meeting for approving the project took place in Fort Wayne.[50] The story of this meeting became a well-known story about the Fort Wayne project. Kahn detailed this in his talk at the Yale School of Art and Architecture on October 1964. The following is the edited version of his talk, which was published in 1965[51]

> I am scared stiff of people who look at things from the money angle. I had to meet some of them the other day at Fort Wayne in connection with an art center I'm doing there—a small Lincoln Center—and I had to say what it would cost. This is a very ticklish situation for me because I wanted them to want a project first, and then to talk about the cost …
>
> I presented the plans to them in as inviting a way as I possibly could …

50 Minutes, August 23, 1963, Box 17, ibid.

51 Perspecta 9/10: The Yale Architectural Journa, 1965, New Haven, Connecticut

> Then when they asked me how much it would cost, I said: Well, gentlemen, I must first introduce the fact that the area which you have asked me to have is the same as the area in my plans. They said, well, all right, but how much does it cost? I said, well, it will cost twenty million dollars.
>
> They had in mind something like two-and-a-half million dollars as the initial expenditure, but the buildings became independent, made it seem quite impossible to begin a meaningful choice with such a low amount. "Therefore, for two-and-a-half million dollars you would probably get the hind leg of a donkey and a tail, but you wouldn't get the donkey."

It became clear that Fort Wayne did not have funds to complete this whole project. I believe it was Kahn's love for architecture and his wanting to help this community reach their noble goal that made him take and start the project.

Two weeks later, FAF informed Kahn that they would be able to raise 2 million dollars.

On September 24, 1963, a new model indicating changes from the last two schemes was presented.[52] Fort Wayne requested the total seating for the philharmonic hall to be increased to 2,500 seats and for the new program to be developed for a new 500-seat proscenium theater. The school of ballet and the fine arts museum continued to be part of the program.

Two weeks later, on October 8, 1963, Kahn's office presented a new cardboard lift-off model to Fort Wayne. Fort Wayne commented the following:

> Architects are to re-examine program for further possible reduction of cubage [sic] and greater space-use

[52] Minutes, September 24, 1963, Box 17, ibid.

economy. Some areas, although they meet programmed requests, are considered excessive.[53]

At this meeting, all participants agreed to prepare a brochure to be used in the fundraising campaign. The brochure would include a philosophic meaning of this project, sketches with photos of the models to convey the spirit of the project.

[53] Minutes, October 8, 1963, Box 17, ibid.

Figure 179. Maquette for fundraising campaign.

On December 5, 1963, a letter from the executive committee to Kahn confirmed and finalized their decision about the project budget and made it official that "it will be impossible … to build the entire group of buildings at one time … The first phase was expected to include a 500-seat civic theater, the art museum (not including the art school), and the fine arts reception center."[54]

This was the collapse of Kahn's intensive efforts to develop a "small Lincoln Center" and of his hopes to make Fort Wayne the only American city to test his civic ideas of comprehensive planning. This must have been a real heartbreaker for Kahn and prompted him to say:

> I was so *ready to give up* the whole commission if they wouldn't build it all.[55]

A month later, in a letter from the office, Kahn reminded FAF that they needed the new and final program:

> Withdrawal of thehistorical society museum and the elimination of the experimental theater will make it necessary …to remake the remaining parts into a new composition to retain the original concept. Mr. Kahn suggested that this is the time to have the professional men, in the remaining member organizations make a final program with which we can work..[56]

A week later, in February, Kahn presented an extensive series of questions requiring answers for reducing areas. By this time, the philharmonic hall and the art school had been eliminated, leaving only the art alliance, gallery museum, and theater (with five hundred seats) in the project.

---

54 Letter from FAF to Kahn, December 5, 1963, Box 17, ibid.

55 Twombly, 2003, p. 165

56 Letter from Kahn to FAF, January 17, 1964, Box 17, Kahn Collection.

Fundraising

Six months passed between this request and the next meeting which took place in Philadelphia. Latz and Shaeffer informed Kahn that they had raised \$2.5 million[57] and were ready to undertake the first phase, which should include the construction of the art alliance, the art gallery / museum, the civic theater, and the court of entrances.

Only East Half

In this meeting, FAF announced that only the east half of the original site was available for the project. (fig. 180).

Figure 180

The east portion of the site had been appraised for \$800,000 and would be available around February or March 1966. It was not clear

---

57 Minutes, September 14, 1964, Box LIK 17, ibid.

whether this amount was part of the building budget, which would make the project budget of $1.7 million for the buildings. However, FAF had stressed that "Mr. Kahn will restudy the entire complex. The tentative schedule was set for redesign and construction through to March of 1966." Though, curiously, annotations on the minutes had *1967* handwritten in the margins.

Kahn had requested FAF to supply the following documents:

a) Site survey, 1"=30' scale, from a city-licensed engineer
b) Program for art alliance facilities and uses

By this time, it had been three years, and Kahn had produced a number of architectural maquettes, exhibited many of the schemes and given numerous talks about them.

Four months later, in January 1965, Kahn presented the civic theater, with a 500-seat capacity. The FAF decided to increase the seating capacity to 800–1,000. Within a few days, Kahn responded:

> Changing the capacity will materially alter the design and will affect the plot plan.

Fort Wayne informed Kahn six months later in August 1965 that there would be "new requirements for the theater, prepared by the newly arrived technical director, Joseph K. Rider, resident designer."

First Phase ($3 Million)

A year later, in January 1966, Kahn informed Fort Wayne that the "first phase is $3 million and includes civic theater, art alliance, gallery, museum, and court of entrances." He urgently requested a professional engineer's survey of the site, which had been requested more than a year before.[58]

---

[58] Letter, Kahn to Ft Wayne, Jan 1966, ibid.

June in Fort Wayne

In a meeting in early June at Fort Wayne, Kahn presented the concept model for the 800 to 1000-seat theater. The meeting minutes indicated the following:

> Nothing conclusive thus far. Architect just wants to show his striving. Architect sees auditorium as though it is a non-flat public square, different from a lecture hall. The audience is interested in themselves as well as play. The most intimate theater, shape and boxes, leads you right up to the proscenium. Epidaurus is a wall of people. Difficulty of above is sight lines.

The notes continued with a description of the design: "There can be 700 people within 60' depth. 1000 [people] would be effective with forward stage. A balcony allows for lesser audience without feeling of emptiness. Interior would be a combination of gold leaf and concrete plus colorful hangings." Fort Wayne noted that "many of the architect's ideas are exciting, but focus is strictly on stage ... Committee likes steep angle floor."[59]

Middle Years (1966–1968)

I started working on the theater at Kahn's office in mid-May 1966. I described this period in parts 4 and 5 of this book. The previous letter referred to was the first introduction document I read. I was completely unaware of the civic design explorations of the preceeding 5 years.

---

59 Minutes, June 7, 1966, ibid.

Last Five Years (1969–1973)

Going through the communications (letters, notes, phone and meeting memos) between Kahn's office and the Fort Wayne Fine Arts Foundation from 1969 to 1973 made me sad. There was a great amount of tension (and disillusionment) that had built between Kahn and the Foundation. In a way, this was a classic disconnect between an architect and the budget-wary client. The ideas of the *small Lincoln Center* and the *court of entrances* were long gone. The Fort Wayne Fine Arts Foundation had started with the grand idea of having a philharmonic hall, an art museum, a fine arts school, and a civic theater, but it was unable to raise the required funds to even purchase the whole site for it. In the end, the theater turned out to be a lonely building sitting on a nondescript site.

Budget $2.3 Million

The civic theater was estimated to be $2.3 million when I left Kahn's office in mid-June '68. A few months later, Tony Pellecchia, a colleague at Lou's office, was appointed to take the lead as the job captain. Tony carried the project until its completion in 1973. He met with the Fine Arts Foundation in Fort Wayne. In three separate meetings, he presented the revised theater, with the volume reduced as requested. He also presented the layout for the school of fine arts. Two days of meetings at the end of 1968 ended with Fort Wayne approving the plan and asking Kahn to proceed with the final drawings.[60]

60 Letter from Miller to Pellecchia (Kahn's office), December 18, 1968, ibid.

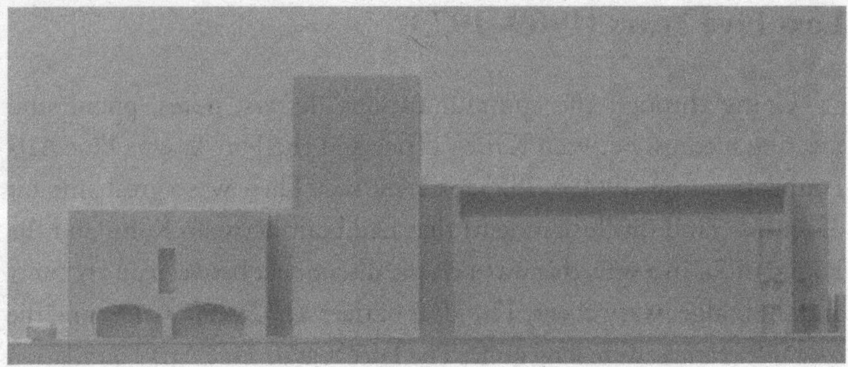

Figure 181.

West elevation, view from the park.

Meanwhile, a copy of the letter of Cyril Harris (acoustical consultant) to FAF arrived at the office. Harris had been engaged by FAF during my tenure of working on the project. In this letter, Harris referred to a long list of his objections to the current design. He indicated what future directions were to be followed in order not to waste a good deal of the work of his office, and he blamed the architect for the lack of communication.[61]

Budget $1.7 Million

A month later, on November 29, 1968, a letter from G. Irving Latz, the president of the Fine Arts Foundation, informed Lou:

> Budget is $1.7 million… and the present estimate of $2.3 million must be reduced.[62]

A few weeks later, on December 18, a letter from the chairman of the building committee, Milford M. Miller Jr., followed. In his

---

61 Letter from Harris to FAF, Oct 15, 1968, ibid.

62 Letter from Latz (president of the Fine Arts Foundation) to Kahn, November 29, 1968, ibid.

five-page letter, Miller listed all the areas that needed to be taken out of the project.[63]

We Will Get Another Architect

A month later, in a call, E. Menerth, the executive director of the Fine Arts Foundation, stated to Tony Pellecchia and D. Wisdom:

> If the changes are not done within a short period, we will get another architect.[64]

Soon after, George Izenour, the theater consultant, submitted his list to the building committee for further cost cutting.[65] Cyril Harris weighed in, hammering suggestions for design revisions, about the opening overlooking the stage at the rear of the stagehouse (the triangular opening).[66]

During the years of the Fort Wayne theater project, many commissions were being worked on in the office such as Phillips Exeter Library and Dining Hall, Maryland College of Art, Indian Institute of Management, Interama Center in Miami, Philadelphia College of Art, and Olivetti Underwood in Pennsylvania and important new commissions were being received such as Kimbell Art Museum, National Capital in Dhaka, Altgar Office, Jewish Martyrs' Memorial, Hurvah Synagogue. These years were the heart of Kahn's professional work and he was becoming well-known. Despite the many variations and limitations put onto the project by Fort Wayne, Kahn had the fortitude to pull the project through to fruition.

---

63 Letter from Miller to Pellechia (Kahn's office), December 18, 1968, ibid.

64 Phone memorandum from Menerth to D. Wisdom and Pellechia (Kahn's office), February 7, 1969.

65 Letter from Izenour to Kahn, February 17, 1969.

66 Meeting notes, Harris and Pellechia with FAF, August 8, 1969, ibid.

Kahn Writes to Harris

Cyril Harris continued his objections and was in sharp disagreement about the opening at the back of the stage. Finally, Kahn wrote a letter to him, dated September 3, 1969, and explained his view of the opening of the actor's house[67] (fig. 182).

> The long triangular opening to the Actor's House overlooking the stage is of importance to me symbolically as a recognition of identity of the Actor's Place behind the stage...To glaze this opening would destroy it completely for its symbolic meaning. It is not there for the show...I will not enclose this opening...

[67] Letter from Kahn to Harris, September 3, 1969, ibid.

LOUIS I KAHN ARCHITECT FAIA

5

Box 18

Ft Wayne

3 September 1969

Dr. Cyril M. Harris
425 Riverside Drive
New York, New York 10025

Dear Dr. Harris,

I was pleased with the report that Anthony Pellecchia gave me of your meeting with him. I appreciate the advice that you have given us which led to the last design.

I have also studied your advice in regard to the mechanical ducts and have found, I believe, a satisfactory answer.

> The long triangular opening to the Actor's House over looking the stage is of importance to me symbolically as a recognition of identity of the Actor's Place behind the stage. I know perfectly well, that this opening can be expected to have a back drop in front of it and then therefore, presents no acoustical problem. Also, I understand fully your apprehension in regard to this opening should it be used as a functional part of the stage in which a person framed in this opening could not be heard distinctly. Let us say this is true. I regard the architectural meaningfulness and stage potentiality of this opening also as important. To glaze this opening would destroy it completely for its symbolic meaning. It is not there for show. Therefore, I will not enclose this opening. What happens to it after the theatre is built I will have no control of.

I look forward to your continued advice.

Sincerely yours,

Louis I. Kahn

LIK:jmh

cc: Mr. Edward F. Menerth
Mr. Milford M. Miller, Jr.

1501 WALNUT STREET PHILADELPHIA 2 PENNSYLVANIA LOCUST 3-9844

Figure 182. Kahn's letter to Cyril Harris.

Figure 183. Kahn's sketch of the long triangular opening at the backstage area.

On a recent visit to the theater that included the back stage area, I was gratified to see that the Actors Porch and the large triangular opening was still there.

Estimate $2.024 Million

In mid-December, 1969, a letter from Kahn to Edward Menerth summarized the current cost estimate[68]:

$2,500,000	A combined cost of the building construction and the special stage equipment [as told to Lou's office by the Fort Wayne Fine Arts Foundation on February 3, 1969]
$400,000	Mr. Izenour's estimate for special stage equipment
$2,100,000	Remaining amount for the building

68 Letter from Kahn to Menerth, December 19, 1969, ibid.

\$2,519,700	February 1, 1969—Office of Louis Kahn estimate
\$2,024,271	December 19, 1969—Office of Louis Kahn current estimate

So the building was now within the requested construction budget.

Harris Resigned

A week later, on December 23, a copy of Cyril Harris's resignation letter to FW arrived at Kahn's office.

In the new year, Kahn, David Wisdom, and Tony Pellecchia arrived at Fort Wayne to discuss various reductions in building materials and cost. All agreed on certain changes in the bid documents.

During the months of February to May, many letters with a nervous tone would be received by Kahn's office, about budget and schedule delays. The preparation of the construction documents and negotiations with contractors proceeded over the next months.

Landscape Sketch

In response to a request for landscaping for the west side of the site, Kahn sent a handwritten letter with a sketch to M. Miller (fig. 184).[69]

69 Letter with sketch from Kahn to Miller, c. February 1971 (exact date unknown), ibid.

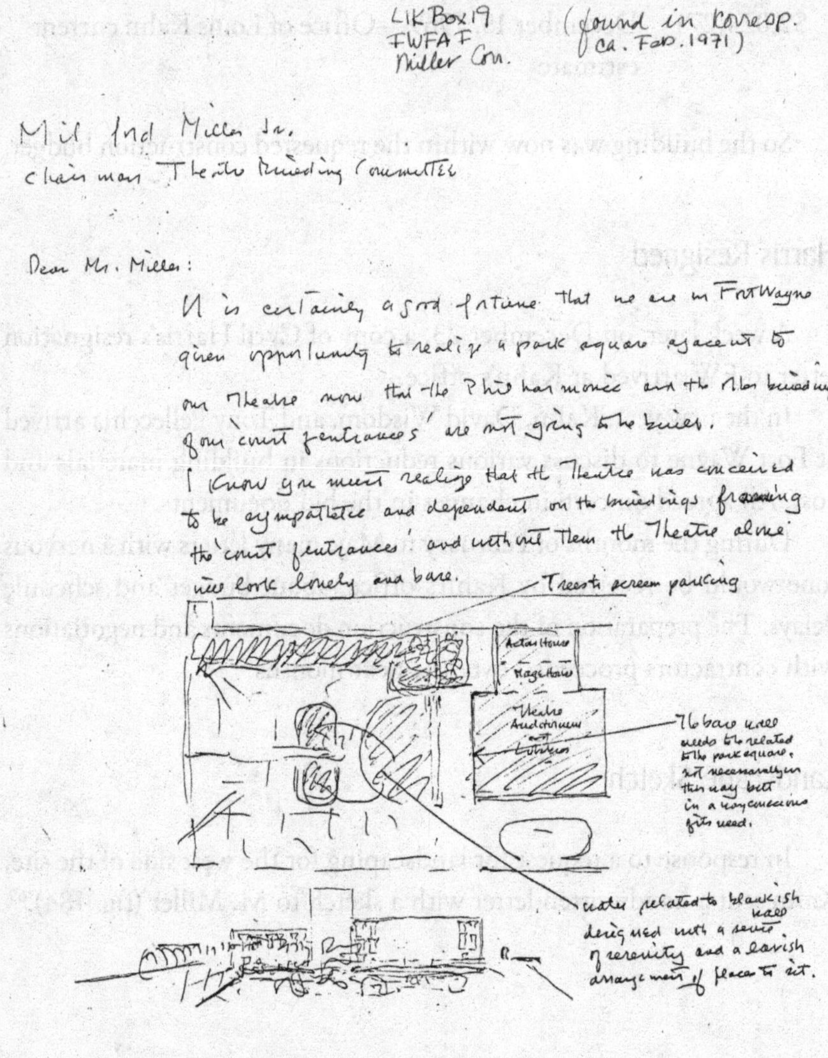

Figure 184

Dear Mr. Miller:

It is certainly a good fortune that we are in Fort Wayne given opportunity to realize a park square adjacent to our theatre now that the Philharmonic and the other

> buildings of our "court of entrances" are not going to be built.
>
> I know you must realize that the Theatre was conceived to be sympathetic and dependent on buildings framing the "court of entrances" and without them the Theater alone will look lonely and bare.
>
> [Notes on sketch]
>
> Trees screen parking
>
> The base will need to be related to the park square, not necessarily in this way but in a very conscience of its need.
>
> Water related to blankish wall designed with a sense of serenity and a lavish arrangement of places to sit.

Rudolf Serkin

During my research at the Kahn Archives in 1985, I found another letter, dated March 8, 1973. The date of it was close to the completion date of the building, and it was handwritten and addressed to Kahn by the previous building committee chairman, Bud Latz.

> Dear Lou, It's beautiful! It's BEAUTIFUL! Really, we are thrilled.
>
> Rudolf Serkin was in Fort Wayne and played a benefit … all Beethoven. He played two concertos! In talking to him later I mentioned Philadelphia, Penn, Kahn, etc. He didn't know of your Ft. W. bldg., so I made arrangements to take him through on his recess from five hours of practicing! … He was so excited

> by the building—your building—that he volunteered to come back for the dedication and play—gratis—in tribute to you! Imagine.[70]

I also found a small handwritten note from Kahn (fig. 209), dated March 13, 1973, in response to Bud Latz.[71]

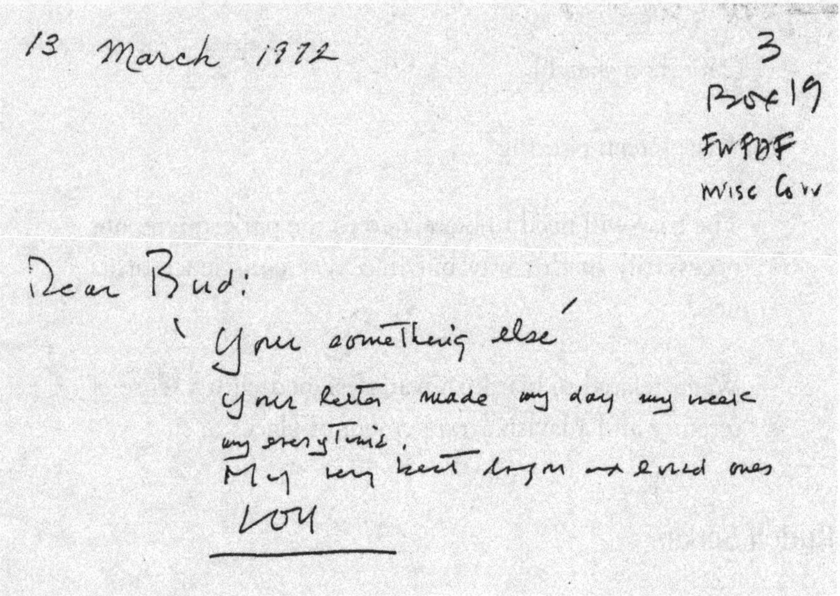

13 March 1972

3
Box 19
FWPDF
Wisc Corr

Dear Bud:

'You something else'

Your letter made my day my week my everything.
My very best to you and loved ones

LOU

Figure 185

> This built my hope that although much had been taken away from the Fort Wayne Theater project, there remained still a legacy that touches the human soul.

---

70 Letter from Latz to Kahn, March 8, 1973, ibid.

71 Letter from Kahn to Latz, March 13, 1973, Box 19, ibid.

Theater Dedication

A few days later, Kahn received an invitation to the dedication and a request for a statement, to be used in their dedication brochure. He responded with the following letter (fig. 186): [72]

[72] Dedication Letter from Kahn, September 20, 1973, ibid.

20 September 1973

RE: Fort Wayne Community Center for
the Performing Arts
Fort Wayne, Indiana

A whisper on the stage must be heard by everyone in the audience. This motivated the thought of the "Violin" and the "Violin Case". The place of the voice is the "Violin"-the stage and the people. The "Case" is the entrance, the lobby and all other outside services.

The auditorium built in concrete as an independent shape and structure, was placed within surrounding space, having its own roof and outside walls. Inner delicate sounds protected from freer and coarser sounds.

3
Box 19
FWFAF
Misc
Corr

Another thought was the invention of the "Actors' House". This was to give the actor his own place, free of the usual backstage chaos. A place of reflection, practice, relaxation, to meet, the fireplace, the dressing room and even, a chapel where he could practice the soliloquy. The "House" had to have a porch. Then the "House" was wheeled to the stage and the porch became the window to the stage.

All the many details of construction, mechanical, electrical, were merely problems, subservient to the central ideas of the Fort Wayne Community Center for the Performing Arts.

When I started this project, I made many studies showing the complete ensemble of the Philharmonic Theatre, School of Art, the Art Alliance Building and the Art Gallery to be composed as a unit with all doorways to these buildings answering to a court, which I named the "Court of the Entrance".

Circumstances made it not possible to include all these buildings but I still harbor the hopeful thought that in time a few of these buildings will accompany this initial structure of the Fort Wayne Community Center for the Performing Arts.

Louis I. Kahn

LIK/kac

1501 WALNUT STREET PHILADELPHIA 2 PENNSYLVANIA LOCUST 3-9

Figure 186. Lou's letter, dated September 20, 1973.

Figure 187. Cover of Fort Wayne theater dedication booklet.

The dedication ceremony took place on October 5, 1973. Kahn and Mrs. Kahn arrived in Fort Wayne at 10:30 a.m. that day. He sat with some civic leaders and some architects around a table in the greenroom, and he gave an inspirational talk. He and Mrs. Kahn returned to Philadelphia that same day on a 6:30 p.m. flight.

Five months and ten days later, on March 17, 1974, Kahn suffered a massive heart attack and passed away in New York City.

REFLECTIONS

Kahn spoke about life routines, a certain cycle of living, about its nature and the essential identities of a place, about the creation of that sense of place and that sense of awe.

What I heard about was that elusive act of understanding, that ethereal comprehension, that knowing, that realization of the art of design, of the art of place-making. All that *experience.* It was not about the brick and mortar of a building, but about soaking in the essence of its story, of its being, of its becoming, of its *soul*, of its *existence will*, of *what it wants to be*—all those nonphysical aspects of a place.

Such inspiration that touches the *heart, like* a word in a poem, a phrase in a song, or a face in a crowd, talks to one's *soul.* These are beyond words, beyond color, beyond sound and touch the most private thoughts, where feelings are. Like that chapel in Crete or that temple in Kyoto - a spirit of a kind, those poetries of life, of art and architecture.

The *soul, will, heart, core,* and *essence* are where *art* flourishes, Heartbeats in a heartwarming song, in a child's laughter, in love, in a scenery, owning and completing art. These bring *art* close to us. They are of emotion, of passion, of love transcending time.

They are in us—in our favorite buildings, our favorite place, our favorite poem, a song. They are special; they are warm.

It is essential to cultivate and bring our spatial emotions to architecture with our intellectual capacity, to the same level as we have done for music and for poetry.

I see places as expressions of ways of life, as sets of human desires and aspirations. I see that every offering to the *"sanctuary of art"* is far above the name or fame of an artist.

I see *Guggenheim Museum* as a *realm of art.*
I see *Farnsworth* as *a desire to live within nature.*
I see *Ronchamp* as being of *purity and spiritual essence.*
I see *Salk Institute* as being of *exactitude, precision, and clarity.*

Any human setting reflects a meaning to that setting in their life, language, culture, music, or tradition. An architect's primary task is to bring out this meaning.

This is *form.*
This is *what it wants to be.*
This is going to the *beginning.*
This is looking to the *nature* of things.
This is *"ask a brick."*

Those were in Kahn's talks, in his directives in the office or with students, in his writings, and in his work. Architecture is meant to bring these into a physical realm, into spatial experience, into life.

Kahn's work is not an architectural style, but an understanding of a way of making a place. This was relevant yesterday, is relevant today, and will be relevant tomorrow.

"What was, has always been.
What is, has always been.
What will be, has always been."

With the greatest joy, I understand, salute, and acknowledge those simple, coherent, and meaningful spatial compositions that enrich our own being, our place on earth, our streets, our neighborhoods, and our cities, bringing lasting joy and progressive civility to our life, uplifting the meaning of architecture and the architect, whose beings and doings are so dear to us.

AND A DAY MORE

It is afternoon, and I am sitting on a stone terrace, a retired architect after fifty-six years of practice. I have worked on projects ranging from 600 square meters to 2 million square meters, from a simple garage addition to giant and prominent international projects. This is a strange profession.

I can see the Aegean Sea. The garden in front of me is in full bloom, overflowing with bougainvillea. The stone terrace is warm and beckoning, fronting our cool stone house, shaded by tall pine trees.

It is early August and I'm thousands of miles and some fifty-four years away from Philadelphia. I am an AIA Architect Emeritus now, and thoughts are flowing in from years ago.

I am hoping that my writings will help students of architecture, young architects, and others. I wonder if my children will read this in amazement. I wonder about my students and the people who have worked with me. Will they be happily amused to know things about my earlier years? Will my writing have any effect in people's minds about how they see architecture or architects? Will it increase or lessen their understanding or love for architecture? And those who were Lou's students or who have worked with him, would they find exaggerations beyond their memory? Would this make people in Fort Wayne realize that a building in Freimann] Square took so much effort, so much struggle? Would an actor performing in that building, or a ballerina or the first violinist gain some new insights into architecture?

Cengiz Yetken
Demir

Vitae of Cengiz Yetken

Cengiz Yetken received BArch (1963) and MArch (1964) from Middle East Technical University in his native country, Turkey and was awarded Fulbright and University of Pennsylvania grants to study under Louis I. Kahn in his master's class. He received his MArch degree (1966) from University of Pennsylvania. After joining Lou Kahn's office, he was appointed as a job captain for the Theater of Performing Arts in Fort Wayne, Indiana and was involved in conceptual design studies, schematics and design development stages giving presentations to the Fort Wayne Fine Arts Foundation on Lou's behalf on numerous occasions.

Mr. Yetken taught Architectural Design at the University of Pennsylvania, (1967-68), Middle East Technical University (1964-75) in Ankara, Turkey, Ball State University, Indiana (1975-77), University of Virginia, (1977-81), and School of the Art Institute in Chicago, Illinois (1984-87). He has lectured extensively in various universities in the US.

After fifteen plus years of full-time academic involvement, Mr. Yetken moved into professional practice and joined Skidmore Owings and Merrill in Chicago (1981-86) as a Senior Designer.

He received his professional license in 1983 and started his private architectural practice (1986-89) in Oak Park Illinois.

In 1989, he joined Perkins+ Will in Chicago where he worked as a Senior Architect on numerous projects in the US and abroad.

He is a member of American Institute of Architects, a member of Turkish Chamber of Architects, and a Fulbright Scholar.

Mr Yetken retired from full-time practice in mid-2005 but continued as a Senior Consultant in Architectural Design at Perkins+Will until mid-2009. Mr. Yetken is married to Carol JH Yetken with two adult children and resides as a US citizen in Oak Park, Illinois.

ACKNOWLEDGEMENTS

My special thanks to William Whitaker, curator, of Kahn Archives for his encouraging comments and point of perspective. Thanks to Julia Converse, former director of Kahn Archives and to Nancy Thorne CA archivist/cataloguer for their kind assistance in my early research. My appreciations go also to Ralph Johnson FAIA, Maria Dering, Sibel Bozdogan, David M. Sokol, and Claude Caswell for their reading the early chapters and offering valuable suggestions.

And to my dear wife Carol Yetken for her support, constant love and inspiration, patiently reading many versions and contributing to the final shape of this book.

PHOTOGRAPHS AND ILLUSTRATIONS CREDIT

Craig Kuhner

110,112,113,116,117, 118, 120, 121. 162.

The Louis I. Kahn Collection, The University of Pennsylvania and the Pennsylvania Historical Society and museum commission

5, 11, 62, 63, 72, 93, 94, 95, 96, 97, 98, 99, 100, 108, 111, 123, 150, 151, 154, 158, 160, 162, 163, 169, 170, 171, 172, 173, 174, 175, 176, 177, 178, 179, 180, 181, 182, 183, 184, 185, 186.

Cengiz Yetken Personal Archive

1, 2, 3, 6, 7, 8, 9, 10, 12, 13, 14, 15, 16, 17, 18, 19, 21, 22, 23, 24, 25, 26, 27, 28, 29, 30, 31, 32, 33, 34, 36, 36, 37, 38, 39, 40, 41, 42, 43, 44, 45, 46, 47, 48, 49, 50, 51, 52, 53, 55, 56, 57, 58, 59, 60, 67, 68, 69, 70, 79, 80, 81, 82, 83, 84, 85, 86, 87, 88, 89, 90, 91, 92, 104, 105, 107, 109, 114, 115, 119, 124, 125, 129, 130, 133, 134, 136, 140, 141, 142, 148, 149, 152, 153, 155, 156, 157, 159, 161, 164, 165, 166, 167, 168, 187.

Perkins+Will/Steinkamp

131, 132, 135, 136, 137, 138, 139, 143, 144, 145,146.

George Alikakos/Yetken

61, 64, 65, 66, 71, 73, 74, 75, 76, 77, 78.

Mark Ballogg / Ballogphoto.com

126, 127, 128.

Neo Take Murrayama, Flickr Creative Commons

4

Muge Cengizkan

106

Cemal Endem

122

Melike Yetken

20

Matthew Carbone, Architect Magazine.com

147

Commercial Post Card

57

INDEX

U

V

W

Y

CPSIA information can be obtained
at www.ICGtesting.com
Printed in the USA
LVHW102347260122
709311LV00010B/250

9 781664 154001